KNOWLEDGE INTEGRATION DYNAMICS

Developing Strategic Innovation Capability

KNOWLEDGE INTEGRATION DYNAMICS

Developing Strategic Innovation Capability

Mitsuru Kodama

Nihon University, Japan

NEW JERSEY · LONDON · SINGAPORE · BEIJING · SHANGHAI · HONG KONG · TAIPEI · CHENNAI

Published by

World Scientific Publishing Co. Pte. Ltd.

5 Toh Tuck Link, Singapore 596224

USA office: 27 Warren Street, Suite 401-402, Hackensack, NJ 07601

UK office: 57 Shelton Street, Covent Garden, London WC2H 9HE

British Library Cataloguing-in-Publication Data
A catalogue record for this book is available from the British Library.

ISBN-13 978-981-4317-89-4
ISBN-10 981-4317-89-6

Typeset by Stallion Press
Email: enquiries@stallionpress.com

Printed in Singapore.

Acknowledgments

This book, which discusses activities related to corporate innovation strategies, was born out of the close observations and analyses that I have built up over many years at my business workplace. I have experience of working in the exciting fields of new product and service development, and internal corporate ventures in the dramatically changing IT and telecommunications sectors. Using my personal experience of business, I felt that the driving power that supports corporate innovation strategy has its starting point as the knowledge held by people and groups, leadership of top and middle management, and the practice process mechanisms of actual business execution. This knowledge, leadership, and practice process go on to formulate and implement the dynamic innovation strategies of companies (or individual organizations).

This book could not have been completed without the painstaking and rigorous interaction that I have had with many practitioners. I would like to extend my gratitude to these practitioners, who are of a number too great to count. Especially, I would like to thank, the senior executives and managers of the companies (high-tech Japanese, South Korean, and Taiwanese companies including NTT, Panasonic,

Cannon, Sharp, Sony, Mitsubishi Plastic, NTT DoCoMo, Nintendo, and Mitsubishi Corporation) that formed the research target of this book. I would also like to express my deep appreciation to Dr. Ikujiro Nonaka, Professor Emeritus at Hitotsubashi University, for contributing numerous stimulating innovation concepts and philosophical insights.

Concerning the publication of this book, I wish to extend my appreciation to Ms. Sandhya and Ms. Alisha, editors at World Scientific, who have provided tremendous supports. Finally, I would like to express my gratitude for a grant-in-aid for scientific research from JSPS. Regarding the publication of this book, I would like to thank for publishing grant-in-aid from Nihon University's head office and Nihon University's College of Commerce.

Mitsuru Kodama

Preface

The Knowledge Integration Firm

Japanese companies are learning how to survive and revitalize in the global markets of the 21st century. This book aims to clarify the sources of competence for Japan's outstanding companies and general trading companies through in-depth case studies of their consumer electronics, communication and telecommunication equipment, machine tools, semiconductor, information and telecommunications. It also considers the *knowledge integration firm* as a new corporate model distinct from Western management model.

The skillful coordination and collaboration of Japan's corporate knowledge and organizational boundaries aimed at technological and marketing innovations both renew accumulated path-dependent knowledge and dynamically integrate diverse knowledge inside and outside the company. They create distinctively new models of Japanese leadership and knowledge integration for business leaders.

The *knowledge integration firm* integrates diverse core knowledge inside and outside the company, and strategically innovates new products, services, and business models. Strategic innovation involves the constant, strategic creation of products, services, and business models to acquire long-term, sustainable, and competitive excellence. It embraces the radical reformation of conventional products and services and the creation of new business models that transform existing business rules. The process of acquiring new knowledge and creating innovations builds up the dynamic organizational capability, which helps to establish a company's position in new markets and technologies. In this book, I use the term *strategic innovation capability* for the organizational capability to realize this kind of continuous strategic innovation.

This book emphasizes how the knowledge held by individuals, groups, and organizations (inside and outside the company) comes to underlie analytical frameworks for grasping dynamic strategic innovation and *strategic innovation capability*. I believe this new knowledge created from diverse knowledge and organizational boundaries (inside and outside these companies) drives strategic innovations arising from *strategic innovation capability*. I consider, especially, that the knowledge integration generated from various boundaries (inside and outside the company), including customers and partners, is a source of strategic innovation. It leads to the *strategic innovation capability*, which creates a sustained competitive edge.

This book presents theoretical frameworks and managerial implications relating to the knowledge integration process in which the knowledge held by people, groups, and organizations transcends knowledge and organizational boundaries to become dynamically shared and integrated. New knowledge (e.g., the development of new products, services, and business models) *strategic innovation capability* are also created. This book also classifies knowledge integration architecture that realizes dynamic knowledge integration at multiple knowledge and organizational boundaries. It presents in-depth case studies to reflect a new, dynamic view of strategy essential to obtain a competitively outstanding *strategic innovation capability*.

Features of Japanese Companies

Outstanding Japanese companies are maintaining and developing organizational culture rooted in the shared values of teamwork

(Kodama, 2001), commitment (Ouchi, 1980), and community spirit (Drucker, 2004). They focus on organizational knowledge creation activities (Nonaka and Takeuchi, 1995) based on accumulated tacit knowledge, while studying the Western management practices (e.g., selection and concentration, strategic alliances, strategic outsourcing, speed management, organizational flattening, knowledge management, re-engineering, and payment by results). Japanese companies are honing their competitive edges by combining the merits of both Japanese management and Western management. Following the Japanese economic crises of the 1990s, some scholars observed the fascinating phenomenon of Japanese firms seeking to revitalize their innovative capacity by applying Western knowledge management practices (Lampel and Bhalla, 2007).

Japanese companies are maintaining technological and service innovations, and market share at top global levels, particularly in areas where the competitive environment is fierce (e.g., digital consumer electronics, automobiles, communication and telecommunication equipment, factory automation (FA), mobile phone services, and game business). The world could learn from successful examples of Japanese companies in these high-tech areas.

Features of Japanese management can be summarized in the following four points:

1. The value chain model of Japanese companies arising from vertical integration encourages the creation of competitively new products, services and innovative business models. This is called the *vertical value chain model*.
2. Coordination and collaboration across industries encourage the creation of win-win business models. This is called the *co-evolution model*.
3. The dynamic knowledge integration process crossing knowledge boundaries inside and outside the company is a core competence of Japanese companies.
4. The *knowledge integration process* of Japanese companies enables the acquisition of *strategic innovation capability*.

The first feature of Japanese management is the creation of good tacit knowledge, which has become the core of the value chain. Leading examples of companies claiming a prominent share of the global market for digital consumer electronics include Sharp for LCD TVs, Canon for digital cameras, and Panasonic for plasma TVs and DVD recorders. These companies daily accumulate and update expertise on marketing, product development and production technology through skillful coordination and integration of knowledge and organizational boundaries among different specialist fields (Brown and Duguid, 2001). At the same time, they optimize the entire value chain crossing vertical boundaries and integrate horizontally to dominate the global market (Kodama, 2007a).

The impact of Japanese companies' core competence management focusing on the development and production processes of core components such as system LSI, flash memory, and analog devices (Hamel and Plaharad, 1994) extends to semiconductor manufacturers in other countries. Business models such as these, which build value chains through vertical integration crossing vertical boundaries, are observed both in high-tech areas manufacturing and distinctive general trading companies. Japanese general trading companies profit as they build win-win relationships among partners aimed at optimizing overall business process value chains ranging from resource development, raw materials trade, manufacturing and processing, intermediate distribution, to retail.

The second feature involves the leadership to build new business models crossing industrial boundaries. Leading cases are mobile phone business (NTT DoCoMo and KDDI), and game business (Sony and Nintendo). These companies are exploring completely new business domains through coordination and collaboration of horizontal boundaries resulting from industry-crossing strategy alliances. The mobile Internet led by i-mode, movie and music distribution, mobile e-commerce, positioning data, and telematics in the mobile phone business, and PlayStation, DS, and Wii in the game business are key examples.

The current situation is that Asian and European mobile phone companies are catching up with the advanced Japanese business models. Meanwhile, Apple's music distribution business has built a new value chain connecting the iTunes music store and iPod platform with music and movie content. iPhone is also building a platform to deliver a range of content to users including voice communications and multimedia data. This Apple business model, however, resembles the co-evolution model of the win-win business ecosystems created by Japan's i-mode (Kodama, 2002; Peltokorpi, Nonaka and Kodama, 2007).

These two features indicate strategic innovation through coordination and collaboration of vertical and horizontal boundaries. They are referred to especially as *boundaries innovation* in this book.

The third feature is Japanese companies' distinctive core competences, which are instrumental in achieving the first two features. It is the *knowledge integration process* resulting from Japanese companies' skillful coordination, collaboration, and integration of vertical and horizontal boundaries. It builds value chains through vertical integration crossing vertical boundaries and new business models crossing industry boundaries. It advances accumulated in-house, path-dependent knowledge, proactively absorbs new knowledge (including path-breaking knowledge) from outside the company (Karmin and Mitchell, 2000; Graebner, 2004), dynamically integrates these different aspects of knowledge, and creates new business models.

The fourth feature is that the *knowledge integration process* drives *strategic innovation capability*. This capability enables the strategic innovation that strategically and continuously generates new products, services, and business models for companies to acquire long-term, sustainable and competitive excellence. Japanese companies have been continuously evolving and developing high-tech product innovations through *boundaries innovation* (mentioned above). *Strategic innovation capability* constantly improves conventional products and services while creating new business models that transform these radical innovations and existing business rules.

In this book, the term *knowledge integration models* refers to the corporate models with these four features. The term *knowledge integration firm* refers to the corporate bodies that apply these models.

The Framework of Analysis

With the *knowledge integration model*, the skillful coordination, collaboration, and integration of vertical and horizontal boundaries promote the dynamic *knowledge integration process*, and build *strategic innovation capability*. They strategically and continuously create new products, services, and business models, and realize strategic innovation. This book will offer an in-depth analysis of Japanese companies' distinctive business models comprising the four features mentioned above.

Dealing with the first feature, the book focuses on describing Japanese companies' skillful integration of knowledge and competence (inside and outside the company) based on vertically integrated value chain models, and the vertical value chain model creating new products and services. To demonstrate the second feature, the book describes Japanese companies' expansion of their own horizontal boundaries, and the co-evolution model creating new business through skillful coordination and collaboration crossing heterogeneous industries. To clarify these two issues, it is necessary to analyze elements of management drivers (Sanchez and Mahoney, 1996) and organizational form of the distinctive Japanese companies that determine corporate boundaries vertically and horizontally as strategic positions.

The focus of the third feature is to clarify the *knowledge integration process* that is also the core concept of the *knowledge integration model*. For this purpose, it is necessary to analyze practitioner thinking and behavior in the built organization form at a micro-level to discover what effectively controls Japanese companies' management drivers. The practitioner thinking and organizational behavior are the areas of formation of dynamic human networks (inside and outside the company) and creation of new knowledge and competences. The *dynamic knowledge integration process* and leadership models created by these practitioners need to be considered.

The focus of the fourth feature is to describe the *strategic innovation capability* created from the *knowledge integration process*. Corporate innovation requires different knowledge integration processes at different stages (from basic research to implementation) and the organizational capabilities responding to these processes. Accordingly, it is necessary to describe the systematization of innovation processes responding to internal and external environments (such as changes in the degree of uncertainty), the specification of elements of individual knowledge integration processes and organizational capabilities responding to situations, and elements of strategic innovation capability by which a company strategically and continuously creates strategic innovation.

Moreover, this book will consider the mechanisms of the *knowledge integration process*, (feature 3) which realizes the boundaries innovation (features 1 and 2) and the *strategic innovation capability* (feature 4). It will clarify the forms of the Japanese company's *knowledge integration model* and the *knowledge integration firm* that embodies it.

The Book's Structure

Part 1 deals with theory. Chapter 1 presents the *knowledge integration model* and its embodiment in the framework of the

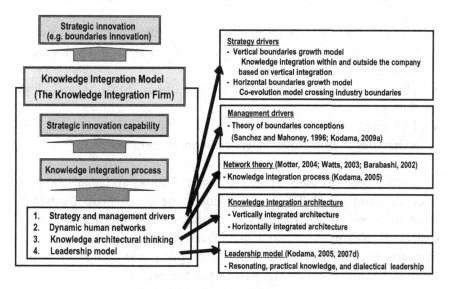

Analytical Framework of this Research.

knowledge integration firm. The framework of the *knowledge integration model* is formed from the concepts of the *dynamic knowledge integration process* and the *strategic innovation capability* that arises from this process. Moreover, the *knowledge integration process* is formed from the individual key concepts of strategy and management drivers, dynamic human networks, knowledge architectural thinking, and leadership models. Here, I will present these key concepts and clarify their relationship with the *knowledge integration process* (see Figure).

Chapter 2 introduces the concept of *strategic innovation capability* created from the *knowledge integration process.* It compares "dynamic capability" (Teece, *et al.*, 1997), which is the forerunner of this *strategic innovation capability*, "MI (major innovation) dynamic capability" (O'Connor, 2008) applying a focus on radical innovation, and "breakthrough innovation capability" (O'Connor, Leifer, Paulson and Peters, 2008). The *strategic innovation capability* proposed in this book presents concepts embracing the four capabilities:

- The management capability of the diverse knowledge integration process in the innovation process responding to object and situational strategies.
- The management capability to realize spiral strategic innovation loops among domains (domains are defined as each development stage of the innovation process).
- The management capability within and among domains (including shifts).
- The integrative competences that co-establish the two different archetypes arising from dialectical management.

Part 2 presents case studies. Chapter 3 looks at Japan's biggest telecom company, NTT, and considers the mechanism by which *strategic innovation capability* is acquired through implementing dialectical management and a spiral strategic innovation loop arising from the dynamic knowledge integration process at each stage of the innovation process, from the past to the future.

Chapter 4 reflects the differences between Japanese and Western business in the consumer electronics, communication and telecommunication equipments, and semiconductor industries. It demonstrates the creativity of Japanese companies and considers the mechanism that realizes the vertical value chain model.

Chapter 5 looks at Japan's machine tool manufacturers to study the organizational strategy and "Ba" management, which become enablers realizing vertical value chain models aimed at continuous innovations of product architecture.

Chapter 6 focuses on Japan's mobile phone business to demonstrate the mechanisms of *strategic innovation capability*, which realizes the co-evolution model arising from dialectic-view thinking and behavior among Japanese companies in these areas.

Chapter 7 looks at the *knowledge integration process* with regard to Nintendo's product development. It also considers how the dialectical thought of markets and technology becomes an enabler acquiring *strategic innovation capability*.

Chapter 8 refers to a major Japanese general trading company, Mitsubishi Corporation. It considers the structure of the business models and personnel management for the vertical value chain and co-evolution models arising from the expression of *strategic innovation capability*.

Part 3 is a general review. Chapter 9 delivers the following three theoretical and managerial implications based on the theories in Part 1 and the case studies in Part 2. The first implication relates to the *knowledge integration process* and related topics. The "knowledge integration firm" constantly generates new product and business concepts from the creation of new knowledge. This concluding chapter demonstrates this relationship of dialectical synthesis among concepts and knowledge, and considers the *knowledge integration dynamics* framework from the viewpoints of conceptualization, dynamic practical knowledge, *strategic innovation capability*, the knowledge integration process, and the new theory of *knowledge difference*.

The second implication is a company's ideal strategy-making process (analyzed at an individual business and project level), the practice process to achieve it, and how the timing and resource distribution of the *knowledge integration process* informs policy and practice. The co-establishment of current and future strategy becomes an important issue in avoiding such problems as path-dependency, competency traps, and core rigidities.

The third implication is the *knowledge integration process* and related topics. It indicates how the knowledge architectural thinking of practitioners can integrate boundaries embedded with valuable and diverse knowledge distributed inside and outside the company. Chapter 9 also looks at how the *creativity* and *dialectic* views, which form distinctive elements of the Japanese company's *knowledge integration model*, have been able to influence leading companies in Asian countries including South Korea and Taiwan. Chapter 10 concerns the conclusions of this book.

About the Author

Mitsuru Kodama is a Professor of Innovation and Technology Management in the College of Commerce and Graduate School of Business Administration at Nihon University. Prior to joining Nihon University, he has been working as a marketer and planning engineer at KDDI, NTT and NTT DoCoMo. He holds the B.S., M.S. and Ph.D. degrees in electrical engineering from Waseda University, Tokyo, Japan. He has published six books including *Boundary Management — Developing Business Architecture For Innovation* (Springer, 2009), *Innovation Networks In the Knowledge–based Firms* (Edward Elgar Publishing, 2009), *Knowledge Innovation — Strategic Management As Practice* (Edward Elgar Publishing, 2007), *New Knowledge Creation Through ICT Dynamic Capability — Creating Knowledge Communities Using Broadband* (Information Age Publishing, 2008), *The Strategic Community-based Firm* (Palgrave Macmillan, 2007), *Knowledge Innovation — Strategic Management As Practice* (Edward Elgar Publishing, 2007), *Project-based Organization In The Knowledge-based Society* (Imperial College Press, 2007).

He has also published over 80 refereed papers in the area of business and management *(Organization Studies, Journal of Management Studies, Long Range Planning, Strategy and Leadership, Technovation, Systems Research and Behavioral Science, etc.)*, information systems and management *(Information Systems Management, International Journal of Information Management, Information Management and Computer Security Business Process Management Journal, International Journal of Management and Enterprise Development, etc.)*, telecommunications *(International Journal of Electronic Business, International Journal of Mobile Communications, etc.)* and solid state electronics *(IEE Electronics Letters, Solid-State Electronics, Journal of Electrochemical Society, Physica Status Solidi, etc.)*. Especially, he received the R&D 100 Awards 2003 from R&D *Magazine* (U.S.).

Contents

The Knowledge Integration Model

1. Background Theory and New Frameworks

In this chapter, I will present the framework of the *knowledge integration model*. This framework broadly comprises the dynamic knowledge integration process and the concept of *strategic innovation capability* that emerges from it. The *knowledge integration firm* applying the *knowledge integration model* acquires and accumulates the *strategic innovation capability* to constantly create new products, services, and business models as new knowledge. It exploits an integration process that dynamically integrates core diverse knowledge inside and outside the company through daily business activities. The organization's *strategic innovation capability* (see Chapter 2 for details) in the form of these accumulated, updated, and evolved intangible assets creates strategic and boundaries innovations (which will be discussed later).

The core engine of the knowledge integration process producing this *strategic innovation capability* is formed from the individual key concepts of strategy and management drivers, dynamic human networks, knowledge architectural thinking, and leadership models.

This chapter aims to describe these four key concepts and clarify their relationships with the knowledge integration process (see Figure 1.1).

I have derived the distinctively Japanese *knowledge integration model* (*knowledge integration firm*) from long-term observation and analysis of ethnography. I have gathered information from in-depth interviews (280 figures in top and middle management) at 56 (corporations in the fields of consumer electronics, communications and telecommunications equipment, semiconductor, machine tools, mobile phones, and general trading) and combined with my own working experiences including 15 years at NTT, Japan's largest telecommunications carrier, 3 years at NTT DoCoMo, Japan's largest mobile communication carrier, and 3 years at KDDI, the second-largest telecommunications carrier.

The *knowledge integration model* fuses heterogeneous knowledge inside and outside the company resulting from dynamic changes in corporate (vertical and horizontal) boundaries. It delivers two new

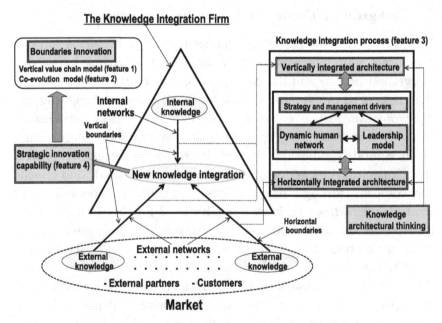

Figure 1.1   The Knowledge Integration Model.

insights regarding new knowledge integration: the realization of new product, service, and business models from Japan's distinctive vertical value chain model (feature 1), and a new win-win business model from the co-evolution model (feature 2).

The *knowledge integration model* involves the knowledge integration process operating through networks inside and outside the company. Specifically, it refers to the integration of internal knowledge through internal networks within the company and external knowledge through external networks outside the company. Through these networks, the model integrates new boundary transcending knowledge arising from the knowledge integration process. In this book, I will use the term "boundaries innovation" (corresponding to the strategic innovation mentioned in the introduction) for the innovation generated from this kind of knowledge integration process. I have inductively derived the four research streams of strategy and management drivers, dynamic human networks, knowledge architectural thinking, and leadership models as the core framework of the knowledge integration process to realize the *knowledge integration model* (feature 3) (see Figure 1.1).

To clarify the core concept of the *knowledge integration model*. I believe that it is important to analyze these research streams for four reasons.

- The close connection of the vertically integrated value chain and co-evolution models with strategy and management contexts.
- The close connection of the knowledge integration process with the human network of practitioners forming inter-organizational networks to integrate heterogeneous knowledge.
- The knowledge integration process through which practitioners link individual knowledge and closely connect it to the architectural thinking that assimilates this knowledge.
- The leadership models of the managers and other leaders, which form drivers as the source of competences to realize the co-evolution of independent vertical value chain models, based on vertical integration, arising from the corporate acquisition of new knowledge.
- Next, I will clarify these concepts based on a key literature.

2. The Four Core Frameworks of the Knowledge Integration Process

2.1 *Strategy and management drivers*

A company's distinctive conceptions of boundary, which determine corporate boundaries as strategic positions (referred to in this book as "strategy drivers"), form a key element by which a company promotes corporate strategy. Such strategy driver functions as an industry value chain (Porter, 1980), which is set up to realize the objectives of corporate strategy. This driver comprises business activities with the objective of forming industry value chains, and is the element that determines a company's vertical boundaries.

A second driver includes elements determining a company's horizontal boundaries, which create new business domains by expanding and diversifying (or downsizing by selecting and concentrating) a company's existing business domains (products, services, and business models), or by integrating different technologies.

Companies must always transform their own corporate governance structures and boundaries to strengthen their strategic positioning under a constantly changing environment (or the environment that the company itself has created). Research of firm boundaries shows that decision making on corporate governance structures and boundaries depends on various elements (the elements determining corporate boundaries are referred to in this book as "management drivers") of boundary conceptions including efficiency, power, competence, and identification. These conceptions have key influences on boundary decisions in any company. The decision making over which activities to implement within the company to enhance the innovation value chain and whether to access external resources through contractual arrangements with the markets form elements of technology strategy at large corporations and venture companies alike (Pisano, 1991).

Companies adopting vertical integration strategies must apply closed, vertically integrated governance structures with internal hierarchies to execute R&D, production, sales, support, and all other business activities in-house. It is also strategically important to exploit potential and form vertically integrated hierarchies of *keiretsu* (conglomerations linked by cross-shareholding) networks, as happened with Japan's auto industry. Meanwhile, companies adopting horizontal specialization strategies, led by IT and digital industries, must designate business activities in their specialist domains in order to license business to, and receive orders from other companies and adopt governance structures characterized by open, flat relationships with other companies. In some cases, vertically integrated companies collaborate with other companies through partnering to realize some business activities structured as a vertical value chain, as the environment requires (Pisano, 2006). In other cases, companies adopt intermediate forms of governance comprising vertical integration to execute outsourcing for some business activities and horizontal specialization. The adopted governance structure depends strongly on its immediate environment and strategic goals. It follows that dynamically transforming corporate boundaries by determining a corporate governance structure appropriate to the environment and conditions is a key theme for the execution of corporate and innovation strategies. After that, the company should define the strategic objectives of constantly competitive products, services, and business models, and implement optimal design (architecture) of the strategy drivers' vertical and horizontal boundary elements to accomplish these objectives.

Generally, for a company's short-term profit orientation, the "efficiency view" is a strong determiner of corporate boundaries. This is based on the thinking of transaction-cost economics and related exchange-efficiency perspectives. For corporate business activities, one element that determines vertical boundaries is the perspective of minimizing governance costs (Williamson, 1975; Coase, 1993; Nickerson and Silverman, 2003). "To minimize governance make or buy" decision costs is also an issue of vertical boundaries between organization and market.

While the "efficiency view" puts great weight on determining a company's corporate boundaries, my surveys have revealed different elements at work among Japanese companies in determining boundaries. Santos and Eisenhardt (2005) considered four management drivers determining corporate boundaries, and proposed non-efficiency conceptions as a new agenda for boundaries research. They discussed the relationship between boundary decisions and organizational features of flexibility, and capacity to inspire, coherence. They also expressed the possibilities for new research in this area. Reflecting Sanrtos and Eisenhardt's study, this chapter proposes the concepts of new creativity and expands the dialectic views for these non-efficiency conceptions.

2.1.1 *The creativity view*

Unlike the horizontally specialized Western model (see Chapter 4), Japan's consumer electronics, communications and telecommunications equipment, semiconductor, and machine tools manufacturers independently create new products from business activities springing from vertically integrated internal networks. In recent years, these companies have also promoted integration of core knowledge outside the company by building external networks to pursue joint development with other companies (including competitors). Moreover, mobile phone businesses led by NTT DoCoMo's i-mode and others are building original business models springing from vertically integrated value chains by constructing external networks of content providers, communications carriers, and vendors, and dramatically growing the market (see Chapter 6). Japan's mobile phone carriers, moreover, create new products, services, and business models through collaboration and joint investment arising from strategic alliances with other industry sectors aimed at expanding horizontal boundaries. These cases involve the corporate strategy view to create new knowledge innovatively, flexibly, and independently that embraces the concepts of flexibility and the capacity to inspire possessed by the corporate organizations above. In this book, I use the term *creativity view* to describe this phenomenon.

The *creativity view* is a key factor in promoting a company's vertical integration. It enables Japanese corporations to upgrade their path-dependent knowledge through vertical integration while absorbing new knowledge and accelerating the integration of their own knowledge through collaboration that builds external networks with external partner corporations. Japanese companies absorb external partners' ideas by assessing the knowledge and business models of other companies based on vertical integration strategies, and raise the originality of products, services, and business models through connect and development strategies (Chesbrough, 2003, 2006; Huston and Sakkab, 2006). In this way, the *creativity view* determines a company's corporate boundaries, and becomes the core concept leading to the vertical value chain model established through vertical integration, which promotes the creation of competitive new products and services as well as innovative business models.

2.1.2 *The dialectic view*

The "coherence" mentioned by Santos and Eisenhardt (2005) corresponds to the notion of dialectical integration aiming to fuse heterogeneous concepts with a sense of harmony and unification. Coherence enables robust business models to be built consistently, promotes coordination and collaboration among stakeholders, and enables the construction of win-win relationships. In this book, the strategy view that leads to corporate strategic behavior creating winwin co-evolutions models based on this kind of coherence is termed the *dialectic view*.

The *dialectic view* is based on the Hegelian approach, which is a practical method for resolving conflict within an organization. Dialectic was applied to organization theory, stimulating discussion based on absolute truths or morality in devotion to the community or in the process of corporate reform. Peng and Nisbett (1999) analyzed the psychological reactions that could easily result from two apparently contradictory propositions while risking crises that allow contradictions. They also proposed 'dialectical thinking in a broad sense' that judged parts of both propositions to be correct. This sort of dialectical thought has also been reported in literature on institutional theory, strategic alliances, and corporate management (Benson, 1997; Das and Ten, 2000; Kodama, 2004).

The *dialectic view* promotes the construction of win-win co-evolution models among stakeholders to build vertical boundaries. i-mode, for example, built a win-win business model around the vertical boundaries of content providers, communications carriers, and equipment vendors, to create network externality effects (Shapiro and Varian, 1998). Sony and Nintendo also created win-win business models around the vertical boundaries of game software manufacturers, game console manufacturers, and equipment vendors (Kodama, 2007c).

Moreover, the *dialectic view* enables the co-evolution models among different industries to create new products, services, and business models and expand horizontal boundaries. Japanese mobile phone carriers, for example, are building business formations that demonstrate mutual business model's synergy effects through joint ventures with portal sites such as Google and record companies in the music distribution business, and alliance strategies and investment alliances with broadcast business aimed at merging communications and broadcasting. Furthermore, while the use of mobile phone e-money and IC cards is spreading in Japan and elsewhere in Asia, Japan's mobile phone carriers are maximizing the value of stakeholders' individual business models through partnership and collaboration vis-à-vis horizontal boundaries with heterogeneous industries including finance, credit cards, retail, and railroads. The creation of new business models from the co-evolution models of co-existence and co-prosperity among stakeholders originates from the strategic behavior of a company's *dialectic view* (see Chapter 6 for details). The *dialectic view* determines a company's corporate boundaries, and forms the core concept leading to the co-evolution model that promotes the creation of win-win business models crossing various industries.

2.2 *Dynamic human networks*

Dynamic human networks operate on a micro-level as a key organizational platform for the knowledge integration process. Studies of network theory shows new findings about it (Motter, 2004; Watts, 2003; Barabashi, 2002). Networks comprising people, groups, organizations, and companies form complementary relationships with formal organizations. These networks become an important platform for practitioners to facilitate knowledge-based activities. Network formation among practitioners, groups, organizations, and companies has a major impact on the integration of information and knowledge (Tushman, 1979; Owen-Smith and Powell, 2004; Lin and Kulatilaka, 2006). The dynamic formation of networks is also essential for companies to constantly acquire new competences (Kodama, 2005). These networks must dynamically rebuild in response to changes in the environment and strategic behavior (Kodama, 2006).

In this book, I will look at "small-world structures" (Watts and Strogatz, 1998) as clusters forming one of the leading network topologies. I will show how networks of small-world structure clusters inside and outside the company drive the strategy and management drivers (the first aspect of the concept) and become key infrastructure enabling the knowledge integration process.

Existing research suggests that networks of people, groups, and organizations are important platforms facilitating information and knowledge-based activities; and the form of organizations and networks has a major impact on the transmission of information and knowledge (Owen-Smith and Powell, 2004; Lin and Kulatilaka, 2006). Network formation is also essential for companies to acquire sustainable organizational capabilities (Kodama, 2005), and these networks must be dynamically rebuilt in response to changes in the environment and strategic behavior (Kodama, 2006).

The network theory of nodes (individuals, groups of people, organizations of groups, and others), network ties, and several network topologies (such as small-world and scale-free structures) imparts important insights into practitioner's behaviors across internal and external corporate boundaries, and the relationships among practitioners. Moreover, the practitioners' thinking and behaviors involved in the formation of human networks propel management drivers and become important triggers for implementing the knowledge integration process.

Networks are broadly classified as centralized and decentralized (Albert and Barabasi, 2000; Ahuja and Carley, 1999). A centralized network suits the vertical and efficient implementation of routine information, knowledge flow and interaction in cases where information and knowledge are sent from central to peripheral nodes (Albert and Barabasi, 2000; Tushman, 1979). Meanwhile, a decentralized network (which may have smaller hubs) may suit network formation facing uncertain conditions and new challenges (Watts, 2003).

Decentralized network formation requires tight clustering and autonomy of work groups. This structural design enhances information and knowledge exchange at the work-group level, and effectively facilitates mutual coordination and adjustments among peripheral local nodes (Tushman, 1979). Such local cluster coordination and collaboration also reduce the information processing load assigned to the central node, as peripheral nodes do not need to communicate directly with the central authority whenever a decision-making situation arises.

Small-world networks featuring a high degree of local clustering with few links between any two nodes, were found to enhance mutual dependence among cluster nodes and facilitate communication, coordination, and collaboration among practitioners, especially when tight collaboration was required to connect value chains among the organizations (Newman, 2004). The availability of such short paths for "bridging" nodes enhances network coordination and collaboration, particularly when interacting among organizations (Watts, 2003; Baum, Rowley, and Shipilov, 2004). Moreover, such network properties are effective when creating new ideas and innovations in complex and heterogeneous organizations (Braha and Bar-Yam, 2004).

Small-world networks also deliver robust network formations to the organization with regard to sudden environmental change and destruction including concentrated information traffic, excessive overload, bottlenecks, and unexpected incidents (Newman, 2004; Shah, 2000). In 1997, for example, when Aisin prominent Toyota supplier, faced a destructive crisis, Toyota and associated suppliers cooperated to build emergent interorganizational networks to avoid disaster. This is a true example Reflecting the action of a truly small-world network formed among suppliers centered on Toyota (Watts, 2003; Nishiguchi and Beaudet, 1998).

Strategic communities (SCs) are formed cross-functionally by practitioners from different organizations and companies. The SCs themselves create small-world structures (see Figure 1.2). The SCs differs from the Communities of Practice (COP) (Wenger, 1998) in the knowledge boundaries (such as different thought worlds and specialist fields) existing among the actors that form SCs. From a social network theory perspective, SCs correspond to clusters and cliques of people as the smallest nodes (Roethlisberger and Dickson, 1939; Roethlisberger, 1977). Cliques are assemblies where practitioners share and exchange information, context, and knowledge, while SCs are assemblies (teams or projects) that conduct simple exchange of information among actors and also give birth to dynamic new context and knowledge in response to any environmental change.

SCs are small-world networks comprising groups of practitioners with diverse specialties who achieve new innovations aimed at solving problems, discovering new tasks, and implementing creative strategies. Small-world networks feature short connections between nodes (people being the smallest node units) and local clustering. Short paths among practitioners acting as nodes attached to disparate organizations enable access to practitioners operating within the company and those belonging to other companies, including customers. Each node in a small-world network is embedded in a local cluster. This local clustering enhances the possibilities of fostering reliable accessibility (White and Houseman, 2003). A small-world network can be formed either by randomly rewiring a portion of an existing regular network or attaching each new node to a "neighborhood" that already exists (Watts and Strogatz, 1998).

Figure 1.2 corresponds what are known in social network theory as the two-mode (bipartite) and affiliation networks (Wasserman, S. and Faust, K. 1994; Faust, 1997; Watts, 2003). I would like to focus, especially, on the dynamically changing SC and networked SC formations that Watts (2003) called "group interlock networks." Watts (2003) used this term based on the actors connected in specific contexts, but in the real business world, actors (practitioners) subjectively and independently form specific-context groups and embed other actors (practitioners) in these groups by extending the

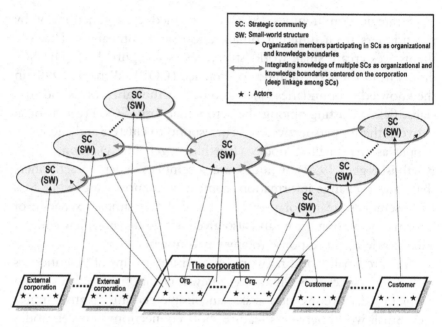

Figure 1.2   Knowledge Integration Through Uniting Boundaries (graphic): Group Interlock Network.

links among them. Accordingly, these SC groups change dynamically in response to context while forming and transforming the networked SC formations.

Practitioners' activities dynamically rebuild SCs on a daily basis. They also participate in multiple SCs to share information, context, and knowledge, and transfer them to other SCs in which they operate to share them once more. This process forms the group interlock network type of networked SC. Within the framework of this network, SCs can be recognized as corresponding to nodes and hubs. Practitioners belonging to SCs as nodes and hubs (inside and outside the company) dynamically bridge the multiple, diverse SCs, and create or link networks among SCs. As a result, multiple SCs become integrated into one network to make new context and knowledge. Practitioners deliberately create networks of multiple SCs among various organizations inside and outside the company, and bind them closely to develop new products and build new business processes (see Figure 1.2).

The creation of SCs among different organizations and specialties within the internal divisions of Japan's consumer electronics, communications and equipment, semiconductor, and machine tool manufacturers integrates internal knowledge and Telecommunications creates vertically integrated business models unique to Japanese companies. The construction of these networked SCs also leads to the absorption of external knowledge (of specialist partners in each horizontally specialized business layer) and horizontal integration of external knowledge. Networked SCs become the basis of the *knowledge integration model*, with which networked SCs integrate knowledge internally and externally (see Figure 1.1). The New IDMs (Integrated Device Manufacturers) among Japan's semiconductor manufacturers (see Chapter 4) also become *knowledge integration models* by forming networked SCs in the same way.

The success of Japan's mobile phone business represented by i-mode and others (Kodama, 2002) owes much to the small-world network SCs inside DoCoMo formed among the entrepreneurial and traditional organizations, and the multiple small-world network SCs formed by external partner companies and companies in different industries. For DoCoMo, the key is in forming small-world network clusters of SCs to extend links with the right external partners. The birth of the i-mode business model arose from the formation of extensive small-world networks among internal and external partners and with companies from different industries, and from DoCoMo collaborating with these networks to co-create new business models. The formation of small-world structure networks (networked SCs) inside and outside the company, based on the case of DoCoMo, accelerated the knowledge integration process and became an important element in co-evolving new business models (ecosystems) in the mobile phone business.

2.3 *Knowledge architectural thinking*

Based on the empirical case studies of the past and those presented in this book, I will explain as well as how SCs and networked SCs form how they integrate different kinds of knowledge. These issues are significant because the network structure of the small-world SCs determines the pattern of the knowledge integration process. I will apply a design concept or architectural focus to consider human and organizational network questions of the mechanisms by which SCs and networked SCs form inside and outside the organization, and the pattern of network formation that practitioners form deliberately. The empirical cases I have examined up to now have shown that knowledge integration broadly comprises three kinds of architecture: vertically integrated, horizontally integrated, and linkage relationship as processes implemented by practitioners' knowledge architectural thinking, and that these can be divided into two separate models.

I will briefly discuss the research process from which the architecture of knowledge integration framework is derived. For the vertical value chain model and linkage relationship architecture, I have analyzed mutual relationships (degree of vertical integration) among business activities within the company, transactional relationships (including contractual content, contract lengths, and power dynamics), sharing of knowledge among companies (degree of information sharing and collaboration), and value networks building business models. For the multi-layered model, I have analyzed the structure of project organizations within the company. For the horizontal value chain and complementary models, I have analyzed business model formations through strategic corporate alliances and joint development, and the processes and the degree of knowledge sharing needed to achieve them.

2.3.1 *Vertically integrated architecture*

Vertically integrated architecture involves the vertically integrated formation of SCs. These can be divided into multi-layered and vertical value chain models (see Table 1.1).

- **Multi-layered model**

A multi-layered model is a strategic community hierarchy where practitioners from various sections within the company form multiple,

Table 1.1 Vertical Integrated Architecture.

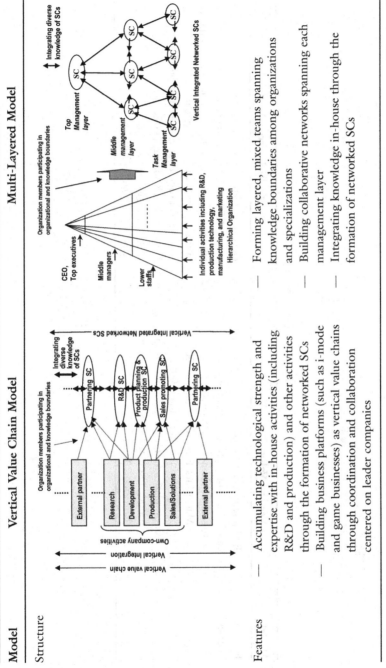

Model	Vertical Value Chain Model	Multi-Layered Model
Structure		
Features	— Accumulating technological strength and expertise with in-house activities (including R&D and production) and other activities through the formation of networked SCs — Building business platforms (such as i-mode and game businesses) as vertical value chains through coordination and collaboration centered on leader companies	— Forming layered, mixed teams spanning knowledge boundaries among organizations and specializations — Building collaborative networks spanning each management layer — Integrating knowledge in-house through the formation of networked SCs

(Continued)

Table 1.1　(*Continued*)

Model	Vertical Value Chain Model	Multi-Layered Model
Empirical cases	1. Building organizational and competitive capabilities through vertical integration of digital consumer electronics — Matsushita Electric (Kodama, 2007a) — Sharp, Cannon (Kodama, 2007c) 2. Business platforms for vertical value chain — i-mode (Kodama, 2002), PlayStation (Kodama, 2007c)	1. Developing i-mode & 3G services — NTT DoCoMo (Kodama, 2007a) 2. Successful examples of new product development in the communications device field — Fujitsu (See Figure 5) – Mitsubishi Electric (Kodama, 2007c) 3. Toyota's TQM promotion activities (Kodama, 2007c)

cross-functional SCs; and these SCs form structuration networks at management level. Multi-layered models are frequently observed in cases of large-scale projects and new product developments (NPDs). With the NPD multilayered model, for example, professionals in various departments and specialist fields develope the target product (such as general architecture design, individual subsystem designs, software and hardware development, and production technologies) and cooperate to form SCs at each management level. These SCs will form further hierarchies. This happens because product architecture relies on function and structure (each component being integral or module, or a hybrid of the two), and the overall system is broken down into numerous layered subsystems (Baldwin and Clark, 2000; Clark, 1985; Simon, 1996).

In the empirical case of Fujitsu's NPD (Kodama, 2005a), knowledge integration of different technology elements were required. They included image and voice compression, semiconductor design and software, communications interfaces, computing software, and human interfaces. Fujitsu has absorbed other companies' technology by collaborating with external partners (US companies) while forming multilayered models within Fujitsu to mobilize knowledge of the disparate technological elements distributed within the company (see Figure 1.3).

Fujitsu's models contain numerous SCs. SC-1 comprises a team of leaders (top management) who are in charge of related divisions at Fujitsu that has complete authority to formulate and execute the new product and service developments. SC-2 comprises a team of senior middle management that pursues studies of system architecture. SC-3 comprises a senior middle management team that examines the connectivity between new products and mobile phones. SC-2-1 and SC-2-2 comprise middle management teams for the studies of software and hardware architecture that form the core of each new product development. SC-2-3 comprises middle management teams that study system integration and application development for new products. SC-2-1-1, SC-2-1-2, SC-2-2-1, and SC-2-2-2 comprise task management teams (including staffs of Fujitsu's subsidiary companies) that study detailed architecture and sub-systems of hardware

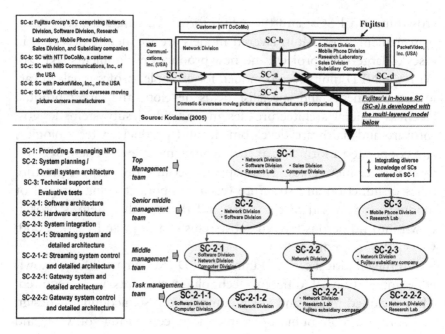

Figure 1.3   Multi-Layered Model within Fujitsu.

and software components forming the core of each new product development[1].

For NTT DoCoMo's large-scale i-mode development and introduction project, DoCoMo has formed multilayered and hierarchical networked SCs that are vertically integrated in-house to create a value chain extending from R&D service introduction (see Figure 1.4).

A cross-functional decision-making team named the Mobile Gateway Service Introduction Promotion Committee (SC-1) was formed from the top management of each section. The team held discussions to determine such matters as i-mode's final service

---

[1] This kind of multi-layered model is observed in manufacturers' large-scale development projects. See, for example, Kodama (2007c) for the case of Mitsubishi Electric's product development.

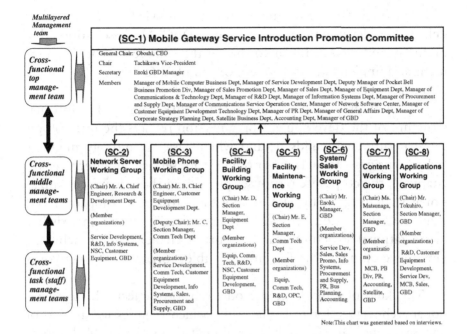

Figure 1.4 Multi-Layered Model within DoCoMo.

architecture, development and facility investments; development schedules and human resources; and selection of development partners and key external strategic alliances. Other teams were created to operate under the final decision-making team (SC-1), which covered i-mode platform architecture development (Network Server Working Group: SC-2); Internet connectible mobile phone development (Mobile Phone Working Group: SC-3); network equipment construction (Facility Building Working Group: SC-4); network operation and maintenance development (Facility Maintenance Working Group: SC-5); marketing strategy (System/ Sales Working Group: scSC-6); content strategy (Content Working Group: SC-7); and applications development (Applications Working Group: SC-8). These SC clusters were formed in layered structures comprising top, middle, and task management teams. The multiple SCs were organically linked and consolidated, and context and knowledge required for service development shared and integrated.

This enabled DoCoMo to create the knowledge for the new deliverable development the i-mode. DoCoMo also adopted a multi-layered model similar to that of the i-mode for the development and implementation system of i-mode's following 3G mobile phone service.

As Henderson and Clark (1990) indicated, the internal structure of the development organization reflects the technological structure that builds it, and when basic technology migrates (when business models or product and service architecture are charged), the corporate responses protecting the existing organizational structure. In by DoCoMo's case, too, the company faced significant limitations to achieve its objectives with an existing organizational structure geared to major challenges, but achieved new development by forming flexible, organic SC networks in-house.

This kind of multi-layered model can form effectively organizational architecture for realizing NPD, which requires integration of diverse technologies (as in the case of Fujitsu) and large-scale business models, such as that of i-mode. With this multi-layered model, autonomous individual SCs comprising groups of professionals guarantee creativity and flexibility when presenting specific duties to achieve new product development or business models. Meanwhile, the SC hierarchies have the merit of implementing duties efficiently with rapid decision-making.

- **The vertical value chain model**

The vertical value chain model involves forming SCs to coordinate and collaborate on individual tasks and then developing them as vertically integrated SCs in order to integrate each R&D, production technology, manufacturing, and management tasks. Empirical cases of networked SCs achieving vertical integration in-house have been reported among Japanese manufacturing companies. The creation of networks among diverse organizations and specialist fields by consumer electronics and communications equipment manufacturers integrates internal knowledge, and creates the distinctive vertical integration of the Japanese corporate model.

This vertical value chain model also functions as a strong-tied intercorporate network for Japan's mobile phone and automobile industries. Leading companies such as DoCoMo and Toyota possess leadership and bargaining power in technologies and markets through networked SCs that build vertical value chain models with high degree of information and knowledge The intercorporate network among Japan's automobile (including Toyota) and parts manufacturers is a prime example of this (Amasaka, 2004; Dyer and Hatch, 2004).

The above-mentioned i-mode business model is made up of vertically integrated value chains comprising DoCoMo, mobile handset manufacturers, and content providers. When DoCoMo was developing its mobile phones, it determined the detailed handset functions, the technology architecture and specifications to achieve them; and the handset manufacturers delivered the completed products to DoCoMo based on these. Information and knowledge was closely shared among DoCoMo and the handset manufacturers through the strong networked SC's links. Moreover, DoCoMo had full authority over what content providers and content to carry on its official i-mode site, and controlled a large number of CPs. Coordinating huge numbers of CPs through vertical integration became a key task for DoCoMo.

Underlying the success of Japan's mobile phone business led by i-mode (Kodama, 2002) was the formation of small-world SC networks among entrepreneurial and traditional organizations within DoCoMo, among handset manufacturers and CPs outside DoCoMo. For DoCoMo, the issue of which external partners to link to and form small-world network clusters of SCs with was significant. The formation of such networks inside and outside the corporation lay at the heart of i-mode's business model. DoCoMo collaborated with external partners to create new business models. The vertical value chain model arising from the formation of networked SCs inside and outside the corporation, centered in DoCoMo, accelerated the knowledge integration process and became a key element in promoting a new co-evolution business model (business ecosystem) for mobile phones.[2]

- **Vertically integrated architecture and the creativity view**

The distinctive creativity view of the Japanese company promotes a vertically integrated architectural structure. Japanese companies, especially, achieve a general mobilization of the knowledge possessed by dispersed individuals and promote its integration by forming net-worked SCs through multi-layered models aimed at original technological innovation. Moreover, Japanese companies are enhancing creativity to develop new technologies and respond to technological change by accumulating the tacit knowledge of experience and expertise among individual tasks through the vertical value chain model. The vertical value chain models arising from networked SCs across companies have become elements in the formation of original mobile phone services, such as i-mode, and the original business platform of Toyota's production system.

2.3.2 *Horizontally integrated architecture*

Horizontally integrated architecture refers to horizontally integrated SCs which are divide into the horizontal value chain and the complementary models (see Table 1.2).

---

[2] The DoCoMo-centered "Small-World Network" (SW) forms hubs, and a structure resembling a scale-free network (Barabasi, 2002) comprising a huge number of links is created. Barabasi (2002) also observes a similar trend, in which 80 percent of all World Wide Web connections are "occupied" by only 20 percent of "hub" websites. Realistically, however, the number of business-related partners is limited. At the same time, a company of micro-practitioners thinking subjectively must discuss the pros and cons as well as transaction costs of building relationships with partners. This is why the networked SC formation differs somewhat (Watts, 203) from the highly centralized, scale-free network (Cole, J.R., and Cole, S., 1973; Barabasi and Albert, 1999); R. Cole and S. Cole, Social Stratification in Science, University of Chicago Press, Chicago (1973); A-L. Barabasi and R. Albert, Emergence of scaling in random networks. Science, 286 509–512 (1999).

Table 1.2 Horizontal Integrated Architecture.

Model	Horizontal Value Chain Model	Complementary Model
Structure	Integrating diverse knowledge of SCs ↕ Horizontal Vale Chain → Horizontal Integrated Networked SCs → SC ... SC Company A ... Company Z Organization members participating in organizational and knowledge boundaries Inter-corporate networks created from different industries	Integrating diverse knowledge of SCs ↕ Horizontal Integration → Horizontal Integrated Networked SCs → SC ... SC Company A ... Company Z Organization members participating in organizational and knowledge boundaries Inter-corporate networks created from the same and related industries
Features	— New knowledge integration through the formation of networked SCs among companies in different industries — Formation of new business platforms (such as mobile-EC services and telematics) among companies in different industry types	— Knowledge integration through the formation of networked SCs with externally distributed and in-house knowledge — New knowledge integration through collaborating in same or related (neighboring business domains) industries

(Continued)

Table 1.2   (*Continued*)

Model	Horizontal Value Chain Model	Complementary Model
Empirical cases	1. Mobile e-commerce — NTT DoCoMo (Kodama, 2007a) 2. Networks among companies in different industries — Network formation centered on NTT DoCoMo and au (KDDI) (see Figure 6)	1. NTT DoCoMo's international strategy — Global development of Conexus Mobile Alliance and i-mode (Kodama, 2007a) 2. Examples of successful new product development in communications device and machine tool fields — Fujitsu (Kodama, 2005)(see Figure 5) — Fanuc, NEC (Shibata and Kodama, 2007) 3. Formation of supplier networks — Supplier's learning networks (Dyer and Hatch, 2004) — The Toyota Group and the Aisin Fire (Nishiguchi *et al*, 1998)

- **The horizontal value chain model**

The horizontal value chain model involves building networked SCs to extend a company's existing business into new domains and build new value chains. It determines a company's horizontal boundaries with regard to the products and services that a company should possess and the kinds of business that create value through diversity. The formation of small-world networks with companies in different industries promotes access to heterogeneous knowledge and dialog at knowledge boundaries. Creative abrasion and productive friction at these boundaries inspires new knowledge and enhances creativity to realize new business models. In recent years, new business models including e-money and credit cards used in mobile phones, integration of communications and broadcasting (merging mobile phone TV broadcasting and the Internet business), and integration of mobile phones and automobiles (telematics) have arisen from the building of horizontal value chains from networked SCs formed across heterogeneous industries (see Figure 1.5).

Japanese mobile carriers DoCoMo and au (KDDI) are actively promoting strategic and investment alliances with the finance, credit card, broadcasting, railroad, retail, advertising, and auto industries while also collaborating with business leaders in the Internet field, such as Google, to learn new, value-added mobile Internet services. The knowledge integration process arising from the formation of business networks, including these cross-industry networks, becomes an important element in the building of horizontal value chains aimed at the creation of new business models.

- **Complementary model**

The complementary model comprises collaboratively networked SCs with relationships equivalent to external partners in the same industries or neighboring business domains. It has few of the hierarchy elements seen in vertically integrated architecture, although it features cases of shared knowledge disseminated among external partners and shared development of new products and services with equivalent

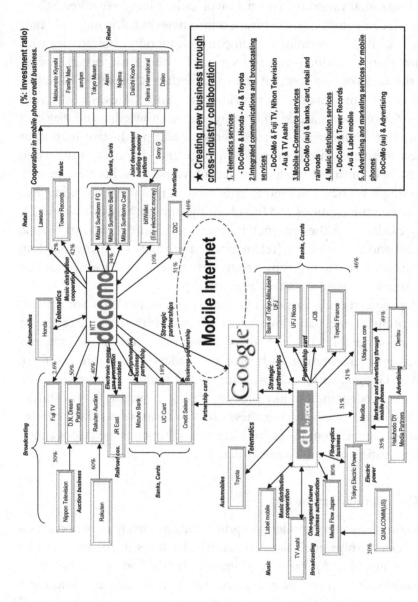

Figure 1.5   Building a Horizontal Value Chain Through Corporate Networks in Different Industries.

connections. DoCoMo, for example, is using this complementary model to extensively spread knowledge of i-mode and 3G mobile phone systems created and accumulated within DoCoMo to communications carriers in other countries. In Asia DoCoMo is forming an Asian-Pacific Mobile Alliance (the Conexus Mobile Alliance) with Far EasTone Telecommunications Co. Ltd. (Taiwan), Hutchison Essar Ltd. (India), Hutchison Telecommunications Hong Kong Limited (Hong Kong and Macao), KT Freetel Co. Ltd. (South Korea), PT Indosat Tbk (Indonesia), StarHub Ltd. (Singapore), and True Move Company Limited (Thailand) Moreover, DoCoMo agrees to cooperate in the areas of global roaming and corporate services. The companies participating in this Asia's largest carrier alliance, which has a subscriber base of around 100 million, are making progress on creating full services for multinational companies and travelers among partner nations and regions, and enhancing convenience for the customer. A further aim is to strengthen the competitiveness of each alliance member.

This complementary model also applies to the new product development of Japanese manufacturers, such as Fujitsu, NEC, and Fanuc (Shibata and Kodama, 2007), through joint development with competitors and associates; the recent case of Sony and Samsung Electronics jointly procuring liquid-crystal panels; and joint development among Japanese manufacturers, such as Hitachi with Canon, and Sony with Toshiba, of organic electroluminescent (EL) next-generation panels. The empirical case of Fujitsu's NPD (Kodama, 2005), mentioned above, achieved success through collaboration arising out of networked SC formation with multiple external partners (see Figure 1.3). Manufacturers such as these in the areas of consumer electronics, communications equipment, and machine tools vertically integrate knowledge arising from the formation of in-house networked SCs, and the structure of the networked SCs reaching outside the company absorbs the knowledge of external partners (specialist partners in horizontally specialized business layers) and integrates it horizontally (see Figure 1.6). The networked SCs in the case of Fujitsu (Figure 1.3) become the basis of the *knowledge integration model* integrating knowledge inside and outside the company. In the automobile

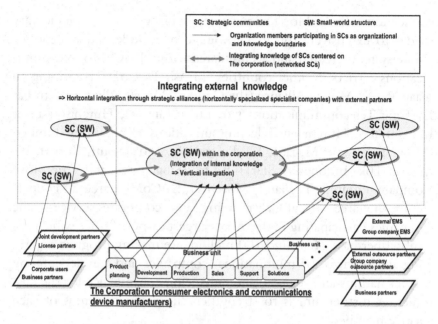

Figure 1.6   Formation of Networked Strategic Communities: Knowledge Integration Model of Japanese Manufacturers.

industry, moreover, the continuously forming learning networks (see the empirical case in Table 1.2) among Toyota's suppliers are an example of the complementary model. The case of other suppliers responding to a crisis — when the factory of Toyota supplier-Aisin-burned down, by cooperating to form small-world network SCs and provide independent backup to Aisin, can also be interpreted as an example of this complementary model (see the empirical case in Table 1.2).

- **Horizontally integrated architecture and the dialectic view**

The distinctive dialectic view of Japanese companies (mentioned above) promotes the creation of horizontally integrated architecture. Japanese companies promote the integration of heterogeneous knowledge by forming networked SCs with partners, including companies from different industries, aimed at building business models with win-win relationships. Moreover, the dialectic view promotes coordination and collaboration among partners (including competitors) arising from the creation of the complementary model, and helps to realize NPDs and joint ventures. Furthermore, co-creation among companies from different industries arising from the building of the horizontal value chain model creates new business models and goes on to promote co-evolution over entire new industries.

2.3.3 *Linkage relationship architecture*

I think of "boundaries" as "knowledge platforms" where practitioners share dynamic contexts (time, place, and relationship) and create new knowledge. SCs as boundaries correspond in space-time to sharing contexts by interacting with others, and transforming production by transforming these contexts. The spaces and times where the sharing of tacit knowledge and dialogues and actions occur are also SCs.

Organizations and individuals are dialectically related. Practitioners transform organizations through the power held by individuals while maintaining circulatory connections between the time-space of "here and now" (SC) and practical consciousness, which comprises tacit knowledge within the motive context, and organizations. People are restricted by the organizations they themselves create, while also holding the practical power to change the appearances of these organizations through their own actions (Giddens, 1984; Giddens and Pierson, 1998). The SCs are the platforms that connect individuals organizations with, and the influence of people's "microexistence" impacts the macro-structures of organizations, companies, heterogeneous industries, and society as a whole through SC formation (or dissolution) and consolidation.

Accordingly, SCs take key positions as micro-macro linkages for social networks and as analytical units from the foci of how individuals operating through relationships with other individuals, organizations, SCs, companies, and industries form and link SCs, and how they influence corporate performance through the creation and accumulation of social capital (Coleman, 1988; Burt, 1997; Nahapiet and Ghoshal, 1998; Cohen and Prusak, 2000); and conversely, how the individuals are themselves influenced.

SC-driven social capital is created as knowledge capital from knowledge management flow. SCs become important in clarifying the process whereby heterogeneous knowledge transcends SC borders and becomes integrated. SCs are also practically significant from the perspective of practitioners somehow creating new knowledge by forming and linking SCs.

A new insight gained from the i-mode development case (see Figure 1.5) is the existence of diverse, layered SCs with constantly changing contexts and network structures that have formed and linked as practitioners subjectively operate on the environment (including customers) and other parties within the organization. Practitioners undertake SC formation and linkage deliberately (or emergently). In the cases of Fujitsu and DoCoMo, especially, new product development in high-tech fields has recently been pressured by the need to merge and integrate heterogeneous technologies. The technological innovations in the past closely pursued and developed specialist knowledge. However. but many cases of merging different technology fields to achieve new product and service development derived from brand-new ideas are now occurring.

A key question is how to integrate diverse, distributed knowledge (from a technological viewpoint, this is also a question of how to integrate knowledge from diverse technological fields). Knowledge integration requires networked accumulation of individual knowledge crossing SC boundaries. In other words, it requires connecting distributed SCs in networks and deeply embedding the distributed knowledge in each SC. As with the dynamic human network mentioned in section 2.2, social network theory also interprets SCs as cliques composed of practitioners (assemblies of actors with close mutual ties), with the network connections among SCs corresponding to ties.

Practitioners committing to multiple SCs play a central role in knowledge integration linking SCs. Integrating heterogeneous knowledge requires practitioners to deeply understand and share tacit explicit knowledge in each SC (knowledge sharing), and the deep embedding of shared knowledge in networks crossing SC borders (the element of deep embeddedness is key) (Kodama 2005a, 2005b).

In particular, the sharing of tacit knowledge requires SCs sharing deep networked contexts to be linked with strong ties.

With i-mode and other cases of service development, SCs bound with strong ties, and deeply embedded diverse knowledge to create new knowledge in the form of new products and services from merged technologies. Thus, building SC networks with strong ties is a key initiative for integrating diverse knowledge; and practitioners take these strong-tied SC relationships into account.

According to social network theory, the weak ties enable bridge-building toward heterogeneous information (Granovetter, 1973). Moreover, Burt's "structural hole" (1992) indicates that actors in weak ties with structural holes are likely to access new information and grasp new business opportunities. Considering the cases where the construction of weak-tied SC networks is an effective means is important (see Figure 1.7).

The i-mode business model arose from the merging of diverse knowledge in such areas as mobile phone, technology platform, and content development. In the first two areas, various SCs were established and strong ties were formed inside and outside DoCoMo organization.

Meanwhile, with regard to the development of diverse content (a wide range including text, games, positioning data, music and video

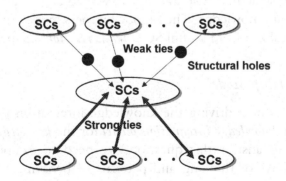

Relationships between SCs

Figure 1.7   Linkage Relationship Architecture.

distribution, and recently 2D bar code, e-money services such as i-mode FeliCa), DoCoMo is no longer building close network relations with specific content providers (although DoCoMo undertakes deep knowledge sharing for content providers on DoCoMo's official i-mode site). It is rather creating SC networks with weak-tied content providers and targeting opportunities for new content business arising from access to new content data.

Looking at the background to the realization of the i-mode FeliCa, the world's first e-money service for mobile phones, rather than begin by sustaining close network relations only with the Sony group that promotes FeliCa to develop new business, DoCoMo has maintained weak-tied relationships with various companies, including Sony, to explore future mobile phone e-money services. By effectively filling this structural hole, DoCoMo and Sony's practitioners can both access new information and knowledge, and create the knowledge to learn new services.

In the area of "knowledge architecture" to achieve knowledge integration, building both strong- and weak-tied SC networks are key initiatives for developing new business; and practitioners need to deliberately consider the co-establishing or exploitation of both strong- and weak-tied SC relationships. I call it the *linkage relationship architecture* of knowledge integration. It involves maintaining strong ties while forming further weak-tied SC networks, and then bridging the structural hole in a timely way to absorb and integrate heterogeneous knowledge. The i-mode business model can be said to have been realized from skillful SC *linkage relationship architecture*.

2.4 *Leadership Model*

What is the source driving the knowledge integration process and building the *knowledge integration model* for the *knowledge integration firm*? To answer this question, we need to examine closely distinctive ways of thinking and patterns of behaving of Japanese people.

Certain conditions that have characterized Japan as a nation, including its climate, have contributed to the formation of an inherent Japanese culture and consciousness. Views and analyses from two research streams can be used to explain the backbone of Japanese consciousness. The first Research stream focuses on Shinto, as described in Japan's classical historical and mythical texts, Kojiki (Chamberian, 2005; Phillippi, 1977) and Nihonshoki (Aston, 2006). Prior to its establishment as a nation state predating the period of Shotoku Taishi, Japan's geographical isolation as an island nation meant that it was rarely exposed to outside influences. In this environment, a localized religion that celebrated the worship of ancestral gods and eventually developed into Shinto was establishing solid foundations. The second Research stream concerns Buddhism (Schock, 2002) which was officially introduced to Japan in 538. Shotoku Taishi (574–622) (Como, 2007; Bodiford, 2003) embraced Buddhism in his youth; and after becoming regent, he incorporated the teachings of Buddha into a constitution (the Seventeen Article Constitution) as a framework for governing the state, thereby establishing for the first time a basic foundation for a Japanese state. This act was a milestone in the establishment of distinctive consciousness and culture of the Japanese people. The constitution was interpreted by some as an effort to integrate, or syncretize Shinto and Buddhism in order to maintain the stability of the Japanese state.

In his examination of the basic structure of Japanese mythology in the Kojiki, Kawai (2003) indicated that "knowledge of mythology" is important in the lives of human beings, and refers to the structure of Japanese mythology as the "hollow equilibrium structure." According to Kawai, the starting point of the concept of the hollow equilibrium structure lies in the "overall harmony" of the human world. This harmony accepts new ideas and contradictions, and allows individual elements to coexist in harmony within the whole. Rather than the integration of the whole under a central authority or principles based on logical compliance, however, overall harmony refers to an esthetic where the balance of the whole is skillfully achieved.

Although this view may appear to be based on dialectical thinking, it is not a Western model of dialectical logic (the processes of Being, Nothing, and Becoming according to Hegel) but instead resembles Eastern dialectical thinking that attaches importance to the "middle way," which psychologist Richard E. Nisbett (2003) asserts and which I will refer to as the "harmonized dialectic."

At the same time, Takazawa (1996) refers to the "logic of harmony" as a unique and independent sense of order in Japanese culture. Takazawa maintains that this logic prevailed in a mostly subconscious manner, and served to maintain order on the basis of Shinto ideals long before Confucianism and Buddhism arrived in Japan. The logic of harmony, with its enshrinement of the principle that "harmony is to be valued" in Article 1 of Shotoku Taishi's Seventeen Article Constitution, also had a significant impact on the formation of the Japanese State. The logic of harmony therefore became the cornerstone in the building of a society based on oneness in body and spirit, and the development of mutual trust between human beings and the resonance of value (Kodama, 2001).

The second stream, as noted above, is the influence of Buddhism. During the reign of Emperor Tenmu in the late seventh century, the political authority of that period reflected the conflict between Japan's ancient Shinto religion and the foreign religion of Buddhism. Although Taishi had deliberately emphasized Buddhism in the Seventeen Article Constitution, it is thought that the Japanese people of that period did not necessarily embrace Buddhism in their entirety, but rather incorporated those aspects that could be accommodated within the scope of the people's views, which were rooted in Japan's ancient Shinto. This attempt to maintain harmony with Shinto while accommodating Buddhism is believed to have spawned the development of Japanese Buddhism. This religion gradually permeated Japan, and gave rise to an era when Buddhist culture and thought flourished.

One of the key concepts of this Buddhism is the view of "nothingness and self-renunciation." It means not having fixed ideas about ways of thinking and acting. Maintaining and adhering to one's views results in bias and rigidity, ruling out the possibility of further progress and development in a one's life. This way of thinking is based on the premise that human beings are flexible and mobile, and can experience progress and development (Mizuno, 1971). Buddhism takes the view that when this idea of nothingness and self-renunciation is firmly established within a person, it naturally leads to the "way of practice," a principle expressed as the "middle way." Buddhism places importance on actions guided by this practice of the "middle way," which means steering away from left- or right-leaning bias while accepting the merits of both and compensating for the shortcomings of each (Masutani, 1971).

In a broad sense, Buddhism is philosophical anthropology (Mizuno, 1971), and its ideas have much in common with the concept of "practical wisdom" ("practical knowledge") (Kodama, 2007b) in Aristotle's Nichomachean Ethics (Aristotle, 1980). It also bears many similarities to the harmonized dialectic of Shinto, which involves a sense of balance.

So Shinto and Buddhism form the backbone of Japanese thinking and culture, to a style of work that is characteristic of Japanese companies. The logic of harmony in Shinto has created vertically integrated businesses based on teamwork across organizations and companies and commitment inherent to Japanese companies, and the overall harmony and harmonized dialectic thinking in Shinto has given rise to the new business models of knowledge integration unifying different specialist knowledge and organizations and industry-crossing ecosystems (including the example of the mobile phone businesses in this book). Moreover, it has created flexible and autonomous distributed organizational structures, including Panasonic's flat and web and NTT DoCoMo's entrepreneurial organizations to realize knowledge integration and new business models. Moreover, the concept of Buddhism has enhanced the quality of innovative activities such as the "evolution of rules" (development and production), a hands-on approach, and continuous improvement based on creative thinking arising from the distinctive "practical knowledge" of the Japanese (see Figure 1.8).

Therefore, Shinto and Buddhism, the basic philosophies of the Japanese, have become the creative sources for each company's distinctive concepts and corporate culture. In the traditional company established by the Japanese founders, for example, Panasonic, Canon, Sharp, Fujitsu, NEC, Sony, Honda, Toyota, tales of entrepreneurial and innovative spirit are inherited as corporate myths, employees passed on and shared among. In fact, the outstanding Japanese

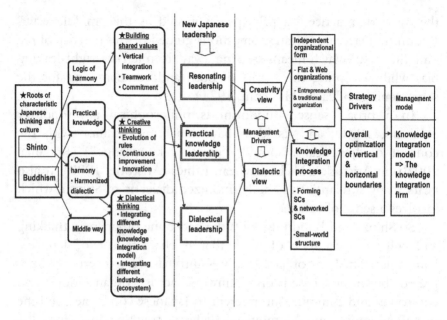

Figure 1.8   Knowledge Integration Model Through New Japanese Leadership.

companies have devoted a significant amount of energy to spread their own corporate cultures and values based on the philosophy of their founders.

Next, from the standpoint of Shinto and Buddhism, this section will examine the leadership styles employed by the business leaders of elite Japanese companies to make corporate myths and stories pervasive and to create, establish, and reform their inherent organizational cultures.

The logic of harmony in Shinto has built trusts and formed shared values among employees, including business leaders, and has become an important element leading to teamwork and commitment which forms the basis of vertically integrated business. These "resonating leadership" elements comprise the thoughts and actions of employees including business leaders, observed at large numbers of Japanese companies. The building of shared value across organizations and companies also promotes creative activities from practitioners and becomes the foundation for dialectically resolving the contradictions of different propositions and themes and positively influences the practical knowledge and dialectical leaderships. The leadership element that stimulates innovative activities from creative thinking arising out of the "practical knowledge" that is the basis of Buddhist philosophy will be referred to as "practical knowledge leadership." This leadership element is frequently seen in areas where Japan currently excels, such as high-tech products, service development, and the manufacturing workplace for consumer electronics, communications equipment, semiconductors, mobile phone businesses, automobiles, and machine tools.

In addition, overall harmony and the harmonized dialectic together with a management philosophy based on the middle-way of Buddhism will be referred to as "dialectical leadership." The element of dialectical leadership comprises business leaders, thinking observed at the development worksites of Japan's cutting-edge hi-tech companies. It also includes the element of organizational capability to simultaneously pursue and synthesize the missions of building *knowledge integration models* arising from coexisting heterogeneous knowledge and ecosystems arising from "win-win" integration across industries.

In this way, "resonating leadership" creates the vertically integrated business structures based on shared values inherent to Japanese companies, and becomes a platform for the *creativity view* of creative thinking and the *dialectic view* of harmonized thinking of business leaders. Furthermore, practical knowledge leadership and dialectical leadership become key elements for stimulating the management drivers, the *creativity* and *dialectic views* (see Figure 1.8). These two management drivers give birth to Japanese companies' specific organizational forms and knowledge integration processes, and generally optimize the strategy drivers for the *knowledge integration firm*.

3 Implications and Conclusion

Japanese companies operating in specific high-tech sectors are globally competitive because they are building their own *knowledge integration models*. Unlike Western management that values horizontally specialized business models concentrating on specific core competences,

Japanese *knowledge integration firms* create integrative competences (Kodama, 2007a) that dialectically integrate knowledge inside and outside the company based on the vertical integration of value chains and industry structures. This is because of the existence of an underlying knowledge integration process through the formation of dynamic and networked SCs, based on the tacit knowledge of the Japanese company.

In contrast to European and American companies, Japanese companies possess a management style that emphasizes tacit rather than explicit knowledge. Japanese management style also emphasizes long-term profits and focuses on creating and sharing tacit knowledge that takes time to acquire, as opposed to Western style that emphasizes the re-use of explicit knowledge in pursuit of short-term profits (Lampel and Bhalla, 2007). The effective sharing of tacit knowledge has been promoted through a common corporate organizational culture and sense of values, and made possible in companies where such elements are widely shared within an organization. This effective sharing in turn promotes the creation of organizational knowledge. In fact, the Japanese companies that achieve excellent results have devoted a significant amount of energy to spread their own corporate culture and values based on the philosophy of their founders.

Sharing the organizational culture and values of a company has created systems and rules particular to that company, and firmly established ways of thinking, views, and patterns of behavior unique to that company in its employees. Toyota's distinctive values, for example, include "wisdom and improvement" and "respect for humanity." Patterns of thinking and behavior have evolved from these values, such as the notion that "water can be wrung even from a dry towel if one applies wisdom," or the idea of "observing production spots without preconceived ideas, as if you are a blank sheet of paper." Again, when considering an object, "One should ask 'Why?' five times over," and "Never be satisfied with a single instance of success but aim higher through continuous improvement." At Honda too, various patterns of thinking and behavior are pervasive among staff, such as the three principles of "Go to the work site, assess the products and conditions, and be realistic." Staff are also asked to "Respect theory, ideas, and time," and to ask, "What is it for, what is the concept, and what are the specifications?" Thus the culture and values inherent to a company create distinctive systems and rules and a distinctive employee style, or mold, which in turn takes root within the organization. Needless to say, distinctive values, culture and style are elements which companies should create independently.

Moreover, the top leaders of any organization are responsible for establishing a corporate culture and promoting the sharing of values among employees; and fulfillment of this role depends heavily on their leadership. Shein (1985) argued that the essence of top-management leadership was to provide management not for the sake of achieving goals but for creating organizational culture, managing it, and even destroying it. Furthermore, Selznick (1957) emphasized the importance of the mythical power of leaders. He argued that the use of myths, stories, and teachings was an effective way to uplift employee's morale and express the company's particular vision and strategic objectives when promoting shared culture and values in an organization. Myths and stories also play a role in creating a decision-making consensus in strategy formulation and implementation in the course of daily corporate activities. Japanese companies' distinctive leadership style, moreover, is rooted in Shinto myths and Buddhist teachings, and has given birth to the "resonating," "practical knowledge," and "dialectical" styles of leadership.

Resonating leadership is the business leaders' ability to establish "resonance of value" and "trust." These qualities form gradually as employees mutually assert their subjectivity and values in the course of dialectical dialog, and discuss strategic visions and goals. A deep dialectical dialog enables the sharing of strategic visions and goals among employees, including the top management. In reality, interpretation differs significantly from one individual to the next, and when this occurs, as in the case of Honda above, management leaders pose the question "Why?" and repeat fundamental questions such as "What is the reason for doing this?." It requires the system to be established and shared among staff. Thus, arriving at a mutual understanding of different interpretations among individuals and sharing values and their resonance generates a sense of unity over the formulation and implementation of corporate strategies.

Practical knowledge leadership, which enables business leaders and staff to practice "what" and "how" and creates new values through the resonance of value and mutual trust, shares high-quality practical knowledge (Lave, 1998; Hutchins, 1991; Brown and Duguid, 1998; Cook and Brown, 1999; Boland and Tenkasi, 1995; Tsoukas, 1997; Spender, 1992; Orr, 1990; Schon, 1983, 1987; Wenger, 1998) among staff, including business leaders, for the purpose of putting into practice optimal decision-making and processes.

The resonating and practical knowledge leadership styles generate knowledge as new value within the organization. These styles can perhaps be viewed as the organizational capability where business leaders form resonance of value and mutual trust, and discover appropriate decision-making and optimal actions, based on practical knowledge, to create new knowledge for implementing individual, specific strategies.

Dialectical leadership, meanwhile, has the aspects of leaders and staff implementing strategies both as a science in an attempt to formulate and implement the corporate strategies analytically and rationally, and as an art and craft to do so creatively and intuitively. Thus corporate management always involves a trade-off between efficiency and creativity, and business leadership aimed at solving this problem is also dialectical leadership.

Business leaders are also required to demonstrate leadership incorporating elements that run counter to the efficiency and creativity of corporate activities. Pursuing efficiency requires the ability to resolve problems and find optimal solutions through an analytical approach, while pursuing creativity requires leaders to nurture the ability to grasp the intangible, imagine and predict, and verify hypotheses through an interpretive or process approach.

When Toyota workers are faced with a discrepancy, they do not adopt an "either/or" but a "both/and" attitude. This perspective enables Toyota to uncompromisingly pursue quality and cost efficiency while successfully producing creative cars like the Lexus, which possess "elegance" and "depth" (Osono, 2004). At Honda and Canon (Kodama, 2007c), Fujitsu (Kodama, 2005), NTT DoCoMo (Kodama, 2007c), Fanuc, and NEC (Shibata and Kodama, 2007), dialectical leadership is the starting point of innovation. The source of dialectical leadership distinct to Japanese companies resides in the dialectical dialog among staff, including the top management, which enables the sharing of deep thoughts and sentiments among staff. In the time and space where the dialectical dialogue transpires, the question, "How will we create it?" is asked rather than the conventional syllogistic, "Does it or does it not exist?" Thus dialectical dialog exploits the productivity of contradiction by delving into the content (meaning). Open thinking among leaders and other staff therefore becomes significant. In concrete terms, it is important to recognize the compatibility of self-assertion and modesty among members. Staff must be aware that they personally make errors and that they use confrontations with others as the medium for developing themselves to a higher level.

This book will take up the future-oriented concept of new Japanese leadership that has been presented in this chapter, and focus on the issue of whether it can be applied to foreign companies. Business leadership is assumed to be affected by environment, business type and style, and traditional organizational culture, and dependent on such factors as the ideas, corporate philosophy, and values of the top management. Meanwhile, it is a fact that Japanese elite companies have achieved success through management based on a sense of values (resonating leadership), practical knowledge (practical knowledge leadership), and dialectical management (dialectical leadership).

The new Japanese leadership examined in this chapter was required both from top management teams and business leaders at the various management levels. The mere presence of a charismatic leader or demonstration of leadership by a top management team is rarely enough for a company to achieve corporate reforms and innovation. Each level of the organization, from the top down, must fulfill its respective role. Business leaders who demonstrate innovative ideas and performance must also be nurtured through practice to establish a management system where multiple business leaders can demonstrate their abilities. This management system relies on the promotion of management based on a sense of values that actualizes the three leadership styles (resonating, practical knowledge, and dialectical management). It is also important to embed deep in organization members the philosophies and visions contained in the corporate myths and stories, based on the ideas of the corporate founders, and so to create, maintain, and transform the unique organizational culture.

2

A Theoretical Framework for Strategic Innovation Capability

1. Radical Innovation and Strategic Change

To acquire a competitive edge and sustain it over a long period, it is clearly important that companies constantly create new products, services, and business models (Jelinek and Schoonhoven, 1990; Morone, 1993; Markides, 2000). Creating and implementing new business models that radically transform conventional products and services and shake up existing business rules induce major strategic changes in the historical flow of traditional large corporations. The major transformation of the mobile phone business with NTT DoCoMo's i-mode (Kodama, 2002; Peltokorpi, Nonaka and Kodama, 2007), Nintendo's DS/Wii game business, and Apple's US developed music distribution business are examples of the creation of co-evolution model, which is a new value chain in the ICT industry.

In recent years, academic research on radical (Leifer *et al.*, 2000), breakthrough (Hargadon, 2003), discontinuous (Kaplan *et al.*, 2003; Laurila, 1998), and disruptive (Christensen and Raynor, 2003) innovation has provided numerous examples of companies taking on challenges to explore new markets and create new technologies. These papers have also presented the accompanying difficulties and the numerous reasons for success or failure. The conclusion is that acquiring the organizational capability to respond rapidly to environmental change, develop new technologies, and promote business development (Broen and Eisenhardt, 1997; Teece *et al.*, 1997; Tushman and Anderson, 1986) is crucial.

Cases have been reported, however, of traditional large companies that were unable to respond well to environment change in numerous industries, including PC markets (Mitchell, 1989), digital photos (Tripsas and Gavetti, 2000), disc drives (Christensen and Bower, 1996), semiconductor exposure apparatus (Henderson and Clark, 1990), and watches (Glasmeter, 1991), and this significantly impacted their performance and chances of survival. The phenomenon is closely connected to the companies' strong dependence on routines that activate specific path-dependent core competences (Nelson and Winter, 1982; Teece, Pisano and Shuen, 1997). If the companies pursue effectively business activities to expand scale and scope, the existing core competences will descend into core rigidities and competence traps and become unable to response swiftly to major environmental changes. (Levinthal, 1991, 1997; Leonard-Barton, 1992; Levitt and March, 1988). Promoting efficient corporate activity restricts task diversity and reduces activities that induce employees to be independently creative (Sutcliffe, Sitkin, and Browning, 2000; Weick, 1995; Levitt and March, 1993).

In the past, a major source of competitiveness for traditional large corporations came from releasing new products by exploiting path-dependent capability and incrementally improving existing products for existing markets (incremental innovation), thereby gaining profits. Meanwhile, radical and breakthrough innovations were a new paradigm shift of new markets and technologies, giving rise to the dramatic expansion of product function, radical transformation of existing markets, creation of new markets, and major cost reductions (Leifer *et al.*, 2000; O'Connor and Rice, 2001). These kinds of radical innovations differ substantially from the path-dependent incremental innovations in the past. To achieve radical innovation, a company requires new knowledge distinct from existing skills and expertise (Dewar *et al.*, 1986; Ettilie *et al.*, 1984; Green *et al.*, 1995).

The reason is that companies and individuals undertaking radical innovations face uncertainty and discontinuity in markets, technologies, organizations, and resources, and while some projects may be able to ride them out, many others are highly likely to stall or fail midway through (Leifer *et al.*, 2000). To acquire a radical innovation capability, a company needs different capabilities (including strategy, organization, resources, technology, processes, and leadership) to the practical management elements nurtured through incremental innovations (Kodama, 2003, 2007a; O'Reilley and Tushman, 2004; Vanhaverbeke and Peeters, 2005).

A large number of prior studies, mostly coming from Europe and the US, looked at the strategic change process and organizational capabilities essential to achieve radical innovations. However, many of these studies focused on empirical or proven case studies of individual research and development or practical projects within companies of all sizes, or else single-item successes or failures from independent venture companies (Miles and Covin, 2002; Howell and Higgins, 1999; Kuratko *et al.*, 1990; Greene *et al.*, 1999). Although this accumulated research is highly important, it is undeniable that companies also rely on the success of individual projects and the special capabilities of the heroes implementing these projects. Thus, with respect to large corporations that do not rely on the capabilities of specific individuals to systematically and continuously create radical innovation, research from the viewpoint of strategy and organization becomes increasingly important. Large corporations can deliver the slack to permit or promote the new routines of experimental and trial-and-error learning that startup venture companies find difficult to implement (Floyd and Wooldridge, 1999; Kogut and Zander, 1992). In the past, however, there is little theoretical or empirical research on large corporations that created continuous, systematic radical innovation, and research from the viewpoint of corporate or management systems to promote such innovation needs to progress (O'Connor, 2008).

Previous research has tried to define innovation. Henderson and Clark (1990) classified radical, architectural, modular, and incremental product innovation at the development level. Davila *et al.* (2005) classified mutual transformation of technology and business models as *radical innovation*, and transformation of either technology or business models as *semi-radical innovation*. Moreover, O'Reilley and Tushman (2004) used the term "radical" for innovation accompanying discontinuous change and "architectural" for innovation accompanying business process change. Garcia *et al.* (2002), moreover, uses *radical innovation* for actions causing simultaneous macro- and micro-level changes in markets and technologies, and defines other new product and service innovations as "really new innovation." Again, based on the classifications of Garcia *et al.* (2002), O'Connor (2008) uses the term *major innovation* for these radical and really new innovations excluding incremental innovations.

Thus, the classification of innovation creating new values outside the range of incremental innovations differs from researcher to researcher. This book seeks to avoid complexity by referring to incremental innovations as the processes of small-scale improvement and business process efficiency improvement without major changes. In general, this is *strategic innovation* creating new value with regard to technologies and markets arising from new changes, but excluding incremental innovation (a meaning shared by all previous research), as mentioned by Davila *et al.* (2005), O'Reilley and Tushman (2004), and Garcia *et al.* (2002). I interpret *strategic innovation* as being almost identical in meaning to *major innovation* as mentioned by O'Connor (2008).

As mentioned in the introduction:

> "*Strategic innovation* involves the continuous strategic creation of new products, services, and business models to acquire long-term, and sustainable competitive excellence. It embraces the radical reform of conventional products and services and the creation of new business models that transform existing business rules."

The meaning of *strategic innovation* as defined in this book corresponds to the *major innovations* comprising the radical and really new innovations above with the meaning of strategically and continuously creating new products, services, and business models, while incremental innovation corresponds to version updates through small-scale improvement of existing products and services. Strategic innovation that strategically and continuously acquires new knowledge to create innovations becomes a key process whereby a company quickly establishes a position in new markets and technologies. *Strategic innovation capability* may also include the organizational capability to achieve this strategic continuous innovation.

As mentioned in Chapter 1, this chapter will present the concept of *strategic innovation capability* created through the knowledge integration process. I will derive a basic framework for creating *strategic innovation* in major companies as well as individual project organizations and independent venture companies. Firstly, I will explain the meaning of *strategic innovation* and present the concept of *strategic innovation capability*, which helps to realize a transition in corporate strategy through *strategic innovation*. Then I will compare this *strategic innovation capability* with the preceding theories of dynamic capability (Teece *et al.*, 1997; Eisenhardt and Martine, 2000), MI (major innovation) dynamic capability focused on radical innovation (O'Connor, 2008), and breakthrough innovation capability (O'Connor, Leifer, Paulson and Peters, 2008).

2. Strategic Innovation Capability

2.1 *What is strategic innovation?*

Markides (1997) defined *strategic innovation* as a dynamic creation of creative strategic positioning from new products, services, and business models, and emphasized that this framework was a dynamic view of strategy by which a company established sustained competitive excellence. To achieve this, a company should not adhere to its existing position (existing business), but always innovate to destroy this position. Moreover, Govindarajan *et al.* (2005) defined it as realizing strategically innovative new business models (including new products and services). This *strategic innovation* refers to business innovation that transforms established business into new business and has a major impact on corporate performance. It is essentially different from the incremental innovation mentioned earlier.

Thus, the *strategic innovation* mentioned by Markides (1997) and Govindarajan *et al.* (2005) can be interpreted as having almost the same meaning as the definitions of the term in previous section. *Strategic innovation*, moreover, refers to the realization of strategic change in both the corporate system and in products, services, and business models. Describing the corporate capability, or the *strategic innovation capability*, to achieve this kind of *strategic innovation* is the focus of this chapter. Next, I will consider this capability in relation to previous research on dynamic capability.

2.2 *The capability map and the knowledge integration map*

The resource-based theories focusing on independent capabilities of companies and organizations (Wernerfelt, 1984; Barney, 1991) have come to develop as strategy theory frameworks from the viewpoints of microeconomics and organizational economics. These resource-based theories and Porter's (1980) competition strategy theory offer detailed analyses of strategic positioning and the relationship between competitive excellence and the internal resources already owned by companies in slowly changing environments and industries. However, it is difficult to analyse how companies in rapidly changing high-tech industries within competitive environments, such as the ICT and digital sectors, create new competitive excellence. Meanwhile, dynamic capability (Teece *et al.*, 1997) is an attempt to build a dynamic theory on existing resource-based theories, and integrate and rebuild competences inside and outside the company in response to environmental changes. The word "capability" refers to business processes for integrating and rebuilding assets inside and outside the company for the purpose of competitive excellence. Dynamic capability becomes the process of improving existing routine capabilities for transforming and exploiting existing corporate assets in response to a changing environment (Zollo and Winter, 2002; Winter, 2003). Process management of existing routines and operations contributes to the incremental innovation of existing business (Benner and Tushman, 2003).

Companies apply dynamic capability, formulate and implement strategies under relatively stable or slowly moving conditions with little business uncertainty. "Learning before doing" (Pisano, 1994) means formulating and implementing detailed strategy planning and policies. It is a key element of this dynamic capability in market structures with clear corporate boundaries and also can grasp the players in value chains.

Later on, a number of researchers have amended and reinterpreted their views of dynamic capability. The most relevant was Eisenhardt and Martine (2000), who made adjustments for tautology problems relating to the interpretation of capability, and presented clear interpretations of the relationship between dynamic capability and competitive excellence. They indicated that dynamic capability is the strategic and organizational processes and the routines of companies that use (integrate, reallocate, acquire, and eliminate) internal and external resources in order to respond to, or create, market change, and inductively derived concepts of corporate dynamic capability essential in both slow- and fast-moving market environments. They acknowledged the importance of "learning by doing" with simple rules to emphasize results rather than prior training and implementation processes, especially in fast-moving environments, where uncertainty rises and an industry's corporate borders become vague (Eisenhardt and Sull, 2001).

This interest in strategy theory has evolved toward a dynamic structure that reflects current corporate activity. O'Connor (2008) respected the dynamic capability theory of Eisenhardt and Martine (2000), and mentioned that a large number of *major innovations* (corresponding to *strategic innovations*), including the radical innovations mentioned above, developed gradually from slow (or very slow) market environments, and were implemented over a period of several years to several decades. Thus, the concept of dynamic capability is described as a theory that can be evaluated and applied around the axes of both market speed and business uncertainty (including risk) characterized by *strategic innovation*.

O'Connor (2008) used the term "MI dynamic capability" for capability that promotes the "exploration" process (1991) and realizes *strategic innovation* under conditions of uncertainty and high risk. MI dynamic capability differs from the dynamic capability theory that emphasizes the evolution of the original "exploitation" (1991) activity process. MI dynamic capability responds to highly uncertain situations, regardless of the speed of market movement, and embraces the concept of dynamic capability in the high-speed markets (also including high uncertainty) mentioned by Eisenhardt and Martine (2000).

Many *strategic innovations* are established through the stages of discovery or invention from slow- and very slow-moving basic scientific research and technological development environments. Later, the developed core technologies and provisional business models based on discovered or invented ideas are adopted and exploited in products and services through improvisation and trial-and-error processes (including the weeding-out process) involving trial manufacture, experiment, and incubation. Product and service markets are gradually established. Then the new products and services anticipated or forecast for the growth markets become the competitive markets for other companies (just when other companies enter the market depends on individual business). The market environment becomes fast-moving, and companies accelerate their investment in necessary resources.

O'Connor and DeMartino (2006) undertook long-term observation and analysis of radical innovation in major US corporations, and indicated the importance of three-phase management (discover, incubation, and acceleration) as a *radical innovation* (corresponding to *strategic innovation*) development framework. They then named the ability to implement these processes the "breakthrough innovation capability," and suggested that building this capability into the company is a key management system leading to successful *radical innovation* (O'Connor, Leifer, Paulson and Peters, 2008).

Previous research, such as dynamic capability and MI innovation capability positioned around the two axes of uncertainty and change led to the situation illustrated in Figure 2.1's capability map, which shows the relationship between those previous researches and the three development phases of O'Connor and DeMartino (2006), mentioned above. Meanwhile, a knowledge integration process supported by the capability map (see the map in Figure 2.2) exists. Here, strategic uncertainty beyond the four elements of markets, technology,

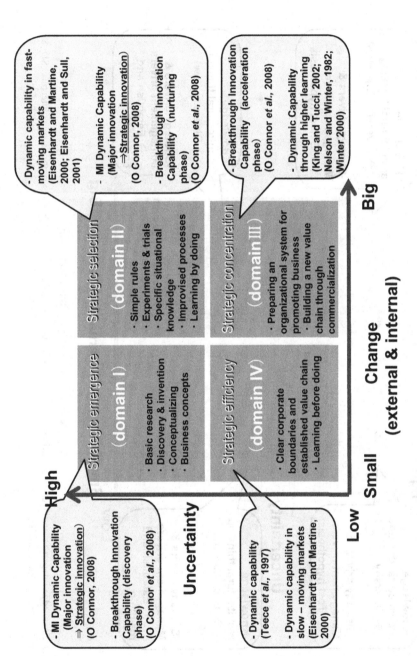

Figure 2.1 Capability Map.

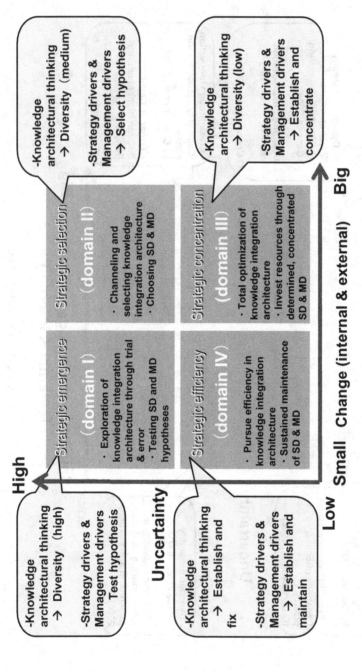

Figure 2.2   Knowledge integration Map.

Notes. Knowledge integration architecture comprises vertical integrated, horizontal integrated, and linkage relationship architecture. SD: Strategy drivers MD: management drivers.

organization, and resources mentioned by Leifer *et al.* (2000) also exists, and change is not limited to the external elements of market speed and industrial technology speeds, but also corresponds to the internal elements of a company's own strategy, organizational revamping, and concentration of resources.[1]

Slow or very slow environmental change with a highly uncertain domain (domain I) observed at the initial stage of *strategic innovation* is the technological creation stage arising from new ideas, business concepts, discoveries, and inventions, and corresponding to the "discovery phase" of O'Connor and DeMartino (2006). In this domain, the exploration process is advanced through the MI dynamic (or breakthrough innovation) capability mentioned above. The basic research and creation of ideas that are the source of new *strategic innovation* require (depending on the field) a longer period of time as the ratio of the scientific element and the degree of technological difficulty rise. The success of this domain relies greatly on creative thinking and action of middle managers and lower-ranked staff in a company's R&D and business development divisions, but strategic participation and commitment from top and senior management is also great. I call this domain strategic emergence.

Diverse patterns exist within the knowledge integration process of this domain. A large number of traditional large corporations are promoting closed innovations focusing on in-house laboratories and development divisions under a conventional hierarchical system. Closed innovation becomes a key process in developing sustained innovation through accumulated path-dependent knowledge. Closed innovation is very important in traditional high-tech sectors, such as heavy electrical machinery, nuclear power station equipment, aircraft, vehicle machinery, machine tools, medical equipment, and semiconductor manufacturing equipment. Meanwhile, technology evolves rapidly in fields such as IT, and the fruits and expertise of outstanding

---

[1] Transformational elements involve external and internal change, and affect management elements that build corporate systems, such as strategy, organization, culture, competence, and leadership. See Raynor (2006) for research regarding strategic uncertainty.

technologies are distributed and expanded worldwide. Adopting open innovation or incorporating some areas of core knowledge from outside, and integrating and assimilating knowledge inside and outside the company under such fast-changing environment makes for an effective *knowledge integration model.*

In this domain, companies must explore business models by asking themselves whether they should:

- Adopt a vertically integrated model arising from vertically integrated architecture (see chapter 1);
- Focus on specific specialist fields through horizontally integrated and linkage relationship architecture;
- Complement their own technologies while exploring strong or weak ties with other companies;
- Build new value chains by integrating and assimilating their own and other companies' strengths through collaboration across industries.

Thus, practitioners must permit expanded diversity for knowledge integration (vertically integrated, horizontally integrated, and linkage relationship) architecture as *knowledge architectural thinking*, and focus on trial-and-error experiments and trial activities.

In any case, companies in the "strategic emergence" domain must hypothetically test the corporate boundaries (strategy drivers) in response to strategy objectives and management environments, and try a range of knowledge integration processes within the trial-and-error process. If a company's own development and production has merit, it is better to activate the management driver's functions that emphasize creativity and build vertical value chain models. But if another company's development results surpass one's own, the company may have to activate the management driver's functions that emphasize efficiency, relinquish independent development, and access and acquire external intangible assets through tie-ups and M&As. Hence, in this domain's knowledge integration process, the practitioners purse knowledge integration activities from the tests of the hypotheses of the strategy and management drivers in response to strategic objectives and diverse *knowledge architectural thinking* (see Figure 2.2).

Next, the core technologies and business concepts that migrate from the slow-moving environment of domain I, with rapidly changing of the in-house (or occasionally external) acquisition of human resources and the maintenance and upgrading of organizations oriented to business incubation to a dramatically transforming domain II environment that sustains speed of change and uncertainty. In this domain, the exploration processes arising from dynamic capability (MI dynamic or breakthrough innovation) based on the simple rules (Eisenhardt and Martine (2000), O'Connor (2008)) are promoted. This domain corresponds to the incubation phase of hypothetical setups, experiments, and assessments mentioned by O'Connor and DeMartino (2006). Learning through trials and experiments also leads to less risk and uncertainty of markets and technologies and greater probability of success for incubations aimed at realizing strategic innovation (O'Connor *et al.*, 2008).[2] Then top and middle management make decisions in selecting and bringing to market the rigorously tested and evaluated products, services, and business models.

O'Connor *et al.* (2008) confines this incubation domain to trial experiment and assessment models, but in many cases, current business activities go beyond trial experiments within the coexistence of uncertainty and dramatically changing, fast-moving environments to the launch of commercial business, where companies may boldly undertake risks with a high degree of uncertainty. The excessive trust and commitment of the leaders lead to strategic activities, based on the creation of business through trial-and-error, while it is still unclear whether the newly developed ideas and prototypes are capable of building new business models and value chains.[3] It corresponds to the cases in the new online business where products are both trialed and launched in dramatically changing domains of generally high risk and

---

[2] Campbell and Park (2005) indicated that since reducing organizational and resource uncertainty is difficult, projects that are high-risk in terms of organization and resources should be rejected after screening.

[3] The likelihood of experiencing a certain amount of failure in the strategic selection domain rises with outstanding leaders and managers. This is also a working hypothesis from my own office experience.

uncertainty. A key question is how to select and implement promising, valuable business. I call this domain *strategic selection*.

In this domain, the knowledge integration process involves selecting and channeling a range of knowledge integration processes tested and experimented with in the "strategic emergence" domain. The next stage enhances the level of completion for knowledge integration as a product, service, and business model. It explains how the elements of strategy and management drivers are generally chosen. Moreover, the diversity of the elements of knowledge integration (vertically integrated, horizontally integrated, and linkage relationship) architecture are reduced in comparison to the "strategic emergence" domain. In some cases, companies review relationships, such as partnerships with other companies, by reconsidering their structural architectures (vertically integrated and horizontally integrated architectures) and transforming their linkage relationship architecture (see Figure 2.2).

New business (including new products and services), which is chosen through *strategic selection* in domain II, shift to domain III, where uncertainty is reduced to some extent while external and internal changes are sustained. Domain III is the stage where the strategic innovation incubated (or partially commercialized) in domain II enters a growth orbit, and corresponds to the "acceleration phase" mentioned by O'Connor and DeMartino (2006). According to O'Connor *et al.* (2008), this is where the exploitation process is promoted by breakthrough innovation capability. This domain achieves the building and optimization of processes and value chains for the selected new business. After that, new business functions are wholly or partially transferred to divisions appropriate to accelerate commercialization (or new divisions are newly established or made independent as external ventures). Resources are intensively invested through the strategic commitment of top and middle management. I will call this domain *strategic concentration*. In the past, a large number of product and service development projects for major corporations (Kodama, 2005; 2007d) invested management resources in commercialization through this kind of shift from *strategic selection* to *strategic concentration*.

This domain is the stage where the knowledge integration process and the management elements (strategy drivers and management drivers) are settled and concentrated, and the completion of products and services is enhanced through commercially oriented knowledge integration. The degree of change in the elements of vertically integrated, horizontally integrated, and linkage relationship architectures is minor compared to the strategic selection domain. Adjustments for overall optimization of knowledge integration architecture is a key theme (see Figure 2.2).

Meanwhile, with the concept of the *strategic innovation loop* (see the next section), companies operating in the strategic concentration domain must strategically and sustainably advance technology and review business models to enhance the value of products and services, and respond to a fast-changing competitive environment. To achieve this, companies must commercialize by shifting new business from domain I through II to III, where a new and updated knowledge integration process appears through new business migrating from the *strategic selection* domain and comprehensive upgrades of existing products and services.

Domain III can be interpreted as a capability to embrace the notion of inherent dynamic capability promoting incremental innovation, perform strongly in response to internal and external changes to create profits by evolving and diversifying operating routines through high-level learning (King and Tucci, 2002; Benner and Tushman, 2003; Winter, 2000; Amburgey, 1993; Nelson and Winter, 1982).

Meanwhile, a great deal of existing business is positioned in domain IV, in slow-moving markets with a low rate of change and uncertainty. Here, incremental innovation is promoted with the aim of systematically enhancing business efficiency through the exploitation process, which comprises activities to improve existing business using mainstream organizations that demonstrate inherent dynamic capability (Teece *et al.*, 1997; Eisenhardt and Martine, 2000). Promoting this domain IV process management accelerates an organization's speed of response to achieve incremental innovation (Benner and Tushman, 2003). I call this domain *strategic efficiency*.

The knowledge integration process of this domain pursues more efficiently existing routines and operations within a framework of fixed established architecture (vertically and integrated, horizontally integrated, and linkage relationship) under continuously sustained strategy and management drivers (see Figure 2.2).

I would like to consider *strategic innovation capability* frameworks to sustainably achieve strategic innovation (the main theme of this chapter) based on the capability and knowledge integration maps of the four domains.

2.3   *The strategic innovation loop and strategic innovation capability*

When considered from the viewpoints of corporate exploration and exploitation, strategic and incremental innovations, and the time axis of business context, the four domains forms a continuous domain loop (see Figure 2.3). The strategic emergence and selection domains are important for strategic innovation processes. *Strategic concentration* is the acceleration phase indicated by O'Connor and DeMartino (2006). This phase rapidly sets up the markets for new products, services, and business models through the exploratory processes of strategic emergence and selection, and shifts the domain from exploration to exploitation. *Strategic concentration* becomes the origin of a new path of newly generated strategic innovation that differs from the existing business of the strategic efficiency domain.

In this *strategic concentration* domain, newly generated business always undergoes major internal or external change in initial phase. At this stage, it transforms internal elements aimed at building optimal values and supply chains in response to external change. Among the *strategic concentration* business, which is subject to major change, businesses that succeed in establishing themselves in the market and achieving stability as mainstream operations shift to slow-moving (or small) *strategic efficiency* domain while promoting still greater operational and business process efficiency measures, and either become part of the existing mainstream lineup or undergo business integration (which promotes still greater business process efficiency).

However, business subject to major external changes of markets and technologies following mainstream growth, and major internal changes in areas such as strategy, organization, resources, and operations

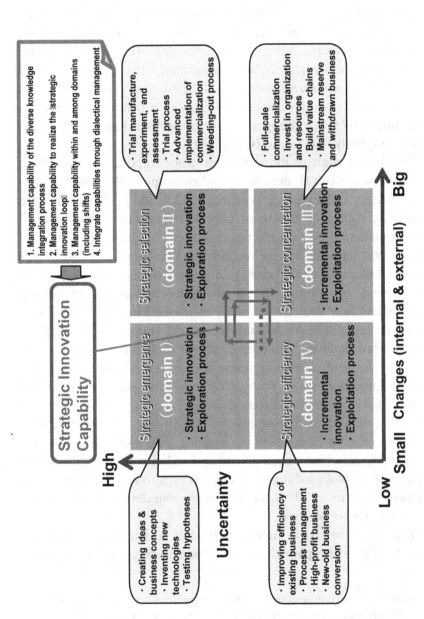

Figure 2.3   Strategic Innovation System.

(e.g., ICT industry involving broadband and mobile phones, on-line business, and digital consumer electronics) always becomes positioned in this *strategic concentration* domain. In other words, business following mainstream direction becomes deployed in the *strategic concentration* and *strategic efficiency* domains. Although new business in the *strategic concentration* domain is the "mainstream reserve," this does not mean that all business can grow in a mainstream environment subject to major changes, and some business have to withdraw. This is absolutely true in the ICT industry.

The flow of strategic innovation for major corporations shifts from domains I to domain II, domain III (where some business undergoing major changes maintain their position), and finally to domain IV (see Figure 2.2). Amid this movement, existing business in the *strategic efficiency* domain may become the target for new/old business conversion with the new path of *strategic concentration* business (or business that shifts from *strategic concentration* to *strategic efficiency* domains) arising from *strategic innovation*. The simultaneous management of existing positions and new strategic positions mentioned by Markides (2001) involves co-establishing in domains III and IV. Transferring from old to new positions involves transferring existing business in domain IV to accelerated, expanded new business in domain III. Although major corporations promote various strategically innovative projects, only some of them survives and succeeds during a natural selection process involved in the shift from domains I to III. Amabile and Khaire (2008) noted a number of cases where outstanding ideas and business models created in domain I have been diluted and ended in failure after a major corporation employs a different managing organization to realize (and commercialize) them.[4] This is one issue surrounding strategic innovation in a major corporation.

The most important inter-domain shift is that from III and/or IV to I. This is the path that creates new strategic innovation (see

---

[4] This is due to the existence of the knowledge boundaries between the product planning divisions that supervise the creation of business concepts and ideas, the development divisions that realize them, and the production and manufacturing divisions. See Kodama (2007a).

Figure 2.2). It corresponds to the process that accelerates environmental and internal interaction and creates new ideas, new technological inventions and discoveries based on high-quality tacit knowledge (Nonaka and Takeuchi, 1995). This knowledge is cultivated through the practice of researchers, engineers, marketers, and strategy specialists in shifting from domains I to IV (accumulating and integrating new practice through existing business practice and strategic innovation) via the "transformational experience" (King and Tucci, 2002; Amburgey *et al.*, 1993) of previously existing business routines and strategic innovation (Kodama, 2007a). King and Tucci (2002) suggested that the "transformational experience" of practitioners involved in the continual (Katz and Allen, 1982) and large-scale (Tushman and Romanelli, 1985; Amburgey, 1993) organizational innovation of product development teams leads to continuous new product innovation and resets rigid organizational intertia. In other words, it enhances potential for embedding new capabilities in organization members aimed at creating new routines to transform organizations and realizing strategic innovation.

Although excessive adherence to existing knowledge to create new knowledge integration becomes a hindrance, the absorption of knowledge from different sectors and industries from a scientific, technological, and marketing viewpoint and the knowledge integration process can trigger new strategic innovations (the i-mode business development in Chapter 6 and Nintendo game development in Chapter 7 correspond to this). Various innovation theories including the importance of shedding the "mental model" (Spender, 1990), the focus on "peripheral vision" (Schemaker, 2004), the challenge of achieving "cross innovation" (Johansson, 2004), and "destructive innovation" (Christensen, 1997) confer insights but more detailed theory building is yet to be undertaken. I consider to work on a hypothesis indicating, that the evolution and diversification of high-level routines through advanced learning in domains III and IV fundamentally promote sustainable innovation (Christensen, 1997) while inducing a shift from domains III and/or IV to I arising from the sustainable innovation of integrating new knowledge inside and outside the company (see Figure 2.2), and raising the probability of achieving new knowledge integration as a strategic innovation.[5]

I would like to explain the following four new insights obtained from this framework, and use them as a basis to explain the *strategic innovation capability*. The first point is that outstanding companies are always inclined toward strategic innovation, and create a diverse knowledge integration process aimed at acquiring new capabilities in each of the four domains. In particular, the shift from domains III and/or IV to domain I induces practitioners' *knowledge architectural thinking* to achieve a new knowledge integration process.

The second point is that outstanding companies possessing the dynamic strategic view deliberately (including some emergent elements) drive loops which include continuous shifts, among domains (termed "*strategic innovation loops*" in this book) from domains I through IV and/or from domain III to I. The dynamic strategy view co-establishes the different modes of the exploratory and exploitative processes and secures long-term corporate growth (March, 1996; Benner and Tushman, 2003; Tushman and O'Reilley, 1997). These two processes (March, 1991; Holland, 1975) do not employ opposing strategic activities. Companies must implement strategy while skillfully balancing the strategic activities in a mutually complementary way (He and Wong, 2004).

Meanwhile, Zollo and Winter (2002) proposed a knowledge evolution process based on adjusted evolutionary theory. The continuous routine activity well-considered within this process can become a trigger to shift from exploitation to exploration. Experiential knowledge accumulated from learning activities also becomes an element in creating new dynamic capability (corresponding to a shift from domain IV and/or domain III to domain I). The authors also explained how the recursive processes and co-evolution of these different modes

---

[5] Numerous studies (Nonaka and Takeuchi, 1995) exist regarding the theoretical frameworks relating to the creation of knowledge such as breakthrough or new ideas. Analysis from various viewpoints will be the subject of future research topics. One such example relates to the creative process for business concepts arising from the synthesis of market and technology paradigms (see Chapter 7).

simultaneously promote corporate challenges and processes (routines). The important question is what top and middle management must do to implement the spiral strategic innovation loop and achieve success.

The third point is that observing large corporations at selected times on a time axis indicates the constant presence of each of the domains I to IV possessing different business contexts. With large corporations, multiple projects oriented to strategic innovation function as layered *strategic innovation loops* on different time axes. Therefore top and middle management must manage appropriately within and among these domains. Different strategies, organizational structures, core competences, organizational cultures, and leadership skills are required within each of these domains. An important question is how the skills and expertise that produce the strategic emergence from accumulated experiential knowledge (which arises from diverse high-level routines through transformational experience via the continuous *strategic innovation loop* (Amburgey *et al.*, 1993; Nelson and Winter, 1982; Winter, 2000) can be created by the knowledge integration process. Moreover, O`Connor and DeMartino (2006) indicated the importance of the relationship between organizational structure and radical innovation capability with regard to the radical innovation development framework of major corporations moving from discovery and cultivation to acceleration (corresponding to domains I to III, respectively).

The fourth point is that analysis of the NTT case study in Chapter 3 suggests that the exploration and exploitation processes are especially interactive. It has been argued that organizations within major corporations undertaking radical innovation should either be isolated both physically and organizationally from the mainstream organization, or else operate as independent venture companies (Hill and Rothaermel, 2003; Benner and Tushman, 2003; Burgelman and Sayles, 1986; Kanter, 1985). However, an appropriate interface with existing organizations is also potentially significant for accelerating strategic innovation from the viewpoint of strategy and resource integration (Heller, 1999; Kodama, 2003). Questions of organizational design (How much should a strategic innovation business integrate with, or separate from, existing businesses? Is it better to have complete separation, complete integration, or something in between?) (Christensen, 1997; Burgelman and Leonard, 1986; Good and Campbell, 2002; Tushman and O'Reilley, 1997) are arguably more important in achieving strategic innovation.

Previous research has discussed management processes and organizational divisions, such as two distinct archetypes-exploratory and exploitative, or incremental or radical (Greenwood and Hinings, 1993; Tushman and O'Reilley, 1997) and the ambidextrous organization (O'Reilley and Tushman, 2004). There is few detailed analysis of the interfaces and interaction among management elements (strategy, organizational structure, core competence, organizational culture, and leadership), each of which differ from two archetypes (Kodama, 2003; Kodama, 2007a). Nevertheless, the co-establishment and coexistence of these two archetypes within the same large corporation, and the skillful management of strategic contradiction (Smith and Tushman, 2005), creative abrasion (Leonard-Barton, 1995), and productive friction (Hagel III and Brown, 2005) are also important elements of successful strategic innovation. The coexistence of contradictions highlights the important roles not only of the top management (Smith and Tushman, 2005; Tushman and O'Reilley, 1997), but also of middle management and staffs (Govindarajan *et al.*, 2005). I call this "dialectical management" (Kodama, 2004; Kodama, 2007a).

Based on the four insights above, *strategic innovation capability* is a concept that embraces the following four competences:

- The management capability to implement a range of innovative knowledge integration processes in response to target and situational strategies
- The management capability to implement the spiral *strategic innovation loop*;
- Management capability within and among domains, including shifts;
- Integrative competences to achieve the coexistence of two different archetypes through dialectic management (see Figure 2.3).

Moreover, *strategic innovation capability* embraces the existing dynamic and MI dynamic capability (or breakthrough innovation capability) concepts mapped in Figure 2.1 while aiming to expand the concept of organizational capability for individual product development projects at large corporations and venture companies in the direction of innovation capability for the corporate or management system. This book calls the kind of management system that uses *strategic innovation capability* to activate the spiral of the *strategic innovation loop,* and continuously co-establishes existing business with strategic innovation business the "strategic innovation system" (see Figure 2.3).

I would like to note the points of difference between the "strategic innovation system" and the "management system" arising from "breakthrough innovation capability" (O'Connor *et al.,* 2008). Since O'Connor's model is sequential, it shifts from discovery through cultivation to acceleration, and it is weak on the positive feedback process of reflection on, and practical application of, the practical knowledge and accumulated transformational experience of in-house expertise, skills, and routines acquired through executing breakthrough innovation and existing business. The sequential model provides a weak framework for shifting to a strategic emergence domain that gives rise to discovery, invention, and creativity. It also provides a weak dynamic strategy view framework for a company to acquire and sustain new strategic positions over many years. The strategic innovation system in this book (see Figure 2.3) comprehensively considers the three points above while creating corporate and management system models for sustainable strategic innovation.

3. Conclusion and Topics

Previously, I have described a theoretical framework for *strategic innovation capability.* The theory of strategic innovation systems will be discussed in details, and a new research approach will be required. One aspect is that most of the strategic innovation research done up to now has emphasized correlations between specific management elements of specific organizations and projects (including strategy, organizational structure and culture, competence, and leadership) with results, and has been limited to analyses of some of the subsystems that comprise the corporate system. However, strategic innovation in the large corporation has a great impact on success or failure, due to complex interaction among the subsystems comprising the corporate system.

Therefore it is necessary to specify the individual subsystems that influence strategic innovation based on strategic innovation systems as corporate systems, and analyze in depth the interactive relationship (such as existing organizations versus strategically innovative organizations) between these features and subsystems, and the dynamic situational changes (balanced or unbalanced) of individual subsystems with the overall (corporate) system responding to internal and external change. System theories (von Bertalanffy, 1960; Capra, 1996) and complex adaptation theories (Morel and Ramanujam, 1999; Stacey, 1996) are capable of inclusively handling the points above. O'Connor (2008) explained how system theory is effective in clarifying a large corporation's radical innovation system, and demonstrates some propositions with respect to the relationship among a number of subsystems.

The second aspect is the research approach from the knowledge-based theory of firm (Nonaka and Takeuchi, 1995; Grant, 1995). Companies that achieve sustainable strategic innovation can implement a new knowledge creation (or integration) chain through a layered *strategic innovation loop* (see Figure 2.3). However, research on *knowledge integration dynamics* is required to answer important questions such as how strategic innovation capability can change the knowledge innovation process occurring within and among domains (including shifts) (see Figure 2.3); how strategic behavior and organizational structure change; and what patterns form the optimal knowledge integration process for realizing strategic innovation. This research, which needs to progress from a theoretical and practical viewpoint, forms the true theme of this book.

3

Strategic Innovation in Big Traditional Companies: A Case Study of Broadband Business

1. Introduction

This chapter presents basic frameworks used by major corporations to generate strategic innovation. Specifically, it considers the strategic change process in the increasingly competitive ICT sector and the mechanisms by employed large corporations to achieve business innovation when taking on the challenge of reforming for the future. The chapter also studies in-depth the mechanisms by which Japan's largest communications carrier, Nippon Telegraph and Telephone Corporation (NTT), targets the future broadband revolution, creates new technologies and services, and strategically innovates.

This chapter summarizes and analyzes the case of NTT's transformation based on the concept of *strategic innovation capability*, (a corporate system capability for companies to achieve strategic change through strategic innovation). It then suggests the mechanisms by which NTT acquired *strategic innovation capability* and shows how NIT implemented spiral *strategic innovation loops* and dialectical management during the dynamic knowledge integration process.

2. Case Study of the NTT Broadband Revolution

2.1 *The ISDN revolution: from phones to multimedia*

In 1994, NTT's president Masashi Kojima declared: "We will transform NTT from a phone company into a multimedia company!" At that time, NTT was facing a major transformation from analogue phones to multimedia. The business environment was one of slowly diminishing income from analogue phones (which had been a mainstay of NTT business) brought about by the entry of new businesses into the market accompanying deregulation of the communications market in 1985, and increasingly competitive phone rates. In 1993, it was hard to decide what kind of strategies and services a communications carrier should adopt to grasp the opportunities presented by the US-centered Internet, which was then beginning to expand.

2.1.1 *Building new organizations from top management members*

Two names are associated with inculcating a great sense of crisis over the future of NTT: president Masashi Kojima and vice president and technology chief Junichiro Miyazu, who took on the post of CEO in 1996. They wanted to transforme NTT's structure to build new, future-oriented business. They came to the conclusion that they should hammer out a future-oriented multimedia strategy and build a new organization within the main organization. Director Shigeru Ikeda became managing director in 1996 and, who NTT-ME CEO in 1998, was charged with creating the new organization, which was named the Service Production Planning Division, and later renamed the Multimedia Business Department (MBD). It launched with 50 staff in 1994; and in 1996, it was expanded to become an organization of 850 members. Top management members, Kojima,

Miyazu, and Ikeda firmly embraced the belief and purpose to break down NTT's traditional organizational culture and exploit ICT to create a new multimedia business market.

Mr. Miyazu demonstrated to Mr. Ikeda his desire regarding to newly structured organizations to create an organization capable of new behavior rooted in new concepts. Mr. Ikeda exploited his previous experience as the head of the personnel division to gather a range of personnel from a setup employing 180,000 people across the country. He picked researchers and engineers with more than a hundred patents or new practical proposals, young people with entrepreneurial experiences, and top systems engineers from the Kansai region. Many of the project leaders who comprised the new MBD organization were upper-level managers from branches throughout Japan that brought a great sense of balance. The capable, multifaceted teams of young staff and veterans exceeded 850 in number at their height (AERA, 1999).

The degree of freedom, speed, and tension within the new organization led someone to remark that: "This organization (MBD) alone is not NTT." MBD contrasted strongly with the traditional, established line organizations within NTT. Naturally, when an organization promoting original business based on new concepts, strong friction with the traditional organization was unavoidable.

Being launched in 1997 as the Service Production Planning Division with around 50 staff, the organization spent the first year in the domain I — "strategic emergence" phase (see Figure 3.1). Mr. Ikeda's key point of "shedding in-house development" was to exploit technology developed by NTT together with outstanding technology developed all over the world, integrate it with NTT technology, and build new business models. Thus, the outstanding researchers who had moved to MBD stopped adhering to NTT's proprietary technology and looked for outstanding technology from the US and elsewhere. At that time, MBD was exploring new business (including products, services, and joint ventures) from strategic tie-ups with leading global partners including Microsoft (including VOD, security, and MSN), General Magic (agent communications business), Silicon Graphics (VOD business), Picture Tel (joint development of TV

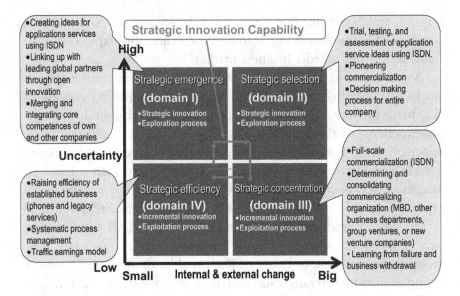

Figure 3.1   Strategic Innovation System in NTT: The ISDN Revolution.

conference systems), Inktomi (joint development of search engines), Apple Computer, and AT&T. MBD pushed for open innovation (Chesbrough, 2003) rather than closed innovation, which is focused on in NTT's internal organization.

O'Connor (2006) noted that "radical innovation must be open innovation." Case studies of US companies demonstrate how open innovation thinking promotes radical innovation. MBD's technology development strategy of the time was close to this thinking. As Figure 3.1 illustrates, open innovation functions as an enabler which creates new strategic innovation shifting from domain III and/or IV to domain I.

The trigger for shifting to domain I related to the conversion of technological thinking possessed by the NTT researchers and engineers of the time. With the exception of access-type optical fiber and next-generation communication systems (including NGN, which will be mentioned later), NTT's digital communications infrastructure development was complete and operational (digitization of the communications network was completed in 1997). Network digitization also shifted the emphasis from the switching hardware of network node equipment to software development. This enabled service functions formerly realized with hardware to be achieved with software. As a result, in 1990s, NTT's switching software development enabled it to realize a range of network services while also upgrading network operations (monitoring and controlling of communication networks). It strengthened the software development capability for its switching and network operation systems. NTT then promoted strategies for in-house development of software for processes ranging from R&D to commercialization and maintenance, and focused on training software engineers. In 1997, NTT established NTT Comware as a wholly owned subsidiary, and proceeded to develop all software in-house, from switching to operation and internal office systems such as ERP and CRM. The change from hardware to software led to a service development mindset based on the software architecture of NTT researchers and engineers, and triggered the establishment of routine processes (domain I→II→III) to smoothly implement stages from R&D to commercialization. It led to knowledge sharing in the R&D and commercialization divisions of the business section and the creation of deep tacit knowledge among organizations, including the involvement of personnel exchange. It also established an organizational environment providing effective feedbacks on new demands from the workplace and the customers to the R&D division. This conversion not only accelerates the shift from domains III and/or IV to domain I (see Figure 3.1), but also transcends the "valley of death" (the shift from domain II to domain III).

Another change in the technological environment occurred during 1990s, when high-tech companies dominated by the US focused on R&D for Internet and multimedia technologies based on client-server technologies and software architecture. In this environment, NTT researchers and engineers had to transform technological thinking from hardware architecture focused on conventional infrastructure to software architecture focused on applications. Then NTT's R&D staff had to convert to software architecture technology thinking aimed at developing allowing new services users to exploit various online applications through a range of terminals and servers.

The trigger that created the new strategic innovation of shifting from domain III and/or IV to domain I (see Figure 3.1) also resulted in conversion from hardware to software architecture to promote the need to develop new services and applications based on such software architecture.

Among MBD projects, those consolidated as especially advanced business concepts and models undertook a shift to domain II "strategic selection" (see Figure 3.1) enabling companies to inspect and evaluate their own projects and business models. In this domain, they generated an expansion of internal change by strengthening organizations and investing in personnel by, for example, increasing the number of staff in each project, thus enabling resource investment for the prototype, trial, and assessment processes to run smoothly. The domain also went through a period when the emergence of various technologies and business models using the US-centered Internet simultaneously generated expectations for major external change in technologies and markets.

Many ideas were tried and tested in this "strategic selection" domain. For example, the Virtual Young Company (VYC) was a project that created a virtual company within NTT. In this way, MBD realized the strategic innovation, which creates new markets by promoting the R&D process in domains I and II (this R&D process corresponds to radical innovation through exploration).

After that, the business chosen carefully via the internal decision-making process (within MBD and at top management level for the entire company) shifted to domain III (strategic concentration), as illustrated in Figure 3.1, and were categorized as business implemented in association with internal, established traditional organizations, new business transferred to existing NTT group companies (subsidiaries), and venture companies independently separated from the main NTT company. Naturally, numerous failures were experienced by previously commercialized services at strategic selection domain II, but MBD nevertheless acquired great skills and expertise while reinforcing the filter function with regard to strategic selection following practical experiences of failure.

In strategic concentration domain III, business linking up with traditional organizations including ISDN service planning and sales;

advertising, publicity, sales promotion, and personnel training facilities; and sales and support businesses for new product terminals and services applying ISDN and the Internet. One product implemented by an NTT group subsidiary at this time was MN128 terminal adaptor, which became a major hit. Other business implemented by independent venture companies by reviewing the funding structure and consolidating among the group business including the current NTT Resonant "goo," NTT Plala net service, and NTT BizLink multipoint TV conferencing service. Failures were also experienced in domain III — the strategic concentration domain. Especially prevalent among these were external joint ventures applying new technologies that withdrew after failing to stimulate demand in new markets. The strategic actions of MBD and traditional organizations in domain III corresponded to the incremental innovation resulting from exploitation and hitched the commercial services determined in domain II to a growth orbit.

Meanwhile, strong friction arose among MBD and traditional organizations in the strategic selection and concentration domains. Numerous issues for consensus arose relating to key macro and micro items of strategy and organization, such as positioning of new business (including new products and services), strategic policy and implementation structures, and personnel distribution. Nevertheless, the top-down communication of vision from the senior members and the promotion of company-wide knowledge management among interacting organizations led to constructive, productive and interorganizational frictions.[1] Then the integration of entrepreneurial and emergent strategies implemented by MBD with the planning strategies worked out by traditional organizations (Mintzberg *et al.*, 1985) created new markets arising from new services.

---

[1] The author worked as section head of a project at the time the Service Production Planning Division was founded (before the MBD was inaugurated). While space is too limited to relate the story here, the new practice was a sustained challenge on a daily basis, and I strongly believe that this organization's surmounting of great friction, as it created large-scale strategic innovations accompanying organizational reform from six years of experience, moved it into a new orbit.

At this time, phone and other legacy services, particularly the traffic profit model of phone service, dominated NTT. Nevertheless, with NTT's full-scale commercialization of ISDN (led by new markets arising from the MBD's strategic behavior), ISDN Internet services spread dramatically throughout Japan, and became the focal point around which the then-core phone and other legacy services gradually shifted to "strategic efficiency" domain IV (see Figure 3.1). Then the traditional organizations that managed the phone services and other core businesses promoted the building and introduction of operation systems through daily business improvement and ICT, and achieved efficient management (corresponding to incremental innovation through exploitation) resulting from thorough process management of core business.

As described above, by shifting through each domain, NTT acquired its own independent *strategic innovation capability* to sustain established core business (incremental innovation through exploitation) while creating new markets (radical innovation through exploration), which new ISDN Internet services (see Figure include 3.1).

2.1.2 *Features of MBD strategy and organizational structure*

MBD business strategy proactively promoted joint development and joint ventures resulting from strategic tie-up with various partners outside the company and incubation through joint trials with specific customers and achieved concrete success. A feature of MBD strategic behavior in the strategic selection domain (see Figure 3.1) is the strong trend toward emergence through the strategic learning process of experiment and incubation.

Various projects were established within MBD regarding such areas as online, search, content, movie, EC, joint venture business. Each individual project strategically formed linked networks or ("strategic communities") (Kodama, 2007a) with respect to online business strategies through external strategic ties and partnerships with specific customers (see Figure 3.2). Then each project leader comprehensively managed and integrated multiple strategic communities to obtain reliable results of the overall synergies of the projects.

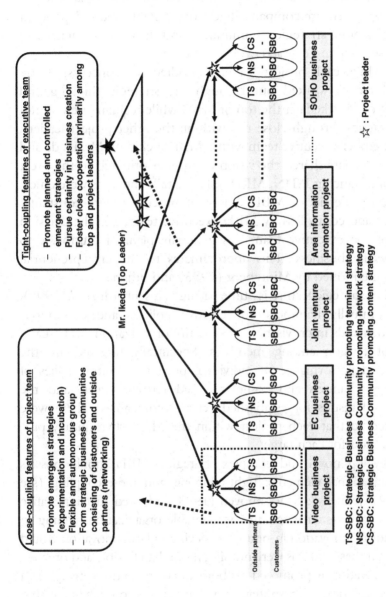

Tight-coupling features of executive team

- Promote planned and controlled emergent strategies
- Pursue certainty in business creation
- Foster close cooperation primarily among top and project leaders

Loose-coupling features of project team

- Promote emergent strategies (experimentation and incubation)
- Flexible and autonomous group
- Form strategic business communities consisting of customers and outside partners (networking)

Mr. Ikeda (Top Leader)

☆ : Project leader

Video business project

EC business project

Joint venture project

Area information promotion project

SOHO business project

Outside partners

Customers

TS-SBC: Strategic Business Community promoting terminal strategy
NS-SBC: Strategic Business Community promoting network strategy
CS-SBC: Strategic Business Community promoting content strategy

Figure 3.2   Organizational structure in MBD.

Source: Kodama (2003).

There are for each project around 30 to 40 employees. These projects promoted much business through rapid decision-making and action for small-scale venture company. They were flexible and independent within and among strategic communities, and the projects themselves had a loose-coupling character.

Meanwhile, each project leader embodied the concepts, strategies, and tactics worked out through the strategic thinking and leadership of Mr. Ikeda at the top of MBD while realizing new strategies and tactics through close ties with all the other project leaders. The 30-member executive team within MBD including Mr. Ikeda and the project leaders shared the vision and values oriented to the great mission of advancing ISDN. MBD policy details and aims were emergent, but the details of MBD emergent processes were constantly monitored and controlled by MBD executive team, and the decision making of the executive team was generally planned cautiously to create specific business. This approximates to the entrepreneurial strategies mentioned by Mintzberg (1985) and others.

Another strategic feature is "time pacing" (Eisenhardt *et al.*, 1998). MBD continually hammers out creative policies and continuous changes, demands improvisation as an entire organization, and creates a state of tension among members. Specifically targeted are the progress and performance of individual projects, monthly tallies of ISDN sales channels and commercialized terminal sales, and the progress and results for established venture companies. These were coordinated so that each project within the MBD rhythmically promoted business for each target.

To develop novel and complex strategies, MBD should possess two organizational elements: tight-coupling and loose-coupling (see Figure 3.2). Jelinek & Schoonhoven (1993) indicated that innovative companies have systematized and accountable organizations aiming to achieve radical innovation in-house. Achieving radical innovation would be difficult if these systems were nothing more than flexible and organic. Radical innovation is promoted by both discipline and creativity. As a formal organization with strategic missions and accountability within NTT, MBD maintained discipline in decision-making while embracing flexibility and autonomy to enhance creativity for each project.

Nevertheless, it is difficult to imagine that the explosive spread of ISDN occurred solely through the strategic actions of an MBD's organization with 850 members. Forming the backdrop to this were the actions of MBD and traditional organizations in creating internal communities and promoting knowledge management throughout the company, which led to the full-scale launch of planning and strategy aimed at spreading ISDN through traditional organizations and the achievement of strategic innovation throughout NTT by integrating these different strategies of different organizations. This stage corresponded to the "strategic concentration" domain presented in Figure 3.1. In this domain, the issue arose of whether the old corporate culture of the traditional NTT organization could be destroyed and NTT somehow launch its activities as one.[2]

2.1.3 *Strategy integration through the MBD and traditional organizations*

While the "consciousness revolution" proceeded throughout the organizations and among all employees, the various policies hammered out by the MBD produced results; and from the beginning of 1996 the number of ISDN subscribers began to rise. As Figure 3.1 illustrates, in the strategic concentration domain, the overheads departments in traditional organizations had to rapidly determine the business, equipment, customer service, and maintenance service to cope with major changes in the ISDN market and target full-scale expansion. Then the measures to smoothly provide ISDN to customers were urgently put in place.

The strategies of the traditional organizations reliably implemented rapid, systematic equipment support (switching equipment and line construction) for the administration and service order sides with regard to customer ISDN demands, and endeavored to enhance

---

[2] See Kodama (2007a) for knowledge management arising from conflict management between the MBD and traditional organizations and the formation of in-house communities.

the quality of customer service. This required highly accurate ISDN demand projections, and here it became necessary to monitor in detail the time pacing strategies hammered out by MBD. Thus, strategies resulting from event-based pacing responding promptly to ISDN customer demand became important (Gersick, 1994).

The advantages of event-based pacing are its great potential for environmental support, and that once policies for the anticipated event are selected, they push forward without change until they succeed. The effects of this pacing are thus demonstrated by securely established, disciplined and top-down organizations, which implement incremental innovations. However, the possibility exists, of mis-timing and thus destabilizes the strategy when reacting to events. By aiming to link up with MBD's time-pacing strategies, the market movements for the company as a whole could be constantly monitored, enabling rapid response to be taken.

MBD considered time restraints and results of creating fixed outcomes within a fixed time frame to establish and popularize ISDN as jointly important positioning. Then MBD deliberately implemented methods to integrate both its own organizations' time-pacing strategies and the event-based pacing strategies of the traditional organizations.

2.1.4 *Linking the continuous and incremental change loops*

Figure 3.3 illustrates this strategy integration process. MBD continuously promoted entrepreneurial strategies based on emergent time pacing, and attracted attention customers' to the ISDN market, which stimulated this sleepy sector. To promote further inducements, entrepreneurial strategy change loops were spirally operated to seek and create new business concepts and ideas (this MBD strategy action is called the "continuous change loop"). MBD then took on the bulk of the responsibility for the R&D processes moving from domain III or IV to I and then to II (see Figure 3.1). As we will see later, MBD took further action to smoothly implement the shift from domain II to III.

MBD's continuous change loop had two implications relating to interface and interaction among both new and old organizations in

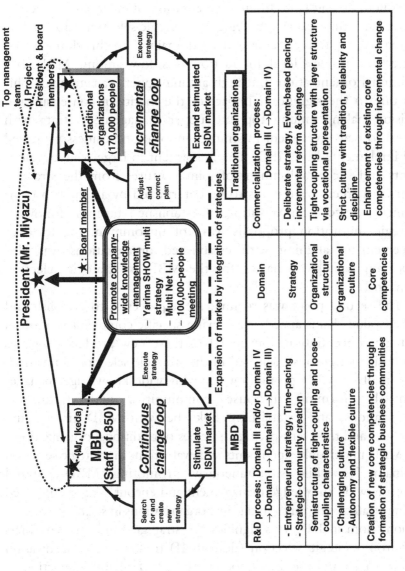

Figure 3.3   Strategic innovation system through dialectical management.

Source: Medtication based on Kedama (2003).

Figure 3.1's strategic innovation system. The first was decision-making processes for new products, services, business, and policy implementation through trial and error, experimentation, and assessment arising from the implementation of emergent, entrepreneurial, and time-pacing strategies at strategic selection (domain II) shifted from "strategic emergence" domain I. In this domain, the degree of business-level interaction was low among MBD and traditional organizations but high among upper management. This was due to the significant impact of the merits of consensus and decision-making among top and upper management strata with regard to new investment in strategy innovation business proposed and implemented by MBD. The investment in large-scale developments and the establishment of joint ventures from the strategic external mergers were items to be determined by all the top management. Since cannibalization of established business following strategic innovation proposals was not uncommon, the form of agreement in aligning with established organizations was also important strategic behavior for the MBD in strategic selection (domain II).

The second point was to implement processes to establish and embed value chains aimed at achieving specific commercialization in strategic concentration domain III of these new products, services and business rigorously selected in the strategic selection domain II. This involved MBD promoting company-wide knowledge management by forming in-house communities with traditional organizations, and establishing links between MBD time-pacing strategies and the event-pacing strategies of traditional organizations.

MBD undertook experiments and evaluations in strategic selection (domain II) while simultaneously promoting MBD-centered company-wide knowledge management and encouraging event-paced pacing strategies through traditional organizations in strategic concentration (domain III). This signifies the strategic innovation business shift from strategic selection (domain II) to strategic concentration (domain III), and the importance of the interface and interaction of strategy behavior among both new and old organizations between domain II and III.

After that, the employees of the traditional organization in domain III (strategic concentration) gradually experienced a revolution in awareness, and the full-scale launch of planning strategy founded on event-based pacing activated by personnel on a nationwide organizational scale led to great expansion in the ISDN market. The process of incremental change implemented through this planning strategy underwent a continuous spiral of planning adjustment and correction (the strategic action of these traditional organizations is called the "incremental change loop"). NTT acquired a strong competitive advantage with a creation of a new market of digital network service and achieved major strategic innovations by linking and integrating each loop through these two strategies.

MBD created new core competences by forming various strategic communities outside the company within a challenging organizational culture, and constantly hammered out creative emergent policies aimed at strategic innovation. Meanwhile, these contrasting, traditional organizations implemented well-planned policies aimed at incremental innovation emphasizing stability and control through a sound organizational culture by enhancing the gradually accumulated core competences. The top teams from NTT management consciously internalized these paradoxical organizations, strategies, cultures, and competences with their internal contradictions, and raised output company-wide by simultaneously launching and integrating these different systems (see Figure 3.3).

The organizational form of Figure 3.3 is analogous to that of the "ambidextrous organization" (Tushman and O'Reilley, 1997), but differs in the following points. In the ambidextrous organizations business-level interaction among new and traditional organizations is extremely restricted, and upper management emphasizes the unification of both organizations. In this case, however, the close interaction (knowledge sharing and collaboration through dialogue and discussion) among the new MBD organizations and the traditional organizations in strategic concentration (domain III) is promoted at each management level (top, middle, and lower). In strategic selection (domain II), meanwhile, business-level interaction among MBD and traditional organizations is small, while interaction and linkage to consensus at a top and upper management working level is great. Another difference is that all the functions of the business value chain for implementing business in the ambidextrous organization (including R&D, sales and marketing, technology, and support) build a dual structure in both old and new organizations. In this case, the division of roles between the new and old organizations is clearly determined, and the business value chain interface is appropriately established.

The case analysis of the ISDN revolution above outlines the flow of each phase from the birth of new business in the strategy innovation loop (strategic emergence — domain I) to fostering (strategic selection, domain II), acceleration (strategic concentration — domain III), and maturity and decline (strategic efficiency — domain IV). The linkage of the continuous and incremental change loops illustrated in Figure 3.3 reflects the features of both new and old organizational strategies, structure, culture, and competence in each of the strategic selection and concentration domains while demonstrating the relationship of strategic behaviours between the two domains. NTT linked two different innovative loops to build the management capability to link up and shift among each of the strategic selection and concentration domains. This corresponds to the strategic innovation capability to create the strategic innovation loop function.

Moreover, this *strategic innovation capability* was highly significant in promoting interaction among the exploratory and exploitative activities of both new and old organizations; integrating strategy, organizational structure, organizational culture, and competence by achieving an appropriate interface with new and established organizations; and then realizing the strategic innovation business of ISDN services and fiber optics. Furthermore, NTT co-established and made to coexist two different archetypes within the same company through dialectical management (a key element of *strategic innovation capability*), and skillfully managed strategic contradiction, creative abrasion, and productive friction. The creation of synergies among both new and old organizations became an important element in the success of the large-corporation strategic innovation.

2.2   The challenge of fiber-optic broadband: More innovation in the strategic innovation loop

2.2.1   Strategic transformation from ISDN to fiber-optic communication

In 1997, MBD undertook a full-scale broadband business through the creation of fiber-optic communications networks. NTT had begun to handle ISDN in 1994, formulating a hop (analog line), step (digital line or ISDN), and jump (fiber optics) scenario. NTT later provided ISDN and ADSL services in parallel, but ADSL was basically an intermediate form until the fiber-optic broadband service was fully commercialized with fiber-optic access. Thus, the promotion of ISDN also led to the fiber business route. At the same time, the fiber-optic cost structure fell, and the systems, equipment, and development necessary for the network structure also progressed.

Moreover, NTT decided to achieve 20 million channels in 2000 through ISDN and promote broadband business through fiber optics. From 1998, ISDN services gradually began to take off at strategic concentration (domain III). To realize its future strategies, MBD converted to a strategy that diverted ISDN application development resources to the new exploratory process (strategic emergence — domain I and strategic selection domain II) of the fiber optic business (see Phase 1 in Figure 3.4). Meanwhile, ISDN services were implemented centered on traditional organizations in strategic concentration (domain III). NTT implemented the dialectical management that used its *strategic innovation capability* to promote the search process (domains I and II) of the fiber-optic business in new organizations and to promote the exploitation process (domain III) of ISDN services in established organizations by adjusting interfaces among new and old organizations.

The project to promote broadband business through fiber optics newly constructed within the MBD was called the "Phoenix project." Passing through strategic emergence (domain I) this project acquired around 250 companies to participate in trials in December 1997, and launched the "Phoenix Promotion Association" to gain experience of experimenting in the strategic selection domain. Then the NTT

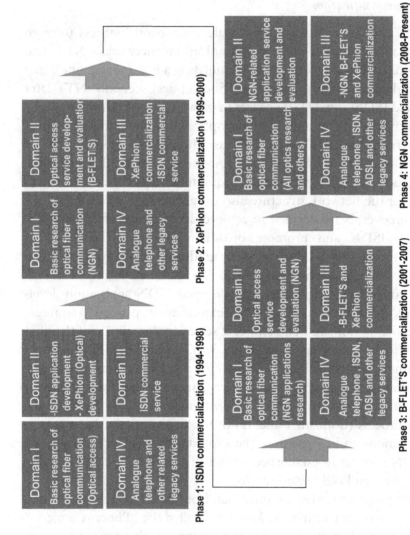

Phase 1: ISDN commercialization (1994-1998)

Domain I
Basic research of optical fiber communication (Optical access)

Domain II
-ISDN application development
-XePhion (Optical) development

Domain III
ISDN commercial service

Domain IV
Analogue telephone and other related legacy services

Phase 2: XePhion commercialization (1999-2000)

Domain I
Basic research of optical fiber communication (NGN)

Domain II
Optical access service development and evaluation (B-FLET'S)

Domain III
-XePhion commercialization
-ISDN commercial service

Domain IV
Analogue telephone and other legacy services

Phase 3: B-FLET'S commercialization (2001-2007)

Domain I
Basic research of optical fiber communication (NGN applications research)

Domain II
Optical access service development and evaluation (NGN)

Domain III
-B-FLET'S and XePhion commercialization

Domain IV
Analogue telephone , ISDN, ADSL and other legacy services

Phase 4: NGN commercialization (2008-Present)

Domain I
Basic research of optical fiber communication (All optics research and others)

Domain II
NGN-related application service development and evaluation

Domain III
-NGN, B-FLET'S and XePhion commercialization

Domain IV
Analogue telephone , ISDN, ADSL and other legacy services

Figure 3.4   Strategic innovation system in NTT Group.

group subsidiary NTT-ME began commercializing (strategic concentration domain) the new service to exploit (XePhion) fiber optics for the corporate user (see Phase 2 in Figure 3.4).

2.2.2 *Broadband business after the division of NTT*

In 1997, division of NTT into holding companies NTT, NTT East, NTT West, and NTT Communication, all the NTT group employees devoted themselves to various domains including research and development and business activities aimed at the corporate vision of realizing broadband services through fiber optics. In August 2001, NTT East and NTT West launched the "B-FLET'S" (B is for "Broadband") fiber access service as a full-scale initiative to create broadband (see Phase 3 in Figure 3.4). B-FLET'S passed through the stage of experimental service in strategic selection (domain II), and is currently commercialized in strategic concentration (domain III). Moreover, in November 2001, the broadband content distribution (BROBA), video communication, and other services launched by NTT Resonant, a strategic company of the NTT group's broadband service (when NTT was divided, part of MBD organization was spun off as the subsidiary NTT-X, which later integrated into other group companies and businesses, and was renamed), was newly trialed featuring a next-generation, 21st century optics vision aimed at spreading NTT broadband.

In November 2002, NTT achieved its next five-year broadband vision titled "toward a world of resonant communication with the next-generation broadband vision for optics," and launched new initiatives aimed at creating broadband through fiber optics. "Resonant communication" implies a natural communication environment amid the flow of innovation from narrowband to broadband Internet arising from the high-quality imaging that narrowband systems such as ISDN were incapable of achieving. "Resonant" expresses the nuances of "resonate," "vibrate," and "resound." "Resonant communication" refers to a next-generation optics communication environment developed in resonance with various individuals of the community, where individuals or companies, use broadband to interactively connect to ubiquitous virtual networks "any time, any place, anywhere." It combines outstanding usability with safety, reliability, and simplicity. It is also a vision that clarifies NTT's *raison d'être* in showing how this proposal would change business, society, and the daily lives of individuals, and the role that NTT would play.

The resonant communication environment enables real, natural communication using, for example, high-quality video that narrowband could not accomplish while also overcoming time and distance as a function of the network itself. Conquering time increases people's disposable time, and conquering distance exponentially expands the range of individual and corporate activities. For real-world activities, rich video communication from the merging real and virtual technologies transcends individuals, organizations, regions, and countries; shares and creates tacit and explicit knowledge by "sharing the realities" possessed by individuals and organizations; and connects to innovative new businesses and social lifestyles.

Realizing the new platform of this resonant communication environment enables support for the creation of various new kinds of knowledge and business models pertaining to individual social lives and corporate activities. Companies can co-create with the customer to enhance corporate creativity and efficiency in areas such as sales, marketing, personnel training, and comprehensive communication and collaboration (including development, design, and manufacturing processes) inside and outside the company while contributing to the creation of new business models. They also help develop the economy and solve social issues in such areas as declining birthrates and the aging society, environment and energy, safety and security, and education and regional disparities.

The new service developments that realized this resonant communication environment were driven by research and development centered on NTT's R&D division, which grew in parallel with the 1990s growth of the Internet. The new services migrated from fundamental research (domain I) through trial evaluation processes (domain II) to NTT's launch of full-scale commercialization (domain III) of Next Generation Network (NGN) services in March 2008 to achieve a resonant communication environment (see Figure 3.4's strategic innovation loop for the shift from domain I in phase 2, through domain II in phase 3, to domain 3 in phase 4).

The NGN service is a sound, secure IP service with four features of open interface, quality of service (QoS), security, and reliability pioneered by NTT first in the world. It combines the flexibility and scalability of the Internet with the reliability and stability of fixed phone networks to deliver an unprecedented information environment. NTT is planning to expand the NGN service nationwide to cover the same area as that of the existing B-FLET'S service by March 2011.

NTT established the "next generation service co-creation forum" to coincide with the launch of the NGN service. This forum enhance thinking of generating new business to interact and build various kinds of collaboration amid the lively sharing of information while also supporting rapid service development and commercialization. It extends beyond the ICT industry to incorporate people connected to various fields, organizations, and industries. It is an open business forum based on the concept of "creating together."

Fiber-optic broadband for the general household is currently spreading exponentially, and Japan's diffusion rate is higher than anywhere else in the world. Despite vocal criticism from journalists, media players, and competitors as NTT set out its fiber optics vision, NTT's envisioned market is now operational. John T. Chambers, CEO of US corporation Cisco Systems, said the following:

> "Surprisingly, Japan has rapidly developed into the world's most advanced network society. Japanese broadband communications are 30 times faster than those in the US, and cost one-thirtieth as much. When NTT first began to pour its energies into fiber-optic communication, the world looked on doubtfully, but now almost everyone says that it was the right move. It is rare for a large number of people to support a great change in the market at its inception, but companies have to have the courage to run necessary risks. Whether or not they can do this determines the future of the company." (Nikkei Business, 2005)

Strategic innovation is high-risk and high-return. The essence of strategic innovation is not to emphasize profit from short-term thinking but to realize strategy for future creation oriented to new business that justifies (or objectifies) the subjective thinking and beliefs possessed by companies and employees. *Strategic innovation capability* is also a dynamic innovation process creates that new knowledge from the subjectivity of people (companies) to discover business opportunities, markets, and technologies with a will to achieve strategic innovation.

2.2.3 *The strategic innovation loop of fiber-optic business*

Each of the new XePhion, B-FLET'S, and NGN fiber-optics services illustrated the strategic innovation loop (domain I–II–III) (see Figure 3.4). In Phase 1 of Figure 3.4 (ISDN commercialization), NTT provided commercial ISDN services in domain III while implementing new trial services exploiting ISDN and implementing the trial of the XePhion corporate fiber-optic communication service in domain II. Similarly, in phase 2 (XePhion commercialization), optics services were launched in domain III while trials of the consumer-oriented B-FLET'S fiber access service were carried out in domain II.

In Phase 3 (B-FLET'S commercialization), under the organizational structure that followed the division of NTT, the NTT East and NTT West companies implemented B-FLET'S commercial optical access services while the R&D division of holding company NTT undertook trials and experiments of the NGN services to realize a resonant communications environment for still more developed next-generation services. In recent years, moreover, in Phase 4 (NGN commercialization), NTT East and NTT West have launched commercial NGN services while NTT's R&D division and the East and West companies' development divisions have taken the lead in promoting domain II activities achieving new business development with trial experiments for services applying NGN centered on the "next-generation co-creation forum." The new XePhion, B-FLET'S, and NGN services were achieved by shifting through domains I, II and III.

Such domain shifts can be explained from historical cases of commercial processes from R&D of NTT's fiber-optic communications technologies (see Figure 3.5). Fiber-optic broadband services have been achieved through the sustained innovation of time and endurance for R&D processes extending over 30 years. As mentioned in Chapter 2, most of the strategic innovations are established through the stages of discovery and invention resulting from basic scientific research and technology development in slow charging environments.

Slow or very slow environmental change with high uncertainty (domain I) observed at the initial stage of strategic innovation is the stage of creating new technologies through new ideas, business concepts, inventions, and discoveries. Fields such as fiber-optic communications technology, which has a high ratio of scientific elements and great technical difficulty, require longer time for basic research to produce ideas that become the source of new strategic innovation. Many Researchers devoted to achieving fiber-optic broadband services by developing core technologies to realize fiber optics communications (long-distance transmission and Fiber To The Home, or FTTH), which is one of the most fundamental key research themes. Development of the VAD fiber-optic manufacturing technology began in 1977. And R&D continued into optical devices such as single-mode fibers, semiconductor lasers, optical connectors, optical splitters and optical switches, and every kind of fiber-optic transmission system (including single channel, multiple channel, fiber access systems, and all-optic networks). The success achieved in domain I owed much to the creative thinking and action of the NTT R&D division's middle management and lower, as well as to the strategic contribution and commitment of top and senior management.

The patterns for the diverse knowledge integration processes required for R&D of fiber-optic communications were present in this domain I. Previously, large traditional corporations had mainly promoted closed innovation centered on in-house laboratories and development divisions under a hierarchical system. Closed innovation is also an important process for developing continuous innovation through accumulated, path-dependent knowledge. While closed

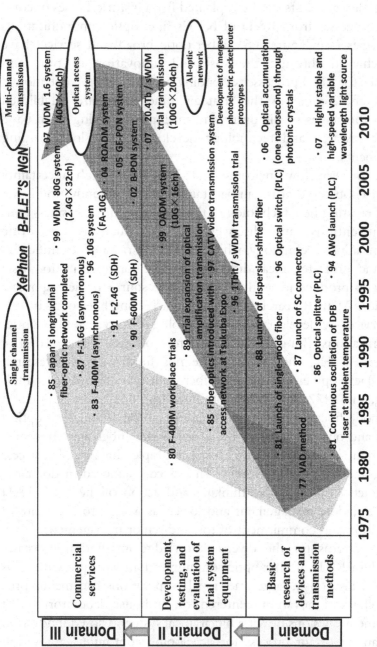

Figure 3.5   Strategic Innovation Loop of Optical Fiber Systems.

Source: Created from NTT's officially released data.

innovation at the NTT laboratories was the main driver behind the development of fiber-optic communications technologies, NTT also dynamically undertook joint development with outstanding Japanese manufacturers — the so-called "NTT family" including NEC, Fujitsu, Hitachi, and Oki.

Later, the development of core technologies and optical transmission systems based on the invention of fiber-optic communication technologies and the provisional establishment of business models for new network services exploiting these systems led to trial manufacture, experiment, and incubation. The NTT's R&D division undertook trial manufacture and development based on developing core technologies in domain I, and performed various trial tests related to fiber-optic transmission in the domain II stage. In this domain, the enhancement of trial manufacture systems raised still further the level of perfection of R&D-division driven trial manufacture systems aimed at commercial services.

The market exploiting and supporting fiber-optic technologies gradually became established in domain II and shifted to the full-scale commercial services of domain III. In this domain, competition among other communication carriers transformed the market to a high-speed environment, and NTT accelerated the investment of essential resources.

2.2.4 *Inter-domain shift among group companies*

The organization committed to R&D processes for fiber-optic broadband services in domains I and II is the "R&D division," centered on laboratories attached to holding company NTT following its re-organization. Meanwhile, organizations undertaking commercialization of fiber-access services (domain III) and various broadband application services (domain III) following the re-organization included NTT East, NTT West, NTT Communications, and the above-mentioned NTT Resonant. NTT East and NTT West focused on fiber access while NTT Communications, NTT Resonant, NTT Plala, NTT BizLink and others focused on broadband applications. Coordination and collaboration among the holding company "R&D

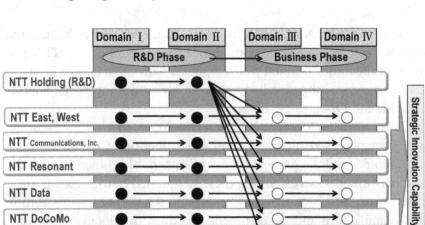

Figure 3.6   **Strategic Innovation Capability in NTT Group.**

Division" and the individual business corporations has become the trigger to smoothly implement a management shift (especially from domain II to domain III) among broadband service domains through fiber optics (see Figure 3.6).

Meanwhile, the main NTT group companies, NTT-DATA and NTT DoCoMo, have proposed new services, such as (FMC) Fixed and Mobile Communications, which merges and integrates fiber optics services with mobile phone services and solutions business exploiting fiber optics infrastructure. Moreover, various core technologies that underwent technology transfers arising from a domain shift (II to III) from the R&D division of the NTT holding company possessed not only fiber-optic communications infrastructure but also various applications technologies. This process will be explained in detail next, but the domain shift is also deeply connected with the knowledge integration process among companies including NTT group members and external partners.

As for the infrastructure development of fiber-optic communications, although the holding company's R&D division took responsibility for domain I and II R&D processes, the business corporations mentioned above (NTT East, NTT West, NTT Communications, NTT Resonant, and others) also contributed to incubation processes (including initial business concepts and ideas development, trial manufacture and experiment) in user-side application and service development. The business corporation side promptly exploited the fruits of the holding company's research and development while participating closely in processes (domains I through III) from product concept development to commercialization for user-side applications exploiting new communications infrastructure including fiber optics.

Business corporations possess R&D functions specializing in application service development. Cost centers specializing in application development business corresponding to MBD in Figure 3.3 (organization names are differed from one corporation to another) exist, and these cost centers as emergent organizations take on the responsibilities of processes through to commercialization (domain I through III). At the same time, the traditional organizational infrastructure of functional organizations (including sales, equipment, maintenance, and procurement) with missions (domains III and IV) for new services to grow into mainstream business by investing in in-house resources aimed at the growth of commercialized services also exists. Coordination and collaboration among these emergent and traditional organizations smoothly operates the management shift among domains (especially from domain II to II). This resembles the ISDN promotion system in Figure 3.3 above (see Figure 3.6).

Meanwhile, although the R&D processes for application services were implemented in numerous trials and new business in domain II, not all business were successful. For NTT, the significance of the trials and pioneering business in domain II was the accumulation of the knowledge (within the NTT group) to discover markets and demand with the potential for future development amid a repeated learning process of withdrawing from and integrating with new business. The processes from R&D to commercialization at each business corporation (see Figure 3.6) sometimes also involved duplicating business ideas (batting and cannibalization). Nevertheless, the top management stratum at each business corporation, including the NTT holding company, accepted a certain amount of "organizational slack" aimed at the challenge of unknown business domains and the accumulation of high-quality knowledge vis-à-vis people and organizations. NTT executed management within each domain and among domains through effective action from diverse knowledge within the group companies, and drove the *strategic innovation loop*. This became the business process that created *strategic innovation capability* throughout NTT (see Figure 3.6).

At the time this fiber-optic service was launched (domain III), the conventional ISDN and ADSL services, along with the declining analog phone services, were already shifting to domain IV and becoming a mature business amid slow market change (see Phases 3 and 4 in Figure 3.4). These services were then replaced and converted to old business as declining businesses with strategic innovation businesses, and new strategic positions formed from the fiber-optics business.

2.3 *Knowledge integration dynamics*

The mission of the research laboratories at holding company NTT was not only to search for the basic elemental technologies to create new principles and products but also to perform basic R & D and shared basic technological R & D aiming to realize new services, and to build bridges between the R&D results and the business departments (building bridges from domain I directly to domains II and III, discussed later). NTT promoted R&D to maintain an edge in the fiercely competitive information communications business (research and development funds amounted to some 200 billion yen a year), retain outstanding researchers to cover a wide range of technology areas supporting ICT (3,000 staff, including 600 with doctorates), and maintain its customary rate of high activity (around 2,600 patent applications a year and 4,600 theses and other external publications).

The fruits of the NTT group's R&D stretching back over 30 years had promoted domestic technologies to the world, starting with digital switch devices, large-scale computers, and high-density magnetic discs, followed by faxes (NTT's image compression technology was used in faxes worldwide), ISDN (its launch was a global first), fiber optics (60 percent global share of production methods) optical connectors (70 percent share of global components), and optical transmission systems (NTT-proposed transmission systems are used throughout the world). In recent years, NTT has promoted the B-FLET'S optical access service, a commercial service for the world's most advanced broadband technologies, the global pioneering NGN service, and next-generation mobile phone services (3.9G mobile phone system) while also focusing on developing Internet business and various application services under the optical, new generation vision mentioned above (see Figure 3.7).

The practical development stage as a research and development theme common to every country exists as a "valley of death" where financing from the market is difficult because it is extremely hard to see whether the technology can be industrialized. This valley exists even for NTT's R&D process due to the deficiencies of industrialization. The "valley of death" exists at the boundaries of domains II and III, and corresponds to the gap between the R&D stages and the market launch. This gap comprises specific organizational initiatives (including investment in commercial products and services) aimed at decision making within the company to judge as a commercial business and commercialization based on the evaluation of trial equipment and performance of trial services. Decision making on commercialization is the final step in domain II, and on the basis of these results, specific action aimed at commercialization is executed in domain III (see Figure 3.8).

Overcoming the "valley of death" is the key to smoothly implement the domain shift (II to III), and bring success to strategic innovation.[3] The infrastructure services of fiber-optic communications and the

---

[3] The next challenge faced by new businesses crossing the valleys of death at the boundaries of domains II and III is to swim through the "Darwinian Seas" (Auerswald and Branscomb, 2003) of domain III under fast-changing environments. The "survival of the fittest" means these companies had to be cost-competitive, either by continually upgrading new products, investing in new products, or methodically enhancing the efficiency of the supply chain to increase the market share of new businesses. The digital consumer electronics business mentioned in Chapter 4 is an example of such a case.

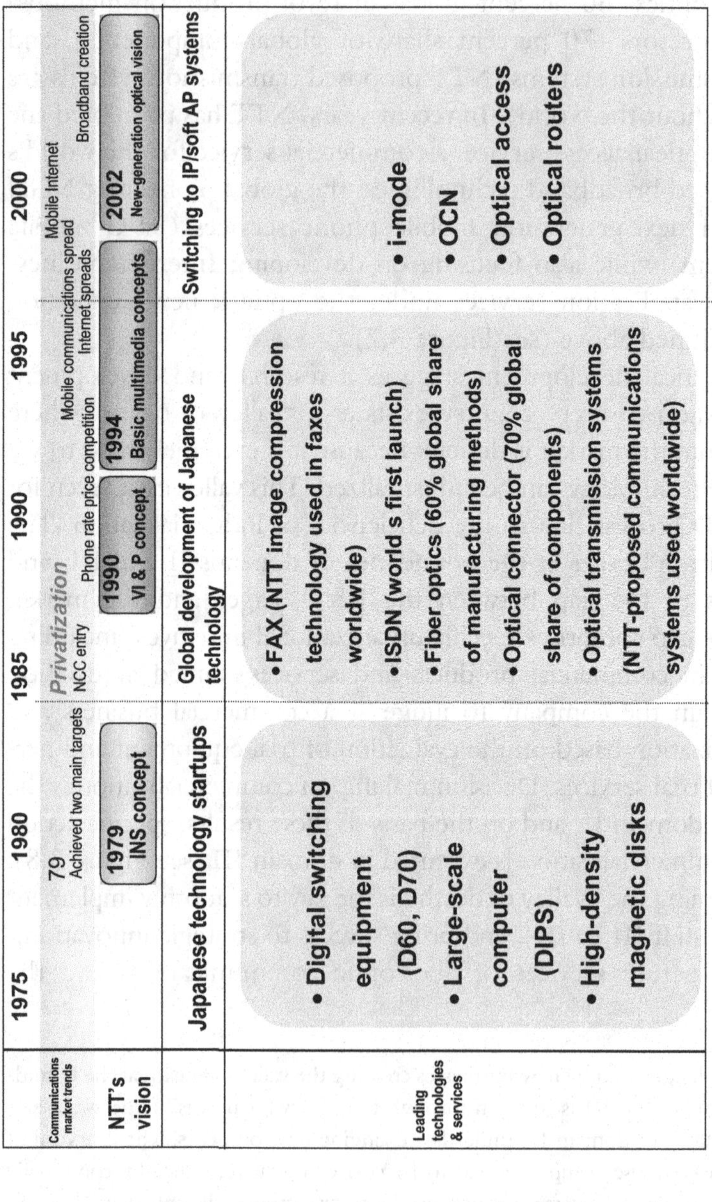

Figure 3.7   30-year Flow of NTT Group's R&D.

Source: Created from NTT's officially released data and interviews with NTT staff.

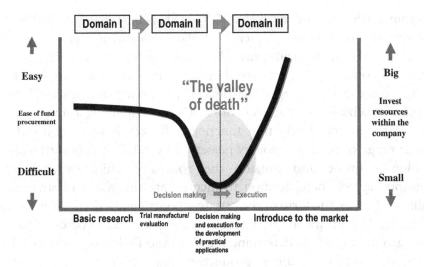

Figure 3.8   The Valley of Death.

process from R&D to commercialization of new application services used by the corporate and consumer users on this optical infrastructure are significant for NTT. The diverse knowledge integration process becomes essential for NTT to smoothly implement this kind of management among domains and conquer the "valley of death." In this regard, I would like to bring up two points. Firstly, NTT's general production team integrates core knowledge inside and outside the company, and the process becomes a framework promoting domain shift (domain II to III). Secondly, it is a framework for promoting domain shift from knowledge and organization integration through the technology transfer of software architecture (mentioned above).

- Knowledge integration through the general
  production team

NTT supported the release of the above-mentioned optical new generation vision in November 2002. In July 2003, NTT arranged the general production function system aiming for further strengthening commercialization of the fruits of R & D. NTT then launched this system in July 2003 to conquer the "valley of death" that lies between R & D and commercialization. The producer designated as responsible for commercialization collaborates with companies inside and outside the NTT group while directly promoting and undertaking commercialization of the fruits of NTT's outstanding research.

With general production functions, the key is to combine the wide range of basic technology possessed by NTT's R&D with technologies inside and outside the company while dynamically promoting commercialization to incorporate the vision of strategic alliance (taking the form of the "strategic communities" mentioned in Chapter 1) both within NTT and with companies and bodies outside the group in order to determine the form and timing of commercialization. Then the general production team picks up marketable technologies from the research institutes and executes missions to build bridges among business themes (candidates) while establishing dynamic partnerships with efficient companies outside the group and targeting the expansion of business domains (not limited to communications services) as the NTT group (see Figure 3.9). The producers set commitments for quantitative business scale (annual objectives that the producers have the responsibility for achieving) to put projects into practice, and become responsible for commercialization. They hold full powers to fulfil their responsibilities, including allocating and reviewing resources and retiring unprofitable projects, and implement projects flexibly. Then they aim to conquer the "valley of death" between R&D and commercialization.

The functions of the general production teams differ from those of the information processing model of organization, which is a leading contingency theory. Examples of existing research including "differentiation and integration" (Lawrence and Lorsch, 1967), "adequate information processing capacity" (Galbraith, 1973), and "coordination theory" (Malone and Crowston, 1994) formed the basis of the information processing model, and described new product development and business process efficiency through adjustment of such areas as communication and cooperation among formal organizations within the company and members of other companies. A great deal of previous

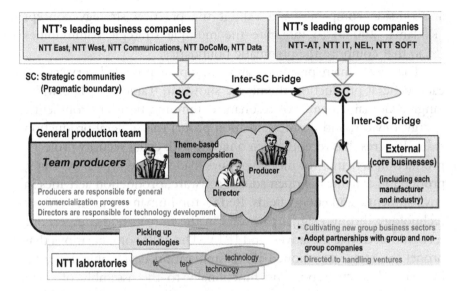

Figure 3.9 NTT Comprehensive Production System.

Source: Created from NTT external public documents and interviews.

research, moreover, suggested the need for smooth communication at cross-cultural boundaries (Allen, 1971; Tushman, 1977; Tushman and Nadler, 1978) and the importance of "boundary spanners" (Brown and Eisenhardt, 1995). The central concept of these theories was to pay attention to the efficient process, transfer, storage, and retrieval functions of large amounts of information and knowledge.

Of course, rules-based internal processes, efficient project management, and information processing approach to implement business processes at the basis of corporate activity are also essential. Strategic innovation, however, tends to arise at organizational boundaries among actors possessing different organizational rules and specialist areas (Leonard-Barton, 1995), and the information processing approach that focuses on efficient information and knowledge processing is unable to sufficiently describe the strategic innovation process at organizational boundaries. Accordingly, the functions of these "general production teams," unlike those of the information processing model, bridge the diverse knowledge boundaries inside and outside companies and exhibit the practical strategy concept (Kodama, 2007a) to integrate the multiple strategic communities (SCs) that comprise the pragmatic boundaries.

The aims, main products, and line-up of provided services for each general production theme are shown in Table 3.1. The wide-ranging domain themes of resonant communication, environmental energy, devices, and business creation propel this general production team. Progress has recently been ongoing with cyber security projects, production activities for mobile phones loaded with Type B IC chips, production activities of open source software, production activities in environmental and energy fields, RedTacton human-area and network technology through signal pathways in the human body, fingerprint recognition device initiatives, and IPTV. The MBD organizations that propel the above-mentioned ISDN application development can be interpreted as corresponding functionally to the assembly of these general production teams.

These general production teams have the function of smoothly driving domain shifts (especially from domain II to III), as shown in Figure 3.6. The teams then promote diverse knowledge integration distributed inside and outside the company aimed at building market and technology value chains. The dynamic changes arising from the general production teams at vertical and horizontal corporate boundaries create new knowledge integration processes (vertical and horizontal integrated architecture and linkage relationship architecture). As a result, the creation of new knowledge merging and integrating NTT's core R&D competences (NGN, optical access service, and various application services) and external core competences (information equipment terminals, software, contents, and applications) enables the creation of a "co-evolution model" arising from the business model's "vertical value chain model" and positive cross-industry feedback (Figure 3.10).

- Knowledge integration through software R&D models

As mentioned above, the creation of R&D software to generate various network services using the hardware infrastructures maintained

Table 3.1　General production Theme Objectives, Main Products, and Service

Production theme	Aim	Main products and services
Resonant Communication	Research and develop upper layer infrastructure technology to realize next-generation NW architecture and new services based on comprehensive design concepts for three to five years from now aimed at achieving a resonant communication environment, which is a pillar of our "optical" new generation vision.	• QoS service • High-quality video distribution NW system • Collaboration service • Community service • High-security NW system etc.
Environmental Energy	Establish environmental and energy related business contributing to socioeconomic activity at an early stage	• Environmental IT software service for public • Multipurpose mobile power supply • Environmental management support system etc.
Devices	Create key devices for development and expansion of the broadband market with major breakthroughs, and accelerate early realization of resonant communication environment	• High-speed laser light source • Variable wavelength light source • Optical router planar light wave circuit switch etc.
Business Creation	Select promising themes linked to new business from core technologies out of R&D, and target expansion of the group's general business domain by creating new business not limited to communication fields.	• Horn method (song synthesizing technology) • Full-duplex codec & LSI for HDTV • Electronic watermarks • Optical ROM etc.

Source: Created from NTT external public documents and interviews.

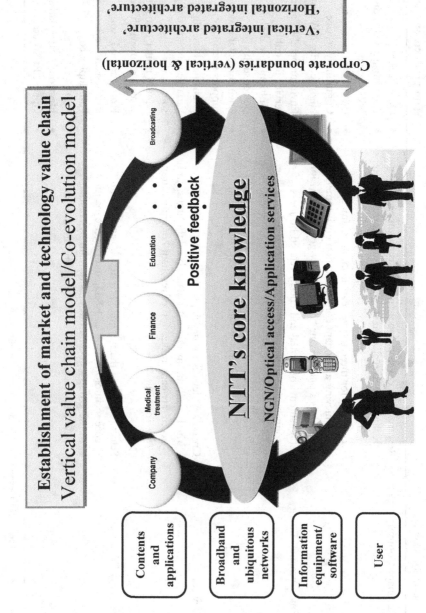

Figure 3.10   Value Chain Concepts from Diverse Knowledge Integration Process.

through the completion of digitization became a key topic. For NTT, another important task was to migrate business providing diverse software-led services under a server and client network environment oriented to the Internet era. In line with this movement, what was asked of the R&D process was the conversion from a hardware to a software model. The software model of R&D does not simply emphasize software development themes; it is a wide-ranging software resource shift that also encompasses hardware development in the shift from circuit design and package systems to architecture and protocol searches. What made the development of switching equipment so urgent, for example, was the migration from a hardware-focused development system comprising switch-circuit designs for circuit connection to a software-focused system developing the switching equipment system architecture, signalling systems, and switching equipment control software to enable a range of network services.

Additional to the development theme of migrating from hardware to software was the change, amid this flow, towards R&D methodologies. Hardware-focused development up to that time had created technical specifications and acquired means of sustaining them in the business division. In these cases, the business and R&D divisions linked with manufacturers to procure hardware (commercial equipment) based on technical specifications. The R&D and business divisions shared explicit knowledge of technical specifications, and were linked only by the manufacturing channel; the knowledge integration process of sharing and activating knowledge was restricted to NTT and specific manufacturers.

When software-centered development changed, however, the two divisions united to enable the business division to use the software developed by the R&D division, and absorbed feedback from the customer needs and worksite while undertaking new service development. The business division then activated core software developed by the R&D division, carried out system engineering (SE) of the entire new service targeted for development, and endeavored to flexibly customize software in response to user needs. Thus, knowledge across organizations was shared, and the in-house knowledge

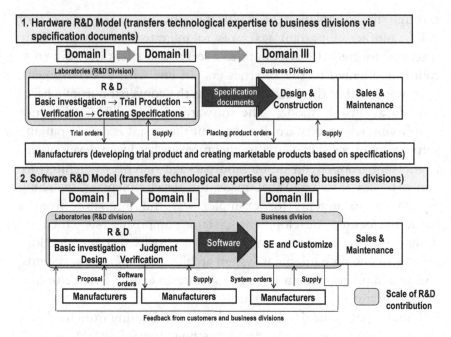

Figure 3.11   Transformation of the R&D Process.

Source: Based on data from Miyazu (2002).

integration process to further develop and activate this knowledge exhibited features of the software R&D process (see Figure 3.11).

Responding to the expansion of Internet business with R&D process steps, many cases also exist of dynamic joint development of software through strategic alliances with external development partners. NTT's internal and external dynamic knowledge integration processes are achieving new services based on software architecture. In this way, the conversion to software R&D processes promotes knowledge integration among different organizations and becomes the trigger for smoothly promoting domain shifts (II to III).

Around this time, in order to minimize time loss in the provision of services, NTT became pressured into organizational reform to bind the R&D divisions, which were positioned as organizations isolated from the then-business division, still closer. NTT targeted new business exploiting the future Internet and multimedia technologies, and in 1993, established the R&D development HQ along with the sales, corporate business, and service production (an organization attached to the service production and planning section that comprised the MBD organization) HQs. This clarified the importance of R&D functions emphasizing software development within the NTT group. NTT's choice of this kind of management formation was made to realize the operation of a huge corporate group as a nucleus of centripetal force arising from the cutting-edge technological capability of world-class R&D centered on software technology in the information distribution age, which was growing ever more globally competitive.

3. Overview

I have highlighted above the specific case of NTT to analyse the strategic innovation system arising from the dynamic knowledge integration process. As this case study shows, companies achieving continuous strategic innovation can be said to have done so by the new knowledge integration chain implemented by the layered strategic innovation loop. To achieve this continuous strategic innovation, companies have to implement optimal knowledge integration processes among different organizations (including partner companies and customers), such as emergent and traditional organizations, in response to conditions within and in a shift among each domain. This is not necessarily an expression of the extremes of closed innovation (or closed knowledge innovation) and open innovation (or open knowledge integration). To build the knowledge integration model mentioned in Chapter 1, outstanding companies activate their own core knowledge while integrating diverse core knowledge distributed inside and outside the corporation through skilful knowledge integration processes based on the thinking of knowledge integration architecture (vertical integrated, horizontal integrated, and linkage relationships).

Nevertheless, the knowledge integration dynamics whereby this kind of knowledge integration process asks how *strategic innovation capability* should be changed or realized, how corporate strategy behavior and organizational structures change, and what the optimal knowledge integration architecture and process patterns for achieving strategic innovation are, can be considered as contingent on the environment and individual companies. In the future, research in knowledge integration architecture, knowledge integration processes, and strategic innovation systems of major corporations will be needed to make further advances through theory, proof, and practical viewpoints.

Chapter

4

Knowledge Integration and Innovation in the Consumer Electronics, Communications Device, and Semiconductor Fields

This chapter presents case studies and analyses of Japanese management in the fields of digital consumer electronics, communications device, and semiconductor. The chapter compares Western and Japanese management styles, and derives from them a knowledge integration framework that enables access to and absorption from external knowledge based on the vertical integration business model practised in Japanese companies.

1. Digital Consumer Electronics and Communications Device Sectors

Digital consumer electronics mainly comprise digital products such as flat-screen digital TVs, DVD recorders, digital cameras, and digital videos. Communications devices are digital network devices supporting

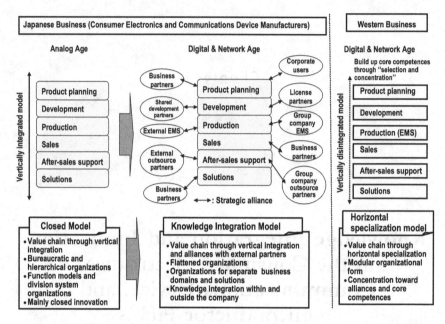

Figure 4.1   Business Models for Consumer Electronics and Communications Devices.

broadband and multimedia. Up to the 1980s, in the heyday of analog technology, a large number of Japanese manufacturers were structured divisionally for separate products, machinery, and tools. These individual divisions consistently created vertically integrated organizational structures and business models for product planning, development, production, and sales (see Figure 4.1). Market changes arising from the development of digital and Internet technologies, media (text, voice, and image) integration through broadband, and new business models crossing industry boundaries accelerated the integration of different technologies. This technological integration and business model diversification led to demands for companies to integrate the range of knowledge distributed inside and outside the company. Moreover, factors such as the acceleration of e-business through the Internet, specialization and division of technology domains, and organizational specialization speeded up the move toward more complex organizational and knowledge boundaries inside and outside the company.

Amid this kind of environmental change, Japanese companies freed themselves from the previous closed innovation model of vertical integration, and came to recognize the importance integrating diverse knowledge inside and outside the company. The corporate knowledge integration process is now, and will remain, one of the most important sales issues (Grant, 1997, 1998).

1.1 *Horizontal specialization model through Western management*

US computer and semiconductor industries have adopted a horizontally specialized business model that helps each company concentrate its core competences in specialist fields. The vertical integration that yielded benefits in the early days of the computer industry (including PCs) has shifted to disintegration through changes in the market and technology business environment (including faster ICT tools and technological changes such as standardization of the technology interface and modularization). As a result, from the 1980s onward, vertically integrated business activities were divided into individual modularized processes, and vertical disintegration and disaggregation in the digital industry accelerated (Sturgeon, 2002; Christensen, Raynor and Verlinden, 2001) (see Figure 4.1). Then the horizontally specialized value chains of the PC and semiconductor industries (described later) arose. The changing environment drastically reduced transaction costs among companies and markets. DELL and other finished product manufacturers were able to efficiently procure products from outside the company, and the finished product manufacturers achieved the transformation of optimal vertical boundaries. Features of this horizontally specialized model are that the interfaces between each horizontally specialized business layer (contract condition interface at order reception level, including product development and manufacture) are made explicit; and each company acts as a modular organization holding specific core competences in each business layer.

In recent years, an increasing number of cases have occurred, in which large, branded corporations, such as Nokia and Apple's iPod in the mobile phones field, have specialized in product R&D and sales and marketing while outsourcing production to EMS companies, large companies such as the US Flextronics and Solectron, and the Taiwanese Arima Communications, which have factories throughout the world.

1.2 *Japanese manufacturers' "knowledge integration model"*

As the 21st century gets under way, Japanese manufacturers of consumer electronics and communications devices have shifted to corporate models that create new knowledge by further flattening the previous vertically integrated organizational structures, skillfully absorbing external partners' knowledge and competence, and combining external and internal knowledge. One of the current strengths of Japanese consumer electronics and communications device manufacturers is the *knowledge integration model* (see Figure 4.1). This model combines constructing value chains through consistent vertical integration business models incorporating basic research, parts development, product development, production, sales, and after-sales support solutions with integrating internal knowledge using outstanding external knowledge held by each horizontally specialized business layer of specialist companies ("Western businesses") in the digital industry. Strategies and aims mentioned with regard to this *knowledge integration model* develop digital and network technologies, realize core Black Box technologies and Only One products[1] (See Table 4.1),

---

[1] The Black Box, named by Matsushita (Panasonic), refers to elemental technology whereby a company adopts its own original technology architecture for the components that make up a product, and plans to differentiate that product from those of other companies. Architectural innovations implementing original connectivity methods among the individual modules that comprise a product or integrating modules to create value that is difficult for competitors to copy, and modular innovation that renews the functions of the modules themselves with original technology are examples of key elements in creating a Black Box. (see R. Henderson, K. Clark, 1990). Only One was named by Sharp. It refers to products utilizing numerous Black Box element technologies that other companies cannot copy. Sharp names its own-company, original products Only One products (see Kodama, 2007a, 2007e).

Table 4.1 The Source of Japanese Companies' Competitive Capability (Highlights of Interviews with Japanese Manufacturers).

Development of 'Black Box' and 'Only One' products	Our number one strategy is to do what other companies don't. I want to focus on the black-box technology sector and build up Japan as an impressive manufacturing country. Core components such as System LSI are one of the significant black boxes. To take the example of Kobe's rice cooker business, IHI heaters (induction heaters) is a black box technology, though low-tech, which is exclusive to our firm. It is our independent technology, which China cannot copy. By making robust black box products in large numbers, Japan will revitalize to become an outstanding manufacturing country (Kunio Nakamura, CEO, Matsushita Electric).	Sharp's DNA derives from the "spirit of manufacturing" of founder Tokuji Hayakawa, who rapidly succeeded in bringing radio and TV products to market. Current management-linked concepts are the "only one" technologies that rivals cannot imitate and "black box" strategies. Among its many "only one" technologies, Sharp has created the Personal Organizer, 3-inch LCD TV, LCD viewcam, Color Zaurus, and mobile phone with camera. Sharp is considered to be a company with the traditional power of harmony, or "Wa." "Wa" suggests a fusion of technologies, which has successfully integrated device products and created mobile phone with camera and "sha mail" picture mail. Communications technologies and image technologies, or word processing and Zaurus information processing technologies have been combined to create the mobile phone with camera and "sha-mail" picture mail. Crystal is made from chemical reactions. I believe new products will be created on the same principle (Katsuhiko Machida, CEO, Sharp).

(Continued)

Table 4.1 (*Continued*)

| Non-separating method of development and production | Complete separation of development and production is dangerous in the manufacturing industry. Cell production teams for DVD recorders, for example, investigate manufacturing processes, and the design side, which makes specification counterproposals for set divisions (development and design divisions) quickly tries to incorporate them. Development and production should be unified. Utsunomiya's TV cell production methods transmit tacit knowledge unified by development and production (Kunio Nakamura, CEO, Matsushita Electric). | Markets move extremely fast. Competition takes place, and that makes the markets move faster still. Complex, fast-moving management is required. More than 2,000 people are involved in digital camera development, including the production force. We can't hire all our personnel in other countries just because labor costs are cheaper there. Going abroad to pursue cheap labor costs can give an edge at certain periods in certain years, but moving factories abroad is not a permanent solution. The key is to somehow establish an optimal production system in Japan under the conditions of Japan's high labor costs. It is important to exploit Japan's technological prowess and expertise in development, production processes, and manufacturing, and for all of this to contribute to Japanese growth (Fujio Mitarai, CEO, Canon). |

(*Continued*)

Table 4.1 (*Continued*)

Promoting collaboration with external partners	In the high economic growth era, business centered on "synthetism," or pursuing the expansion of business scale based on a company's own resources. In the economic recession that followed, a shift occurred toward "selection and concentration," the dynamic outsourcing and control transfer of non-core business to enhance core competences. Business processes that were difficult to differentiate began to be outsourced. Now, amid increasingly fierce competition, companies are pushing "selection and concentration" still further, and are searching for new models to develop business dynamically through collaboration that strategically combines a company's own strengths with those of its external partners. These new business models create new corporate value and enhance competitiveness by integrating multiple strengths through flexible collaboration with companies, especially client companies. To achieve this, a company must respond to drastic environmental shifts and change partners when necessary. Always aim to optimize the value chain while changing the forms of dynamic collaboration. NEC calls this "dynamic collaboration." (Akinobu Kanesugi, CEO, NEC)

develop products supporting multiple product types, produce cells as manufacturing innovations, develop and apply ICT, and develop sales systems and new solutions to dominate world markets.

Core technology developments such as Matsushita's Black Box and Sharp's Only One products are implemented in-house and contribute to the accumulation of expertise. They also promote collaboration with other companies by implementing joint development with outstanding external partners and dynamically adopting external partners' outstanding technology. Integrating heterogeneous technologies is especially important to realize multimedia services through advanced broadband services and mobile phones, and collaborate with external partners possessing leading technologies is an urgent task (See Table 4.1).

The *knowledge integration model* incorporates elements of dynamic collaboration among these partners. The *knowledge integration models* of Japanese consumer electronics and communications device manufacturers go beyond deepening and refining a company's core competences (path-dependent resources) to create new competences by acquiring new knowledge (including path-breaking resources) across technology and industry boundaries.

On the subject of production processes, Japanese companies implement thorough "selection and concentration." The manufacture of core products that can be differentiated from those of other companies, such as Sharp's and Matsushita's flat-screen TVs and Canon's digital cameras, is mainly undertaken in-house (mostly within Japan). Meanwhile, non-core products (those that cannot be differentiated from those of competitors) are driven by dynamically outsourcing to Electronic Manufacturing Service (EMS) For example, Canon's Oita factory, which produces digital camera cells, systematically endeavored to speed up the dispatch of new products in accordance with market demands. In recent years, digital cameras have miniaturized and incorporated advanced features at ever-faster speeds, making it essential for Canon to load high-density components has become essential. The company has encountered many similar problems in the manufacturing process for new products. On one occasion, advanced assembly expertise was needed to incorporate a single small spring. Canon's head office product technology center developed a new production method exploiting ICT, and the production technology division of the factory responsible for developing manufacturing equipment contributed its diverse experience and knowledge, considered original, independent assembly equipment and tools for the manufacture of each new product, and communicated its expertise to the assembly division. The capacity to pursue speed and flexible support for this kind of production technology can also become the capacity for competitive survival in the field of digital consumer electronics (see Table 4.1).

While the creation of routines and established manufacturing methods raise efficiency, the excessive stress on production efficiency in horizontally specialized business among Western management has a negative effect on product innovation, and can create a production dilemma among manufacturers (Abernathy, 1978; Qiang and Bianca, 2006; Westerman, McFarlan and Iansiti, 2006). A common feature of Japanese manufacturers' basic structure, the vertical integration business model, is the unification of development and production processes. This unification concept results in new product innovation brought about by the advance of technology. New design rules impact existing production rules, and new production methods impact existing design methods. Accordingly, development design and production engineers always need to dynamically implement deep sharing of information and knowledge (see Table 4.1).

The development of digital consumer electronics incorporating cutting-edge technology elements, as in the case of Matsushita, has been structured by the high integrity of the vertically integrated organizational system crossing work functions and specialist fields (Wheelwright and Clark, 1992; Kodama, 2007b). Canon's CEO Fujio Mitarai emphasizes that "development and production should be unified". Canon, moreover, does not just unite development and production for digital cameras, but also gathers the development and production organizations for the shared major component of lenses in devices such as digital cameras, printers, and copy machines in one physical location, and creates development and production scenarios. This unification, or integration of organizational and knowledge boundaries, leads to the evolution of new development and production rules and becomes a trigger sparking the necessary creativity among engineers.

1.3 *Basic differences between Japanese and Western management*

The fundamental difference between Japanese and Western companies is the difference in thinking relating to business activities that determine the vertical value chain (integration or unbundling). In recent years, the unbundling of function (R&D, production, and sales) against a background of ICT development has boosted the efficiency of transaction costs among a large number of companies. As transaction and interaction costs fall, the simultaneous pursuit of the three different economies (speed, scope, and scale) becomes difficult, and companies learn to strengthen business domain specializations through concentration and selection (Hegel and Singer, 1999). This is the correct argument for implementing strategy under fixed conditions. A large number of Western and Taiwanese companies, especially in the ICT and electronics industries, have exploited the merits of this unbundling and developed core competences through concentrating and selecting resources. As described in 3.3, Japanese companies also have a tendency to form integrated organizations that vertically merge the different business activities and specialist fields, while Western companies, especially in IT and digital industries, tend to form specialized modular organizations in domains where business activities and fields are horizontally specialized.

Taken from a knowledge management point of view, however, even if unbundling is able to handle speed economies, the companies that exploit this unbundling may not be capable of building competences to create high quality products and services or adding values such as total solutions by exploiting the synergies of each R&D, production, and sales functions. This is because the principle of self-sufficiency (internal production) is fundamental to building the intellectual capital that enables a sustained competitive edge (Teece, 2001).

Toyota Motor Corporation, one of Japan's outstanding companies, expands economies of scale by pursuing lower costs and higher quality through its own advanced production methods while also pursuing economies of scope through its global production and marketing system. Moreover, the global development and production system of the Innovative Multipurpose Vehicle (IMV), which aimed to establish a simultaneous development and production system on a global scale, has further reduced the life cycle of new products while achieving *economies of speed* for the development of the world-leading hybrid automobile. Moreover, Matsushita Electric, Sharp, and Canon, which earn profits and market share in the digital consumer electronics field, are pursuing economies of scale through revolutionary cell production innovations, economies of scope through simultaneous vertical launches on a global scale, and economies of speed by rapidly developing new products from core Black Box technology. Building and accumulating precious intellectual capital that exploits the features of business activity bundling and the simultaneous pursuit of the three economies through "integrative competences" (Kodama, 2007a) are both features of Japanese companies.

Creative and productive friction and interaction among bundled business activities transcends existing core competences to obtain new competences while incorporating the potential for creating new innovations (Hagel and Brown, 2005; Leonard-Barton, 1995). Many of the outstanding companies in Japan's high-tech business fields do not determine costs simply from interaction costs within and among companies, but also consider the source of innovative creation. This is a feature that differentiates Japanese from Western companies.

2. Semiconductor Business Sector

2.1 *The semiconductor industry as a model for horizontal specialization*

A major business innovation in the semiconductor industry was the separation of semiconductor design and manufacture. This resulted in the development of the horizontal specialization system in the 1990s, especially in the semiconductor industry, and companies specializing in areas such as semiconductor design, manufacturing, and design tool development (Ferguson, 1990; Florida and Kenny, 1990; Florida and Kenny, 1991; Gilder, 1988).[2] Instances such as the US companies Qualcomm, which has a monopoly in semiconductors for mobile phones in North America, nVIDIA, which has a global share of semiconductors for graphics image processing, and e-Silicon, which implements development coordination for iPod's LSI, are known as fabless-specialized companies focusing on the semiconductor design business without owning semiconductor plant equipment. Design houses specializing in circuit design also exist. Moreover, the Taiwanese semiconductor manufacturers TSMC (Taiwan Semiconductor Manufacturing) and UMC (United Microelectronics Corp.) are working out new business models comprising semiconductor manufacture platform solutions, known as foundries (Chen and Sewell, 1996; Chiang, 1990). TSMC and UMC specialize in manufacturing extremely low-cost semiconductors.

Meanwhile, a new player named IP (Intellectual Property) Provider has emerged, offering a link between the separation of semiconductor development and manufacture. IP Provider undertakes license sales for the core technologies of large-scale circuit blocks, including MPU microprocessors, and specialized design technologies. Examples include the UK company ARM, which provides MPU cores using SoC (System on chip, also known as System LSI) for a large number of mobile phones, and the US company Rambus, which has a great impact on the internal structure of PCs. The re-use of inspected IP blocks to complete increasingly complex and highly integrated SoC designs in a shorter time frame is becoming a hot topic.

In this way, technology innovation has split the business structure of the semiconductor industry centered in the US and Taiwan from vertical integration comprising the business elements of product planning,

---

[2] See R Burgelman C. Christensen, S. Wheelwright and M. Maidique (2003) and R. Burgelman and A Grove (2001) for literature relating to Intel as a semiconductor IDM that concentrates resources in microprocessing R&D, production, and global sales and marketing.

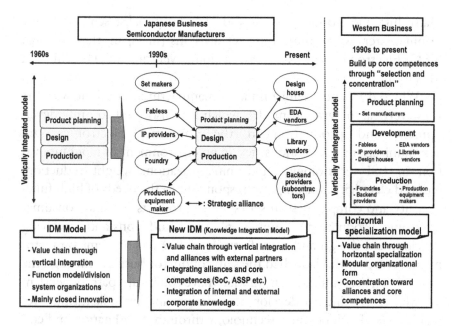

Figure 4.2   Semiconductor Sector Business Model.

semiconductor development (design), and semiconductor manufacture toward horizontal specialization that is independent and open for each business element (see Figure 4.2) (Kodama and Ohira, 2005). Current participants in the industry are players with diverse specialist technologies in each business layer who develop competitive and collaborative business with each other player. These players are also virtually integrated through strategic alliances exploiting features of the modular organizational form among heterogeneous business structures.

2.2 Japanese companies' semiconductor business model

Meanwhile, Japan's Matsushita Electric, Toshiba, Fujitsu, and other companies are vertically integrated semiconductor manufacturers called IDMs (Integrated Device Manufacturers) with the interactive functions to provide semiconductors oriented to the company's original system (set products) and sell semiconductors to other companies. Similar to integrated system manufacturers with semiconductor divisions like

Matsushita and Toshiba, IDMs also include specialist semiconductor manufacturers with no in-house set divisions (in Japan, these include NEC Electronics and Renesas, a joint venture of Hitachi and Mitsubishi).

Why did Japanese semiconductor manufacturers continue with the IDM vertical integration model, which was also used to unify development and production in the consumer electronics and communications device industries, in an environment of rapid innovation in LSI technology, rapid miniaturization, weight reduction, reduced electricity consumption responding to the needs of high functionality and compactness in set (system) products (such as consumer electronic products and mobile phones), and constantly evolving development design and manufacturing rules? Japan's semiconductor manufacturers, who launched the semiconductor business through the original vertical integration model, have built up path-dependent knowledge relating to development design and manufacturing over many years, developed new technology through coordination and collaboration with development design and manufacturing divisions, and dynamically trained engineers. Rather than emulate the Western management style of selling low-profit businesses and restructuring personnel while innovating in digital technologies, a large number of Japanese semiconductor manufacturers accumulate intangible assets, such as technological prowess and training personnel, from a tacit knowledge focus. During the second half of the 1990s, on Japan's semiconductor manufacturers kept up traditional IDM while promoting collaboration with external partners possessing specific specialist technologies and shifting toward the knowledge integration model, dubbed the "new IDM", which will be discussed later (see Figure 4.2).

2.3 *The new phenomenon of the semiconductor business in the 21ˢᵗ century*

In the twenty first century, LSI design development and manufacturing enter a new stage. The small-scale, diverse production of SoCs (today, large scale, diverse production is generally deemed necessary) has developed from the mass manufacturing era of MPU and DRAM (standard, all-purpose semiconductor components), broadband and high functioning mobile phone services have also developed, and markets for vehicle-oriented LSI and the integration of communications and broadcasting quickly become established. Alongside this, LSI integration and microprocessing technologies have developed rapidly, and stronger links have been pursued between semiconductor design and manufacturing with regard to process boundaries, which separated in the 1990s.

Engineers, especially, have not had to design semiconductors while considering the manufacturing processes that follow. It has become clear that it is not enough for LSI, with its nanosize microdesign, simply to feed back and optimize data among adjacent processes for conventional semiconductor design and manufacturing. This has triggered the great changes in LSI design and manufacturing rules as practiced previously. As mentioned earlier, the TSMC and UMC foundries established a business model based on the separation of design and manufacture. What is important in a business model pursuing SoC development in the twenty-first century is not a separation through simple design and manufacturing interfaces arising from explicit knowledge, but an approach that emphasizes the interdependence of the design and manufacturing processes.

Japanese IDMs responding to this kind of environmental change are shifting their business models as semiconductor processes grow more detailed. For example, Fujitsu's "new IDM" is not limited by previous IDM functions, but shifts to a model emphasizing external partners. Highly specialized technologies including IP, libraries, and EDA (Electronic Design Automation) design tools, have spread through external specialist companies rapidly developed with the integration of LSI over several years, and have demonstrated the limitations of a company supporting the entire burden of its growth (especially development costs). Meanwhile, IDMs have come to recognize the importance of satisfying customer demands while exploiting their IDM strengths by efficiently adopting intellectual resources from other companies. External specialist companies (including fabless, design house, IP providers, and EDA vendors) can provide discrete specialist technology. Ultimately, all IDMs possessing

specialist technology can offer total solutions for customer requirements and SoC usage methods to achieve the SoC that the customer
demands.

Accordingly, Fujitsu maintains conventional IDM functions while
responding rapidly to diverse customer needs (support in response to
several contracts in areas such as set design, software development,
and LSI design) by dynamically incorporating in-house the knowledge and competences of external partners, including Fujitsu's group
companies (fabless, design house, IP providers, EDA vendors,
foundry, backend, suppliers, and manufacturing equipment vendors),
while working together with Fujitsu's internal network and external
partners' external network. This approach lies midway between
closed innovation through own-company development and open
innovation activating specialties with external partners. This is similar
in thinking to the previously mentioned *knowledge integration model*
of consumer electronics and communications device manufacturers
(see Figure 4.2).

3. Consideration and Discussion

3.1 *Boundary conception: The distinctive management drivers of Japanese companies*

What determines the elements of Japanese companies' independent
vertical and horizontal boundaries, as shown in case analyses?
Santos and Eisenhardt (2005) suggested four distinct determining
conceptions: efficiency, power, competence, and identity. These
four conceptions test managers on the fundamental organizational
issues of cost (efficiency), autonomy (power), growth (competence),
and coherence (identity) with regard to corporate activity, and
form important elements determining the corporate boundaries of
Japanese companies. Organizational boundaries arising from recent
strategic outsourcing aimed at cost reductions, especially, raise the
efficiency of corporate activity. The building of *keiretsu* networks
rooted in long-term relationships of trust with subcontractors in
Japan's automaker, electronic consumer, and communications

device industries also promote influence and autonomy by maintaining the power of corporate activity. DoCoMo's i-mode business model, with its internal and external networks, is building a co-evolution ecosystem with CPs and development vendors and making an impact on the mobile phone industry (see Chapter 6). The *knowledge integration model* of acquiring new competence determining corporate growth has become a source of new dynamic capability among Japanese companies. A coherent Japanese corporate identity incorporating resonance of value (Kodama, 2001) and teamwork is giving rise to continuous improvement and other incremental innovations. The four boundary conceptions are elements influencing corporate boundary management as *it* relates to strategic management.

As I mentioned in Chapter 1, I would also like to suggest two new conceptions of management drivers characteristic of Japanese companies not mentioned by Santos and Eisenhardt (2005). The first is the *creativity view* for cultivating advanced technology sectors and new business. The *creativity view* of new business innovation through product innovation in the consumer electronics, communications device, and semiconductor fields and coordination and collaboration among industries in the new and mobile phone business fields arising from Japanese companies' characteristic vertically integrated organizations is an important management driver determining vertical and horizontal boundaries. The second is the *dialectic view* aimed at coexisting and prospering with heterogeneous concepts. The *dialectic view* of compatibility between a company's internal and external knowledge forms an important element in building a corporate *knowledge integration model*. Moreover, the dialectic view is building win-win relationships through a co-evolution model of ecosystems among mobile phone carriers and partner companies (CPs, development partners, and companies in other industries) observed in the mobile phone business in Chapter 6. These creative and dialectic conceptions determine the corporate boundaries of Japanese companies, and form elements important to building independent value chains and business models (see Table 4.2).

Table 4.2 Management Drivers, Organizational Forms, and Knowledge Integration in Japanese Companies.

Research Context / Business Sector	Strategy Drivers	Conceptions of Management Drivers	Organizational form	Knowledge integration	
				Internal network	External network
• Consumer electronics • Communications devices • Semi-conductors	• Vertical boundaries growth model => Building value chains through vertical integration => Horizontal integration of external knowledge	*Creativity-view* • Product innovation through integrating development and production *Dialectic view* • Coexistence of internal & external knowledge • Coexistence of vertical integration & horizontal specialization	• Vertically integrated organization & semi-structure model of module organization • Flat & web type organizations	Knowledge integration through networked SCs within and among business units	Knowledge integration through networked SCs of specialist companies at each layer of horizontal specialization

3.2 Conceptual framework of the creativity view: The theoretical background of the relationship between vertical integration and creativity

I would like to consider why *the creativity view* promotes a value chain model through vertical integration from the viewpoints of competitive technological excellence and knowledge integration. Existing research emphasizes that companies should not implement vertical integration in industries where the rate of change is high (Harrigan, 1984; Hill and Hoskisson, 1987). From the viewpoint of transaction cost economics, the disadvantage of business processes operating through vertical integration that adheres to unchanging and outdated technologies is clear (Williamson, 1981, 1985; Afuah and Bahram, 1995; Balakrishnan and Wernerfelt, 1986).

Nevertheless, for companies that want to lead the way in new technology markets, vertical integration also confers the advantage of "early adoption" for companies that introduce new technology, enabling them to respond to new technological change or create their own technological change. Vertical integration thus becomes an effective technology strategy for a company to establish superiority over rivals through its original technology and early establishment of *de facto* standards (Afuah, 2001; Pisano, 2006; Fine, 1998, 2000; Harrigan, 1984).

Pisano (2006) suggested that vertical integration may not be a mistaken relic of the past. According to Pisano's technology strategy research in the pharmaceutical and biotechnology fields, the vertical integration model should be adopted for extremely innovative development in the scientific and technological aspects of pharmaceutical products. R&D and manufacturing technology for innovative products requires tacit knowledge comprising creativity of scientists and developers. The transfer of tacit knowledge among companies is especially difficult, while vertical disintegration raises transaction costs and acts as a disincentive to new innovation. Accordingly, vertical integration can be said to function advantageously in realizing high-tech products that require creativity. The behavior of Japanese companies in building value chains through vertical integration, to obtain a competitive technological edge to realize successive new products exploiting creative technologies, was observed from interview data related to *the creativity view* (see Figure 4.3).

The second focal point is knowledge integration. Interview data and existing research have clarified how Japanese companies possess the natural features that facilitate the routine formation of mixed cross-divisional teams (possibly including external partners and customers) aimed at achieving new targets and solving problems (e.g., Kodama, 2007c). In-house vertical integration systems built from diverse specialist fields and routine business also serve as knowledge capital platforms (resources with value) for forming mixed teams that can flexibly cross divisional boundaries as required without experiencing sectionalism, and can trigger action aimed at novelty and uncertainty. The mixed teams that overcome organizational and knowledge boundaries among practitioners can also trigger creativity and new knowledge inspiration (Kodama, 2007c, 2007d; Leonard-Barton, 1995; Stacey, 1995).

Moreover in high-tech fields, the interdependence of R&D and manufacturing functions is strong, and tacit knowledge (including experience and expertise) among researchers, developers, and manufacturing engineers is shared and accumulated. This high degree of "information stickiness" (Hippel, 1998) makes the transfer of tacit knowledge to external companies difficult, and also makes it difficult for high-tech companies to separate R&D and manufacturing. As mentioned earlier, building a vertically integrated knowledge capital platform accumulated from experience and expertise works advantageously for companies in the areas of responding to technological change and resolving new issues, which require speed and creativity. It follows that the actions of mixed teams with vertically integrated systems become the foundation for integrating the knowledge of various practitioners.

As seen above, cases of positively unbundling specialist fields to reap efficiency and cost savings through simple rational judgment, with the aim of creating new technologies and products, are seldom seen among outstanding Japanese companies in high-tech fields. Japanese high-tech companies have the idea of pursuing the fruits of new knowledge integration while taking risks through vertical

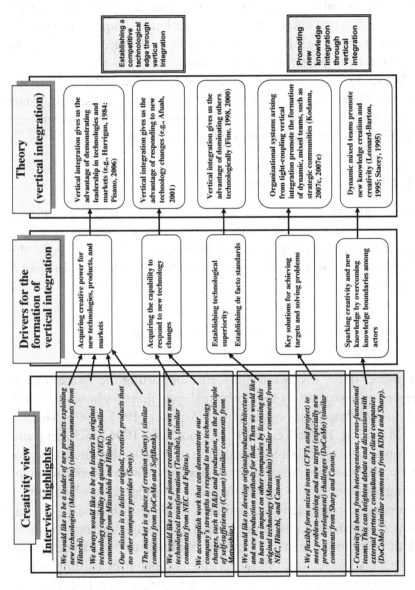

Figure 4.3 Theoretical Background of Relationship Between Vertical Integration and Creativity.

integration in the pursuit of creativity. Comments from senior managers at leading Japanese companies Sharp ("We are putting our efforts into product development that emphasizes new concepts") and DoCoMo ("We want to establish the kind of organizational culture that hones the capacity for creativity and independence") also underline the importance of the *creativity view*.

Thus, the drivers that promote vertical integration in Japanese companies have their origin in the *creativity view*. This element results in the establishment of new technology, support for new technology change, and promotion of knowledge integration.

3.3 *Organizational form*

Next, I will consider organizational forms determining the corporate boundaries of Japanese companies. The *creativity view* and *dialectic view* of the management drivers considered above help to build the organizational form of Japanese companies' distinctive *knowledge integration firm*.

3.3.1 *Consumer electronics, communications devices, and semiconductor business sectors*

One aspect of the organizational forms supporting the Western management style that drives the horizontal specialization business model is the use of "modular organization" (Sanchez, 1995, 1996; Sanchez and Mahoney, 1996; Lei, Hitt and Goldhar, 1996); Schilling and Steensma, 2001). Modular organizations enable the integration of diverse, advanced specialist technologies and delivery of products supporting customers' diversified demands through a combination of resources and competences distributed inside and outside an organization. Companies that have established technological standardization, including component modularization, are likely to build these modular organization sectors. Moreover, for competences existing within the company only, it is important to integrate external, diverse, in-house competences in cases where new innovation is impossible. In the high-tech sector, especially, the modularization of the corporate internal organization and the dynamic, flexible combination and recombination of modules as organizations supporting environmental change form the elements giving rise to dynamic capability (Teece *et.al.*, 1998; Insead and Eisenhardt, 2001). Another way of thinking about modular organizations is through the processes by which companies individually modularize multiple projects within the company, reorganize projects supporting market change, and build project networks (Kodama, 2007e).

Among computer, consumer electronics, and semiconductor manufacturers whose processes have been accelerated by horizontal specialization, US and Taiwanese companies focus on development or in-house competences in EMS and foundries, while external partners undertake other competences in modular form. Coordination with these modular organizations through external networks is emphasized, and digital industries are developed. US and Taiwanese business strategies have skillfully activated the business models of horizontally specialized industries, adopted modular organizations, and created a business model similar to the open innovation model (Chesbrough, 2003) that manages and coordinates knowledge and competences distributed within and outside an organization. In order to realize this kind of business model, it is important to define the specialist fields of a company's own competences, and coordinate by building external networks with external partners (see Figure 4.4).

Meanwhile, the knowledge integration-based firm is indicated as a *knowledge integration model* that drives independent development while positively promoting strategic alliances among outstanding partners the world over (see Figure 4.4), enabling Japanese manufacturers to respond to technological change and diverse customer demands in the digital and network era. The principle of self-sufficiency through closed innovation enables customer solutions to be provided by companies developing all highly specialized technologies independently and coherently integrating design and manufacturing. The *creativity view*, which is one of the management drivers of Japanese companies, promotes unification of development and production, creates rules for new product innovation, and realizes Black Box and all-in-one products. A company's expertise in all specialist

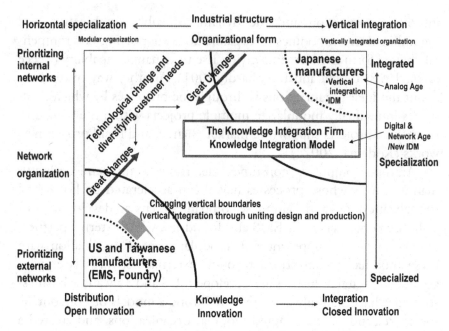

Figure 4.4   **Shift to the Knowledge Integration Firm.**

fields and its coordination and collaboration of internal networks become important elements in realizing the business model. At the same time, Japanese manufacturers are promoting innovation management as a midway form between open (distributed knowledge) innovation exploiting specialization with external partners and conventional closed (integrated knowledge) innovation by means of incorporating an external partner's (horizontally specialized company) knowledge and competences in-house in modular form, and co-establishing internal and external networks. As an organizational form, this involves a shift to a semi-structure model of tightly-coupled elements within companies possessing vertically integrated organizations and loosely-coupled elements among companies possessing modular organizations (see Figure 4.3).

Organizational structures differ from manufacturer to manufacturer, but common elements include construction from business units, HQs of individual business domains and in-house companies, and the flat and web-type organization of the individual business units. The flat and web organizations (Kodama, 2007c) designated by Matsushita Electric grasp the World Wide Web (www), which shares the transmission and reception of information and knowledge, and implement overall knowledge sharing and integration of value chains (planning development, production, sales, support, and solutions) based on flat organizational structures (an average of five layers from top to lower management) across organizations. Flat and web organizations also closely share common knowledge relating to development and production among each business unit within the company. In this way, flat and web organizations hold special qualities as vertically integrated organizations crossing each specialist field. These organizational structures also behave as modular organizations by which a company possesses special core competences, absorbs core competence knowledge (including path-breaking knowledge) held by external modular organizations, closely integrates knowledge as in-house modules, and creates new knowledge.

Flat and web flattening confers autonomy on organization members and promotes faster decision-making. Moreover, the web orientation creates strategic communities and networked strategic communities based on the formation of *Ba* (Nonaka *et.al.*, 2000) inside and outside the company, and promotes vertical integration of value chains and knowledge integration within and outside the company. In this way, Japanese manufacturers do not simply adhere to independent development through closed innovation. Rather, the strategic behavior of absorbing the world's outstanding knowledge promotes a *dialectic view* management driver with the aim of coexistence of knowledge that simultaneously exploits in-house and external competences.

New organizational forms as a new phenomenon:
Changes in Western management

Meanwhile, in response to recent changes in technology and diversification of customer demands, US and Taiwanese EMS and foundry companies promoting horizontal specialization business models are incorporating self-sufficiency elements, as management emphasizes coordination with external modular organizations having individually divided functions. For example, the EMS companies Flextronics (US) and Arima Communications (Taiwan) are progressing from contract manufacture of set products, such as consumer electronics and mobile phones, to more lucrative, highly creative design work, such as mobile phone design. In order to provide customers with services at every stage of the product development cycle, from product planning to market introduction, Flextronics is buying and acquiring the intellectual resources of several high-tech companies with design capabilities. Flextronics is also shifting from horizontally specialized, in-house strategy drivers to a vertical orientation (a vertical integration model comprising design, engineering, and manufacturing services) aimed at full turnkey product development.

Moreover, foundry companies such as Taiwan's TSMC aim not just to enhance cost competition in a similar manner to EMS companies, but also to promote support for increasing mutual reliance on boundaries as they relate to semiconductor design and manufacturing processes together with LSI miniaturization. Specifically, this is a shift in strategic behavior toward positive participation for the foundry companies' design business. The company itself implements the previously outsourced manufacturing post-processing (including LSI packages), and is able to offer customers a full turnkey service over the whole value chain, from semiconductor design to manufacturing. This means that self-sufficiency elements have been incorporated from the previous modular organizational form in a similar way to that of the EMS.

EMS and foundry companies, which are always under cost-competitive pressure, are focusing on the idea of responding to market and technological change by moving into more lucrative, high value-added business domains requiring creativity and shifting the company's own vertical boundaries. EMS and foundry companies are coordinating more closely with external partners, and refining the new knowledge and competences (such as full turnkey services including design skills and expertise) of the companies' internal divisions while promoting knowledge integration through internal networks. This thinking includes the mind-set of incorporating the closed innovation elements of in-house self-sufficiency into open innovation thinking. It also incorporates vertical integration elements aimed at integrating design and manufacture as an organizational form in the in-house organization. This indicates that the horizontally specialized business model is slowly trending toward vertical orientation through the integration of design and manufacture (see Figure 4.4).

As described above, US and Taiwanese companies have transformed the rules relating to manufacturing development and production in order to respond to profit expansion and diverse customer demands with technological change. They consider both the functions of the modular organizations and the ideal state of the new organizational structures. They have become robust organizations responding to dynamic environmental change (markets and technologies) and incorporating the mutual benefits of modularity and integration. These corporate models skillfully and dynamically build and rebuild internal networks within the company as well as external networks with external partners (including customers), and give rise to dynamic capability integrating corporate internal and external knowledge.

The corporate *knowledge integration firm model* of Japanese manufacturers also includes organizational entities that simultaneously promote closed and open innovation: the former through internal corporate networks, and the latter through external networks among companies (including customers). US and Taiwanese manufacturers also keep an eye on *knowledge integration-based firms*, but as a point of departure, Japanese manufacturers are shifting away from a vertical integration model while US and Taiwanese manufacturers are shifting away from a horizontal model (see Figure 4.4).

4. The Strategic Innovation Capability of Japanese Companies in the Consumer Electronics, Communications Device, and Semiconductor Fields

Figure 4.5 illustrates the strategic innovation system of Japan's high-tech manufacturing industry. Features of the product and component

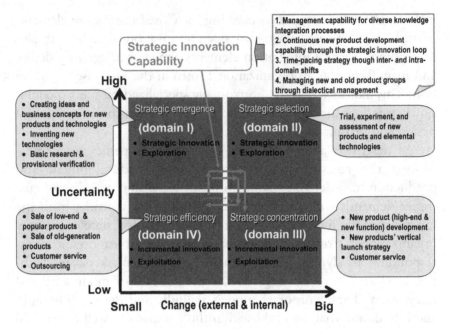

Figure 4.5   Strategic Innovation Systems in High-Tech Manufacturing.

development strategies in the consumer electronics, communications device, and semiconductor industries are the simultaneous advance of exploration and exploitation processes and the close linkage of the process cycles. The strategic emergence and strategic selection domains are exploratory processes at the core of strategic innovation for research and development and for trial, experiment, and assessment of new products and elemental technologies. Strategic concentration is an exploitative process for quickly establishing markets for new product, service, and business models passing through the exploratory process of strategic emergence and selection. This strategic concentration formed the origin of new path emergence arising from newly generated strategic innovation that differs from the existing business (products, services, and business models) of the strategic efficiency domain. These four domains form a continuous strategic innovation loop in the capability map, and create sustained new product development capabilities (see Figure 4.5).

In the high-tech fields of digital consumer electronics, communications devices, and semiconductors, the strategic concentration domain exists as a product business domain where the external transformation of markets and technologies and the internal transformation of strategy, organizations, resources, and operations for leading products continue to be significant following growth. Accordingly, the new-function and high-end products arising from the new elemental technologies within this product group are always positioned in this strategic concentration domain. Meanwhile, low-end, commonly distributed, and old-generation products shift from the strategic concentration to the strategic efficiency domain after the development and sale of new products. In this way, the innovation process flow for the high-tech manufacturing industry shifts in succession from domain I to domain IV (some of the most advanced products are retained in domain III).

The form of the knowledge integration process is also different in each domain. In Japan's high-tech manufacturing business, the exploratory processes of domains I and II are mainly propelled by knowledge integration arising from vertical integration architecture. In recent years, however, several cases have arisen of new technology development propelled by collaboration and M&As resulting from association with external partners through complementary models of horizontal integration architecture (mentioned in Chapter 1) responding to conditions. In some industries, product groups requiring knowledge integration from traditional closed innovation also exist. The domain III commercialization process also involves cases of commercialization based mainly on vertical integrated architecture where other companies' core knowledge is incorporated as required. Domain IV mainly promotes efficiency. In recent years, Japan's manufacturing industry has applied the horizontal specialization model of US and Taiwanese companies, and promoted outsourcing to an EMS or foundry for older product groups that do not possess core technologies (components) while dynamically exploiting knowledge including other companies' expertise.

Managing the smooth shift within and between domains that is one aspect of *strategic innovation capability* promotes time pacing strategy (mentioned later). Moreover, the element of dialectical management that coestablishes exploration and exploitation promotes the smooth management of new and old product groups (see Figure 4.5). A key focal point here is the phenomenon of linkage and synchronization for the exploratory and exploitative processes — the elements that link time pacing strategy and dialectical management. R&D supervisors and marketers engaged in exploratory processes always commit to next-generation product planning, development, and R&D of elemental technology, and need to promptly transfer the results to the commercial development, production, sales, and other divisions.

Linkage and synchronization are elements that smoothly execute management of the domain shift from strategic emergence through selection and concentration to efficiency; implement research and development of next-generation products (including the new products and technologies of the future) while bringing existing products to market; and enhance the management capability in each domain for specialist organizations in each sector to promptly and smoothly migrate to new-generation products. Linkage of exploratory and exploitative processes corresponds to implementing domain shifts from exploration to exploitation. Synchronizing exploration and exploitation means adjusting the timing for migration to new-generation products at each specialist organization and executing in a timely manner. In other words, the linkage and synchronization of exploratory and exploitative processes signify linkage and synchronization among domain boundaries, which can be interpreted as the boundaries of each specialist organization. Linkage and synchronization at these boundaries form a key element in the creation of *strategic innovation capability*.

4.1 *Linkage and synchronization of boundaries*

I would like to consider a new perspective on sharing related to new product development processes in the fields of consumer electronics, communications devices, and semiconductors from the concepts of linkage and synchronization at the boundaries. In Japan's high-tech manufacturing industry, various actors spanning organizations including research, product planning, development design, production technology, manufacturing, sales, and customer service execute business through close interaction. In the digital consumer electronics business, with its environment of dramatically changing markets and technology innovation, Japan's digital consumer electronics manufacturers must continuously invest in new products with good timing in order to acquire market share.

Among the strategies to achieve this is the vertical launch strategy[3] as a time-pacing strategy.[4] The time-pacing strategy is the strategy for competing through regular, rhythmical scheduling at predictable fixed times amid a market rendered largely unpredictable by sudden change. It is also a management technique for skilfully managing the transitional phase from one new product development project to another, creating one's own market lead rhythm and strategically exploring new markets.

The formation of networked SCs as platforms for the deep sharing of context and knowledge is a key action for staff operating in different specialist fields at different organizations in the process of creating new products. As Figure 4.6 illustrates, SCs for R&D, production, product planning, and sales are formed within the projects for the creation of new products (see Figure 4.6). Japanese manufacturers form R&D SCs

---

[3] A vertical launch strategy aims to sell in large volumes at the launch of a new product, and acquire a high share of the market at a stroke (within a month or so). When sales of this model weaken, the next new product is launched at high volume. This is a speed-dependent sales strategy that involves successively acquiring market share through repetition. Japan's major digital consumer electronics manufacturers are mostly advancing market share expansion by promoting these sales strategies (Kodama, 2007a).

[4] A time-pacing strategy is a strategy for competing through regular, rhythmical schedules at predictable fixed times amid a market rendered largely unpredictable by sudden change. Such strategies developed mostly in the US' IT industry from the second half of the 1980s. They skillfully managed the transition period from one project to another, created their own rhythms to take market leads, aligned with the external rhythm of seasonal change and supplier cycles, and generated an efficient, advantageous pace. The top companies implementing these strategies did not lag behind but maintained their positions, strategically created market pace, and are continuing to win. For details, see Eisenhardt and Brown (1998).

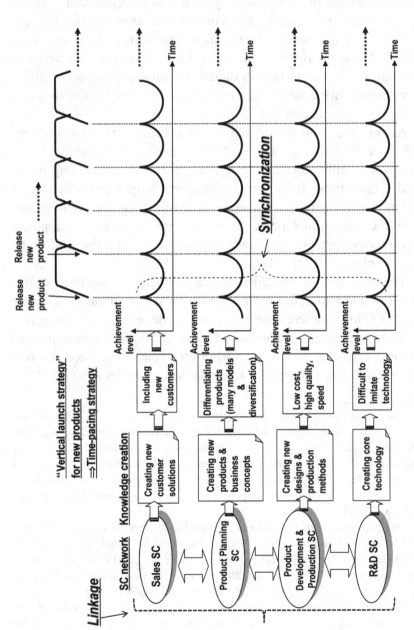

Figure 4.6   Boundaries Linkage and Synchronization.

among members of laboratories and product development divisions, create core Black Box technologies (such as system LSI and other semi-conductor chips) for digital consumer electronics products, and go on to acquire a superiority focused on technology strategies that other companies cannot easily emulate. Product development and production SCs are formed from members of product development, production technology, and other departments. By specifically implementing development and production techniques based on new product design concepts, they create a competitive edge in terms of quality, cost, and speed. The strong link between these two SCs generally optimizes the R&D and production business processes. Here the laboratories are mainly responsible for the R&D of next-generation technologies, and mostly in charge of the strategic innovation business that makes up the exploratory processes in Figure 4.5. Meanwhile, the product development and manufacturing technology departments take charge of the latest new product development and production, and mainly oversee the incremental innovation of the exploitative process based on accumulated technology. These departments operate in different domains, but the formation of SCs and networked SCs achieves the linkage of business executed both within and among the domains.

Moreover, the strong linkage of product development and production, product planning, and sales SCs builds a value chain stretching from R&D to product planning and sales while implementing inter-domain linkage (especially strategic selection and concentration) aimed at realizing new products. The formation of these SCs and networked SCs strongly links sales and marketing power to create new, differentiated product concepts based on potential client needs, and achieve dominant global market share by co-establishing the diversification capability and speed for the technologically realized product.

The new product development capability of Japan's manufacturing industry has these SC formation and network linkage capabilities as boundaries at its source.[5] With vertical launch strategies implemented

---

[5] Carlile (2004, 566) says that instead of viewing the firm as a bundle of resources (Wernerfelt, 1984; Barney, 1991), it will be viewed "as a bundle of different boundaries where knowledge must be shared and assessed."

simultaneously on a global scale, staff at various organizations are implementing business (time-pacing strategies) around the core of individual SCs up to the launch of new product sales. The employees in individual SCs decide on specific strategies and tactics broken down into individual employee roles, and fulfill their own roles aimed at the goal of launching sales.

Operations determined by individual SCs, however, cannot be separated from overall SC optimization, even if *implemented incompletely on separate time axes.* Senior managers (extending to SC project leaders and middle managers), participating in multiple SCs have to transmit and share information and knowledge among employees in different organizations and specialist fields. The management thus dynamically shares context and knowledge among SCs, and fulfills its own goal-oriented work role while demonstrating creative collaboration and supporting other personnel. This kind of "creative collaboration" (Kodama, 2007c) not only partially optimizes SCs but also overall enables SC optimization by creating rigid networks for SC linkage. In other words, the degree to which operational targets are achieved by individual SCs also determines the partial optimization of SCs and overall optimization as network SCs through mutually rhythmical synchronization. SCs and networked SCs link different specialist domains and organizations, and promote the sharing of knowledge among actors in each domain. They share and adjust items such as the timing for commercialization and development among individual organizations. As mentioned in Chapter 1, the knowledge architectural thinking of the actors building vertical value chains and multi-layered models of vertical integrated architecture, especially, promotes linkage and synchronization among individual organizations and management layers (see Figure 4.6).

How can we pin down this concept of synchronization more specifically? What specific action Japan's manufacturing industry should take to realize a global vertical launch strategy for new products is a subject of debate among staff in various organizations. A huge number of action items comprising overall strategy and tactics are broken down into actions for implementation in numerous sections, such as marketing, advertising and publicity, sales, product planning, development, production technology, manufacturing, and distribution. Among this huge number of actions, an especially important element is those action items that cannot be completed through the operations of an organization alone. The range of examples extends to items to implement through adjusting and linking with other organizations and those to implement at an organization based on output executed at other organizations.

All the action items that cannot be completed by operations in an organization alone must be performed by forming SCs transcending organizational and knowledge boundaries. Staff in the SCs debate and arrive at consensus concerning matters of specific objectives, meanings, timelines, and means or in other words, the questions of who, what whom, why, when, and how. These are the micro-units of policy and implementation for the specific strategies and tactics that comprise the employees' practical strategy behavior. This behavior, moreover, is a dynamic element implemented while practicing trial and error within the transformation of time. Employees must always possess a dynamic strategy perspective and implement deliberate strategy alongside flexible, resilient emergent strategy. Employees must also cope by improvising in dramatically changing situations (Kodama, 2007a).

In SCs, the deep sharing of context and knowledge through employees' creative dialogues implements strongly interdependent action items with other organizations. The employees implement practical strategy action items determined at each SC, and constantly monitor the degree of completion of these processes. Each SC implements items of practical strategy behavior amid a state of interdependency. This is because the items of "when," "who" and "how" require adjustment and collaboration among the employees of different organizations.

Accordingly, employees (especially senior managers) who participate in multiple SCs and commit to objectives must align on a temporal axis with the pitch and rhythm for completing each operational objective (practical strategy action) at each SC aimed at achieving the overall project target (realizing vertical launch strategy arising from new product development). The mechanism that aligns the employees' pace and the operation of practical strategy action with fixed pitch and rhythm at each SC is linkage and synchronization. This boundary is a key mechanism for realizing time-pacing strategies.

SCs and SC networks are knowledge platforms that share dynamic contexts and create new knowledge among employees. SCs share, create, discuss, and practice tacit and formal knowledge in time and space. A new perspective gained from cases of new product development in Japan's manufacturing industry is that diverse layered SCs and their SC networks possessing different contexts and knowledge are always forming, and are also formed and linked by employees independently encouraging others within an environment (comprising clients, for example) or organization. Employees deliberately form and link (or create networks) teams of boundaries (ToBs), but SC and SC networks assembling employees from different specialist fields is a key focus, and it is here that the knowledge boundaries at the source of innovation lie.

These knowledge boundaries take on the character of pragmatic boundaries while increasing the uncertainty and novelty factors in new product development (Kodama, 2007a). To convert the energy generated at these pragmatic boundaries into innovation requires a strong common intent among employees. This strong common intent rooted in shared values (Kodama, 2001) is a key element additional to the existence of boundary objects as tools to promote innovation and of common language, meaning, interest, and knowledge among staff (Carlile, 2002; Cramton, 2001; Star, 1989). In Japan's manufacturing industry, the presence of employees' strong common intent forms strong SCs and SC networks, and leads to the success of new product development and vertical launch strategies implemented simultaneously on a global scale.

Chapter

5

The Strategic Innovation Capabilities of Machine Tool Manufacturers: A Case Study of Mitsubishi Heavy Industries Plastic Technology Co., Ltd.

1. The Importance of Manufacturing and New Organizational Strategies

Manufacturing is the jewel in the crown of Japanese companies. The increasing competitiveness of Japan's manufacturing in the latter half of the twentieth century turned Japan into a leading industrial power. In recent years, however, this situation has been changing as new markets and competitive environments appear, and the connection of corporate performance with high-functioning, low-cost development and production of outstanding products and technologies has become looser. The case of digital consumer electronics in Chapter 4, especially, illustrates the increasing intensity of product commoditization arising from growing competition and modularization of digital product features.

Obtaining profit in the manufacturing industry requires skilfull organizational strategies for the manufacturing process. In a fiercely competitive environment, it is important to maximize the manufacturing industry's value-added driven by strategic and organizational management relating to organizational capability and product architecture. In this chapter, I will examine the Japanese machine tools manufacturer Mitsubishi Heavy Industries Plastic Technology Co., Ltd. (Mitsubishi Plastic in short) to consider the knowledge integration process arising within the company itself through strategic tie-ups with external partners, and *strategic innovation capability* creating product innovation through unique product architecture (hybrid architecture). Then I will analyse the knowledge integration architecture and the creation of *Ba* as an element promoting Mitsubishi Plastic's own knowledge integration process.

This chapter begins with a description of injection molding machines, which are leading products of Mitsubishi Plastic, and goes on to describe the product architecture of injection molding machines together with Mitsubishi Plastic's product innovation development process. Then I will consider the mechanism by which Mitsubishi Plastic realizes independent product architecture through organizational dynamism inside and outside the company and the knowledge integration process.

2. A Case Study

2.1 *Injection molding machines*

Injection molding machines (see Figure 5.1) are tools for efficiently creating plastic components. They heat and melt plastic granules, and inject the molten plastic into a mold under high pressure, filling the desired spatial configuration. Upon hardening, the mold is opened and the object extracted. Put simply, the creation of plastic products involves three basic operations of melting the plastic materials, molten flow, and hardening to create shapes. Injection molding machines are transverse or upright. In transverse machines, the molds open and close horizontally, and in vertical machines, they open and close

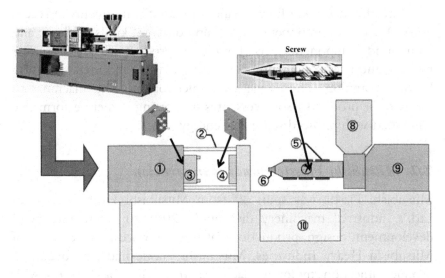

Figure 5.1   Diagram of an Injection Molding Machine's Basic Structure.
Source: Mitsubishi Plastic's publicly released materials.

vertically. Many of the plastic unit component shapes are executed by transverse machines. While upright machines have advantages for insert molding and automated systems, transverse machines can automatically release molded objects. There are two types of machine: the hydraulic injection molding and the electric injection molding machine. They are categorized by size (small, medium, or large) according to mold clamping force measured in tons (tf).

Today, the vehicle components (including bumpers and instrument panels), electrical machinery, office automation devices, cameras, computers, and other products are following a high-functioning, miniaturizing and low-cost trend. Most of them use injection-molded components. In recent years, the manufacture of general-purpose components has shifted overseas, and Japan's domestic manufacturing has had to develop high value-added products differentiated by size, accuracy, design, and performance while supporting low-volume production of diverse product lines and shortening delivery time to meet needs.

With the increasing functionality of plastic components in recent years, the use of components combining different kinds of plastic and compound components (insert molding products fusing dissimilar metallic and plastic elements) combining plastics and metals has also become common. The demand for injection molding machines to create these products also necessitates supporting higher performance combined with reduced space and energy.

2.2 *Mitsubishi Plastic's product innovation*

Mitsubishi Plastic was spun off from Mitsubishi Heavy Industries Ltd.'s industrial machinery division in 2005 to create integrated development, design, production, sales, and services. As a division of Mitsubishi Heavy Industries, Mitsubishi Plastic had first begun to produce injection molding machines in 1961 in association with National Automatic Tool Company (NATOCO) of the US. In the following year, it launched its type-I mid- and large-sized machines fitted with a variable delivery pump and with a mold clamping force ranging from 300 to 1,450 tf.

Mitsubishi Plastic mainly developed and manufactured mid- and large-sized injection molding machines, but once the NATOCO tie-up concluded in 1976, it proceeded with independent development. From 1986 onward, its product series comprised small, energy-saving molding machines with variable delivery pumps and mid-sized machines using direct-pressure clamping and achieving the world's smallest space. Mitsubishi Plastic also developed the world's smallest space capability for its signature large-scale machines through its clamping structure as similar to mid-sized machines. The machine were a great hit in Japan, where factories have little free space.

From 1998 to 2002, Mitsubishi Plastic created each of the mid- and large-scale product lines and continuously sold a super large-scale machine as the MM III series. During this time, the market for injection molding machines was undergoing a major shift from hydraulically to electrically driven. Electric injection machines accounted for about 70 percent of the domestic manufacturers' shipping volumes for small-scale machines. Aiming to expand this market share, Mitsubishi Plastic is selling Mitsubishi Plastic–Fanuc machines through an alliance with Fanuc for domestic market, and OEM machines from Toyo Machinery and Metal Co., Ltd. for oversea market.

A key factor for this alliance is, first of all, where Mitsubishi Plastic is to procure the drive-train components. Mitsubishi Plastic purchased servomotors from Mitsubishi Electric but determined that future purchases would be based on the basis of cost. Mitsubishi Plastic determined that Fanuc's technology, which was strong in the area of drive trains, would complement its own strengths in body design.

Another aspect was the separation between hydraulically and electrically driven machines. Mitsubishi Plastic manufactured and sold hydraulic injection molding machines exerting a force of 80 to 6,000 tf, but a focus on energy saving led to a rapid shift toward small-and mid-sized electric injection molding machines. Fanuc noted that virtually all the small-scale machines were electrically driven, and proceeded to steer its business to produce electric drives for the mid-sized machines also. Mitsubishi Plastic and Fanuc each held around 10 percent volume share for the domestic market and ranked fifth to sixth in the industry. Both companies' volume-based market share amounted to around 20 percent, similar to that for major manufacturer Nissei Plastic Industrial Co., Ltd. The market for injection molding machines was worth around 200 billion yen. Since 2000, the domestic production value has risen 20 to 30 percent a year on the back of a sudden rise in demand for production of information communications devices such as notebook PCs and mobile phones.

For mid-sized machines, Mitsubishi Plastic launched its ME series in 2000. These machines accelerated the electric drive trend, and achieved high injection rates using Fanuc's servomotor with toggle-type clamping. The result was a dramatic rise in Mitsubishi Plastic's market share (especially in domestic market) focused on automobiles and consumer electronics. In overseas markets too, the demand for electric drive trains was growing. There was great anticipation of higher orders from notebook PC ODM manufacturers in Taiwan and China, and for the liquid crystal TV industry.

For its large-scale machines, the Mitsubishi Plastic parent company enlisted the cooperation of parent company Mitsubishi Heavy

Super-sized em Series (3,000 & 3,500ton)   3000emR Electric Double Injection Molding
electric injection molding machine   Machine with Rotary Platen System
    (3,000 ton)

Figure 5.2   Super-sized Electric Injection Molding Machines.

Source: Mitsubishi Plastic's publicly released materials.

Industries laboratories at Nagoya and Nagasaki to develop the "em series" Electric Double Injection Molding Machine with Rotary Platen System (see Figure 5.2) and achieve the super-sized electric injection molding machine with the world's smallest space. To differentiate itself from its competitors, who had all adopted toggle-type clamping, Mitsubishi Plastic adopted its own world-first clamping mechanism (double-platen clamping) and orders rose, centered on the automobile industry.

Today, the manufacture of plastic components and products is seeing a growing demand for electrically driven injection molding machines, which are cleaner and use less energy than conventional hydraulic machines. First used in small-scale machines, electrically driven trains have recently been adapted for large-scale machines producing more than 1,000 tf, but servomotor capacity and machine size constraints limit use of the drives to the 1,500 ton class. For large molded objects used in vehicles, led by bumpers, major themes include the "high cycle" linked to higher productivity, thinner panels that reduce vehicle weight, and higher plastic content in body panels and modular components. Future developments anticipated for large-scale, electrically driven injection molding machines are the shaping of stable, highly accurate, high-quality products in larger and more complex forms.

These expectations have led Mitsubishi Plastic to develop the 3000 emR large size co-injection molding machine (see Figure 5.2), the world's first electrically driven rotary platen model, with a maximum clamping force of 3,000 tf. This advanced machine can process two different kinds of plastic into one molded unit, greatly boosting the production of large plastic components. Its outstanding defect record when compared to the conventional hydraulic-driven machine, moreover, enables it to respond to the demand for lighter vehicle components as a core technology.

In recent years, against a backdrop of rising environmental awareness, lighter vehicle bodies for enhanced fuel efficiency have joined the development of hybrid, electric, and other eco-cars as major topics in the vehicle manufacturing industry. Creating plastic windows is one effective means of reducing vehicle weight. However, the production process took up much time with the assembly of the transparent glass of the window and the strength required for the frame. The large-size co-injection molding machine demonstrates the machine's problem-solving power.

Mitsubishi Plastic's development of the 3000 emR has enabled the production of lighter vehicle-related components, simplified the assembly process, and improved design capability. Since demand from outside the automobile sector is also anticipated, development of the 1450 emR, with a clamping force of 1,450 tf, has been added to the product lineup. Creating the product series has become the key to the modularization of the injection molding machines (discussed later). Modularization enables great reductions in the time needed for adjustments to verify inter-component compatibility, lower costs, and enhanced design and development efficiency.

In the future, the field of medium- and large-size machines will see an acceleration of the trend away from metal to plastic and from hydraulic to electric drive. Recognizing this, Mitsubishi Plastic anticipates increased orders for the "me" and "em" series of medium- and large-scale injection molding machines both at home and abroad, especially since enhanced product precision has become a given in recent years, and high-cycle, low-energy production to give a costing edge has become a condition for competitive superiority. This is why the mold processing industry is increasingly demanding electrically driven injection molding machines, and why the expectations have grown that Mitsubishi Plastic's electric drives will differentiate it from the competition. Furthermore, Mitsubishi Plastic aims to become the world's top manufacturer of electrically driven machines for the automobile sector, where large-scale hydraulic machines are widely used, by investing in the market for large-scale electric motors.

2.3   *The product architecture of injection molding machines*

2.3.1.   *Basic structure of injection molding machines*

Figure 5.1 illustrates the basic structure of the injection molding machine, which is common for both the electric and hydraulic machines.

1. The mold clamping mechanism
   This is the mechanism that opens and closes the mold. It must be strong enough to withstand high pressure when the injection molding machine is filling. Direct pressure, toggle, and other types of clamping mechanism are used.
2. The tiebar
   The tiebar supports the molding machine template, guides the mold's opening and closing operation, and acts as a column absorbing the clamping force. Generally, four tiebars are used as one unit.
3. The mold (movable side)
4. The mold (fixed side)
   The mold (see Figure 5.1) plays the most important role in the creation of plastic products, and is produced in alignment with the required product. Even for plastic products with the same purpose and configuration, changing the mold design and production method alone can lead to differences in mold costs as well as production quality and volume. Producing large volumes of a product over a long period of time, for example, requires

durability, whereas boosting productive capacity by the hour requires the design of molds capable of diverse production in single runs.

5. Band heater

   The band heater is a kind of electric heater used to adjust and set heat-applied materials. It is fixed in a sheet on a metal board by means of embedding heat-producing resistance wire of Nichrome or similar material in mica or another heat-resistant insulator.

6. Nozzle

   The nozzle is an injection opening in the molding machine connected to the molding sprue for injecting molding materials into the tip of the calefaction cylinder.

7. Heating cylinder

   The heating cylinder is a calefaction tube to fuse, plasticate, and transports molding materials. A band heater is attached to the periphery with a screw inside (see Figure 5.1). When heat is transmitted to the molding materials from the outside, the shear force of the rotating screw applies heat, and plasticizes effectively.

8. Hopper

   The hopper is an opening attached to the molding machine for injecting molding materials. In many cases a hopper drier (a drying device attached to the machine) is used.

9. Injection unit

   The injection unit plasticizes and ejects the molding materials. Along with the clamping device, the injection unit is a major component of the injection molding machine. Injection devices include plungers, screw PRIPRA, and inline screws.

10. Controller

    The controller is a device for controlling the individual settings (such as injection speed and pressure) of the molding machine.

2.3.2. The product architecture of injection molding machines

Product architecture is a basic design concept of how to divide a product into modules, connect to individual interfaces, and divide up product functions. The product architecture of injection molding machines is dominated by closed modular configurations assembled in-house by each manufacturer. Injection molding machines are sold as combinations of clamping side and injection side components. Put simply, they are products for standard design structures, and can be said to combine standardized interfaces with modules featuring high functional independence.

The word "interface" as applied here for molding machines refers to the clamping structure (bolt nut or ferrule), and corresponds to the socket or connector of electrical components. It is also a product that ensures prior clarification (standardizing) of connectivity rules with other components by independently setting each component or module, and combines and coordinates them for the functioning of the entire system.

Nevertheless, detailed scrutiny of the product architecture for each component of the injection molding machines reveals the existence of both integral and already modularized components. The product architecture features for the individual components of injection molding machines are as follows.

1. Open modular architecture as modularized products comprises heaters (cylinder-heating components), hydraulic switch bulbs, pumps, and motors. The control panels and units are closed modular architecture.

2. The two components of clamping and injection mechanisms exist as integral components. The clamping mechanism corresponds to the platen, links, tie bars, and other clamping machine components used to generate clamping force and the components used in machines for melting and extruding plastics. The injection mechanism corresponds to screw, cylinder, housing, and other components. Moreover, parts adjustment among injection molding machines involves a large number of integral elements, and a great interreliance of length, level, and positional adjustment.

In the future, modularized components will comprise mold heating control systems (parts that control the heating of metal molds to influence molding quality) and electric drive systems (drive mechanisms combining motors, amps, and ball screws), and these are being developed as product series. While each manufacturer is different, product series are generally integrated in-house by the manufacturer. One of the keys to modularization is management that outsources through effective specialization. To achieve this, it is important to combine work for subcontraction into one package as far as possible, eliminate as far as possible the complex interrelationships involved in entrusting operations among the subcontractor and the company itself, and create interface rules. Endeavors such as these have the effect of promoting product modularization. By modularizing product architecture in injection molding machines, Mitsubishi Plastic is creating industry standards and interface rules with suppliers by, for example, effective outsourcing for the development of mold heating and electric drive control systems.

Existing research shows that product architecture originated as an integral model, and is gradually modularizing in every industry. The speed of modularization development and the degree of modularization have been strongly influenced by the nature of the industry. The automobile industry is also moving in the direction of long-term modularization, but not at the same speed as the electronics industry.[1] The following research suggests why industries are developing toward modularization.

First is the high design rationale of modularization. Modular architecture has many advantages and some disadvantages (see above), but its key benefit is that it allows greater design consistency than integral architecture. This is why companies incline to put their design efforts into enabling modular architecture. Design rationale and strategic rationale do not always coincide, however. A strategy focus may sway management to choose integral over modular architecture.

---

[1] Today, the automobile industry is energetically searching for new sources of motive power to replace the internal combustion engine and so reduce the carbon risk. Replacing the conventional combustion engine with an electric or alternative motor is anticipated to dramatically increase vehicle modularization by greatly reducing complexity. Selecting design rules for this modularization is easier, because the complexity of the vehicular product system is reduced.

Second is the logic that a customer's evaluation standards change in response to product lifecycles (Christensen, 1989). All new products have a low capability in the initial phases, and are unequal to satisfying the criteria of customer demand in terms of performance and function. During such periods, companies try to fulfill the criteria by optimizing product performance that leads to integral product architecture. Since that modular architecture is constrained by design rules, it is not necessarily appropriate for performance optimization. With rapid technological progress, however, product performance overshoots customer demand, and the customers' basic evaluation shifts from performance to other criteria. Technological developments mean that modular architecture can also deliver product performance to satisfy customer demand, while other criteria, such as rapid, flexible product development, grow more important, and companies select outstanding modular architecture holistically. The perspective of changes in customer evaluation thus demonstrates how new products emerge in integral form and gradually shift to modular.

Third is the logic of an effective relationship with suppliers (Fine, 1998). In current time of relentless technological and market change, it is almost impossible to carry out all product development in-house; and effective outsourcing management is required. It is important for a corporation to combine as much subcontraction work as possible into one package, and to do its best to eliminate complex interrelationships with subcontractors over commissioned business. Endeavors such as these promote product modularization and openness. Attempting to regulate and raise the efficiency of relationships with suppliers leads to product modularization. IBM's open modularization for PCs can be remembered as the result of a short time frame for development arising from effective outsourcing. Existing research backs up this example to indicate that industrial architecture gradually modularized for rational reasons.

Meanwhile, the efficient, effective adjustment of injection molding machine components with integral elements requires processes to create optimized, advanced technological architecture while circulating modular and integral designs using methods such as processing through self-manufacture, tolerance analysis through design (components always have variable measurements and forms, and dispersion also occurs during assembly of these variable components. Tolerance analysis estimates the variability beforehand), tolerance analysis through production technology and prior site assembly (determining compatibility of machine and components), and functional analysis (classifying necessary and unnecessary functions and then optimizing) considering the user's method of application.

In this way, combining two components in a product always involves tolerance of size and adjustment for required accuracy. It is impossible to accurately complete parts processing on the basis of a single measurement. Rather, it is determined according to the leeway allowed with regard to standard measurements that become the processing criteria supporting the component's application objective. The difference between the maximum and minimum permissible measurements for large and small sizes, respectively, is called the "tolerance of size". Tolerance of size allows adjustment using spacers (gap insertion adjustment) alongside machine processing adjustments. Spacers adjustments occur during assembly operations, however, and this extends lead times. In contrast, tolerance analysis for machining can do away with the need for adjustment by analyzing tolerance quality. By enabling the common use of molding machine components, self-production of modules is extremely efficient from the viewpoint of materials procurement and reducing the design burden. Mitsubishi Plastic undertakes to modularize with consistent manufacturing innovation. The manufacturer's mission highlights quality, cost, and delivery (QCD). In-house modularization is also an improvement activity satisfying all aspects of QCD.

The fruits of Mitsubishi Plastic through these kinds of modularization activities are also the fruits of developing organizational capability cultivated by product development arising from the integral architecture of the past. Generally, modular architecture design requires a higher level of organizational capability than that for integral architectural design (Baldwin and Clark, 1997). This is because modular architecture requires that each module be designed in parallel, followed by final verification to ensure that all the modules operate as an integrated, organic system. Whether the previously established design rules can operate well is, in many cases, not known until integration is actually attempted. Sometimes an unanticipated inter-reliance of the modules first becomes clear at the final verification phase, creating the pressure of requiring redesign. Avoiding such an outcome involves setting effective design rules that take a prior overview of the whole system. This is no easy matter, as it also requires rich experience and knowledge of the entire system.[2] Considered from this perspective of corporate organizational capability, companies become capable of modular architecture design after gradually building up knowledge and experience from integral architecture design.

Meanwhile, injection molding machines may also shift from modular to integral through innovations in injection technologies as regards screw development and the first active thermoregulatory systems. Reason for this shift is that the reputation for product performance based on a new technology system focusing on innovative elemental technology turned out to be a key value for customers again. In these cases, companies shift product architecture toward integral in order to achieve overall optimization of integral rather than modular architecture, which is easier (Christensen and Raynor, 2003). The second reason is that the knowledge and expertise that companies accumulate to achieve modularity becomes ineffective when innovative elemental technologies are adopted. Adopting these technologies requires a new partition of sub-system interfaces, which at once invalidates the knowledge, expertise, and experience accumulated to realize modularization (Shibata *et al.*, 2005). The company has yet to accumulate sufficient knowledge and expertise to achieve modularization based on a new technology system. However, as a result, it has no choice but to re-adopt integral architecture. In industries such as injection molding machines, when companies adopt innovative elemental technologies, product architecture shifts in the opposite direction from modular to integral.

Coordinating the product architecture thinking of injection molding machines leads to the following. As product architecture progresses toward closed and open modulars, the molding machine

---

[2] The many difficulties faced by IBM when achieving system 360 modularization in 1964 graphically illustrate it (Baldwin and Clark, 2000).

components change from integral to modular in response to the flow of time and changing technologies and market trends (or customer needs); and a partial shift from modular to integral occurs in response to wide-ranging technological innovation.

In the future, product architecture for medium- and large-scale injection molding machines, especially, will see the continuance of integral components for the core components (technologies) of the screw and clamping device together with the development of modularization due to the demand for speed and efficiency (cost-cutting) from industry standardization and the assembly process for common components. Examples include the creation of open modules areas for mold thermoregulatory systems capable of contributing to molding stability and reduced defect rates, and closed modules of systems driving injection devices. Among these, accordingly, the product architecture of mid- and large-scale injection molding machines can be called a hybrid model of product architecture combining integral and modular elements (see Figure 5.3).

Hybrid product architecture is a robust product concept combining the strengths of integral (accumulation and enhancement of core technologies and design development expertise) and modular (enhanced design and development efficiency through industry standardization and unified design rules) components.

2.4. *Future product development and business process strategies: MC & MD*

In recent years, the automobile industry has kept a close eye on modular products as weight-reducing technologies and metal substitutes aimed at the trend toward plastic product development for electric vehicles. In this regard, Mitsubishi Plastic has added to its role of manufacturer of injection molding machine hardware by undertaking the development of new molding techniques aligned with user needs. Thus, it is promoting the development of technologies to improve the surface of plastic foam molding for weight reduction and to plasticize resins, including the main modular component of continuous glass fiber.

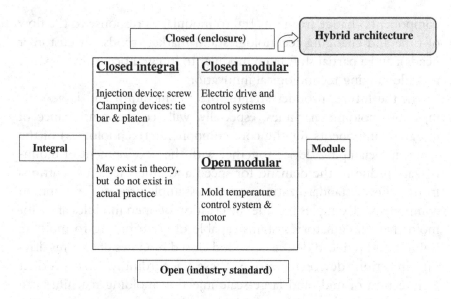

Figure 5.3   Product Architecture for Mitsubishi Plastic Mid-and Large-Sized Injection Molding Machines.

Source: Material created by the author with reference to shibata, Yano, and Kodama (2005).

Note: Mitsubishi Plastic creates all injection modling machine components in-house, with the exception of motors (shared-use with Fanuc).

Today, production for delivery on very short timescales has become a potent weapon for ensuring a competitive edge in the component business for injection molding machines. To achieve this, Mitsubishi Plastic has re-structured its supply chain management (SCM) and dramatically transformed production methods from the manufacturer-led "push" model emphasizing efficient production to the customer-led "pull" model maximizing throughput. Specific initiatives of actions to unify the trinity of business process reform, IT strategy action, and product system reform around a core of reformed employee awareness, and gaining dramatic results for shorter production lead times, fewer unfinished goods, and enhanced compliance with delivery times are key themes at Mitsubishi Plastic. Another fact of these actions is to reform the corporate climate, and large-scale changes in the business process are accompanying the conversion from a conventional case-by-case design model for accepting orders to a mass-production system for products created with a minimum of diagram drawing. Be that as it may, products unaligned with customer needs will not sell, and can create no customer value. In this regard, Mitsubishi Plastic has introduced the concepts of mass-customization (MC) and modularization (MD).

MC and MD represent a way of thinking that gathers and analyzes customer needs, separates common and individual components, and executes design and manufacturing accordingly. It realizes the coordination of client needs with systematic standardization and commonality at the component level. In this way, component types and volumes can be reduced. The benefits of MC and MD are diverse. Exploiting a supplier's standard components, for example, enables minimization of design areas. Since it also facilitates bulk buying and advance logistics, procurement costs can fall. Design standardization also sets corresponding parts of the blueprint to make it easy to build long-term relationships with suppliers, and shortens the lead time to manufacturing. With the new product series of injection molding machines, Mitsubishi Plastic has achieved drastic standardization after thoroughly analyzing customer needs. This has led to shorter lead times.

Mitsubishi Plastic's parent company, Mitsubishi Heavy Industries, brings not only injection molding machines but also MC and MD concepts to the factory worksite. It creates patterns of customer needs, divides equipment into multiples of units, and standardizes those units. Even if the plant configuration changes depending on the business item, the company tries to use standardized units. Putting the MC and MD concepts into practice enabled a dramatic reduction in the overall process for a carbonized sludge plant led by Mitsubishi Heavy Industries.

Low-cost Asian competitors are making roads into the Japanese market for injection molding machines and threatening Mitsubishi Plastic's market share as customer demand grows for low-cost, short-cycle products. In response, Mitsubishi Plastic has launched SCM projects and enhanced the efficiency of the molding machine assembly process while promoting component modularization (standardization and commonality). The production scheduler also enables simulations to be carried out using actual data and the acquisition of verification results enabling production with targeted lead times.

At the November 2008 International Plastics Fair exhibition (IPF), the new product development project announced by Mitsubishi Plastic: the Electric Double Injection Molding Machine with Rotary Platen System, the world's first large-size co-injection molding machine-modularized injection molding technology and component assembly and processing under the core concepts of "high quality, high efficiency, low energy", thanks to Mitsubishi Plastic's technological collaboration with Kyowa Industrial Co., Ltd. and Konan Tokusyu Sangyo Co., Ltd. The project achieved a 30 percent reduction of manufacturing and development lead times and 25 percent monthly reduction of inventory holdings, with a 40 percent rise in the delivery compliance rate to the customer.

In the future, the transmission of users' operational expertise as production bases migrate overseas will become a major issue, and Mitsubishi Plastic is also endeavoring to develop user support structures exploiting IT technology and expert systems.

2.5 *The structure of Mitsubishi Plastic's product development*

Mitsubishi Plastic has inherited Mitsubishi Heavy Industries' technological prowess as the integrated specialist manufacturer of injection molding machines while supporting speedy decision making and response, and systematically advancing product development through selection and concentration. As the specialist developer and manufacturer of the medium- and large-scale molding machines, Mitsubishi Plastic's product positioning delivers to customers some of the world's fastest ultra-large-scale electric molding machines as well as the globally unique large size co-injection molding machine, and thermoregulatory system products for high-quality molds. In April 2008, Mitsubishi Plastic had 226 employees; its organizational structure is illustrated in Figure 5.4.

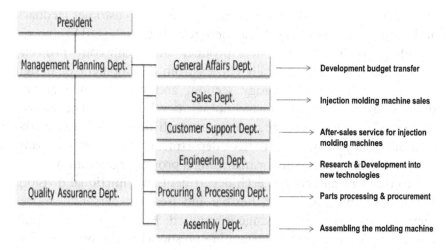

Figure 5.4 Mitsubishi Plastic's Organizational System and Unified Management.

Source: Mitsubishi Plastic's publicly released materials.

The company's organization is basically an organization of functional divisions. The organizational chart in Figure 5.4 shows many points that differentiate it from a normal company. The management planning department not only formulates overall business planning, production, development, and sales strategies, but also integrates organizations with specialist development, sales, and production functions. As the general manager of Mitsubishi Plastic stated: "our organization has no walls", each organization is always taking unified action, and could be called a boundary-less company. Problem-solving organizational behavior has become established; employees of all divisions share information with regard to the various issues and customer needs; and members transcend the different divisional walls to become united. Accordingly, the improvement of everyday routines and product series as well as solution businesses such as customizing is implemented mainly at the functional organization in Figure 5.4.

Meanwhile, when developing or introducing new products (e.g., injection molding machines or molding technology), the technology, customer support, and sales departments factor in customer feedback and needs, and go on to form a "design built team", (DBT), (corresponding to SC) for the new product and technology projects. Project managers are generally chosen from development or design groups within the technology section, and create new planning designs for new model and technology developments. The project managers' role is to exchange opinions with those in charge of the sales and component procurement departments within the company. The most important issue for managing a project organization well is not to build a wall between each department and functional division. When many projects occur, flexible and frequent personnel movement and organizational change is required. Each organization must also dynamically dispatch outstanding personnel to the projects. The existence of walls among organizations prevents this from being implemented smoothly. Nevertheless, at Mitsubishi Plastic, this kind of problem rarely appears. This is considered to be because the organizational group of the community of practice (CoP) transcends disparate functions and deeply shares information and knowledge, and the division-spanning project teams are created in a medium that facilitates their formation (Kodama, 2007c).

When developing injection molding technologies and machines within the company, Mitsubishi Plastic's project teams absorb the fruits of elemental technologies R&D at Mitsubishi Heavy Industries' research laboratories in Nagoya while implementing design business through tie-ups with group companies such as Mitsubishi Electric and Churyo Engineering Co., Ltd. (see Figure 5.5). A feature here is that Mitsubishi Plastic (sales, development, and production plants), Churyo Engineering (wholly financed by Mitsubishi Heavy Industries), and Mitsubishi Heavy Industries' Nagoya laboratories share the same site (see Figures 5.6 and 5.7).

Within this site where members share information and knowledge, Mitsubishi Plastic is unifying its injection molding machine operations from R&D through product assembly, component procurement, and business sales to after-sales service. In order to survive in the cutthroat business environment as a manufacturer, it accurately grasps customer needs, and rapidly delivers and maintains original,

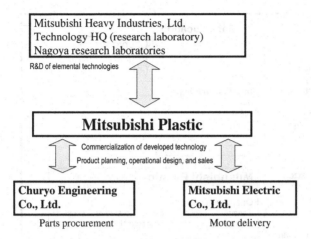

Figure 5.5   Mitsubishi Plastic's Component Development System.

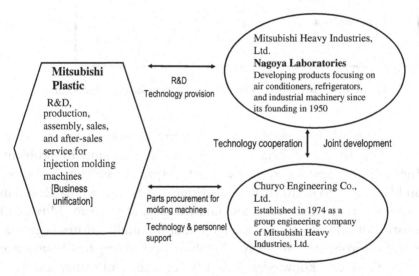

Figure 5.6   Collaboration among Mitsubishi Plastic, Nagoya Research Laboratory, and Churyo Engineering.

unique products and services. The sharing of information within the same site and office space promotes the formation of *Ba* (Nonaka and Takeuchi, 1995: Kodama, 2009a) in the sharing of dynamic new contexts.

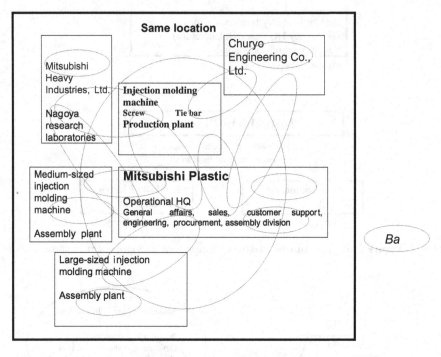

Figure 5.7   Mitsubishi Plastic's *Ba* creation in the same location.

The knowledge management of *Ba* formation is a means of strategic organizational management for solving this kind of problem. Innovative companies create *Ba* in virtual space by utilizing real space and ICT, and go on to create knowledge and SCs (Kodama, 2008) in order to constantly create new knowledge and wisdom. Mitsubishi Plastic not only creates knowledge but also skilfully creates organizational environments to share, distribute and utilize this knowledge and *Ba* to create knowledge. This is a key feature of management.

Mitsubishi Plastic's building of "knowledge-creating *Ba*" promotes the formation of knowledge and SCs that collaborate through communication among people and divisions as required, regardless of the organizational framework. Here the managers of each organization are required to have the coordinative strength to link as required the various groups within the organization and the manifold knowledge activities at various *Ba*. Accordingly, *Ba* is one of the sources of knowledge integration. It promotes the creation of SCs and networked SCs (see Chapter 1), and leads to skilful knowledge architectural thinking among managers. Mitsubishi Plastic then builds a series of vertical value chain models (see Table 1.1) from research through marketing, development and design, manufacturing, and sales to support through the knowledge integration process arising from vertical integrated architecture.

2.6 *Mitsubishi Plastic's new innovation project*

At the International Plastic Fair (IPF) held in Makuhari Messe, Chiba, from November 7 to 11, 2008, Mitsubishi Plastic announced the world's first large scale Electric Double Injection Molding Machine with Rotary Platen System (3000 emR). The new product development concept was manufacturing that is kind to the world, with the aims of developing products and technologies that protect the environment and contributing to building a sustainable society.

The name of the 3000 emR development project is the multi-material integration process. It is a project implemented through a two-year strategic alliance of Mitsubishi Plastic, Kyowa Industrial Co., Ltd., and Konan Tokusyu Sangyo Co., Ltd. (see Figure 5.8). Mitsubishi Plastic's project leaders collaborated closely with their counterparts in associated companies to build this project aimed at new technological challenges. This kind of new joint-development project with other companies differs from Mitsubishi Plastic's traditional system for developing new products (see Figures 5.6 and 5.7 for the development system comprising Mitsubishi group companies in the same location) in that it based on strategic collaboration with competitors in the same industry. SCs centered on Mitsubishi Plastic's development team leaders form to target the major theme of uncertainty in taking on the challenge of new technology developments (see Chapter 1). SC formation is based on *Ba* formation. It enhances the intrinsic motivation of the members by promoting the sharing of new contexts among different companies and building value and trust among development members with regard to high development objectives.

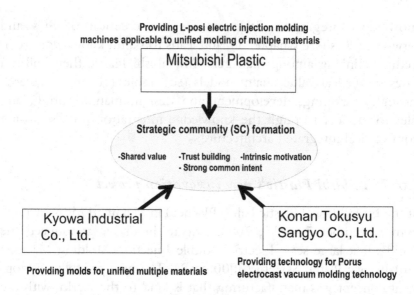

Figure 5.8   Formation Through Strategic Cooperation Among Companeis.

SC formation leads to skilful knowledge architectural thinking among development managers. Mitsubishi Plastic not only builds the vertical value chain model through the vertical integrated architecture of the knowledge integration process within the Mitsubishi group, but also absorbs knowledge from other companies for strengthening its own core competences or for additional strength through the knowledge integration process (arising from horizontal integrated architecture) to build a complementary model (see Table 1.2 in Chapter 1).

Specifically, Mitsubishi Plastic is supplying the L-position (L-shaped deployment of injection apparatus) model of injection molding machine and LFT screw applicable to its own core competences of integrated molding for multiple materials. Kyowa Industrial Company is supplying unified molding dies for multiple materials realizing its own core competence of multiprocessing with a single model. Konan Tokusyu Sangyo is supplying its core competence of the porus model of vacuum molding technology indispensable in the manufacture of preformed sheets. The modular based product architecture of this new injection molding machine combines the qualities of integral and modular models as general product features through integrating each companies' core technologies. Accordingly, it is also a hybrid model of product architecture.

In the field of injection molding machine technology, strategic joint development with other companies will be a main channel of project success. Each company mutually provides core technologies; and the question of how to demonstrate maximum merging and integration of these core technologies is significant. Mitsubishi Plastic has succeeded with the *knowledge integration model*, a model that merges the vertical value chain model arising from vertical integrated architecture that determines its own core competence and the complementary model arising from horizontal integrated architecture to absorb the core competence that comprises other companies' core knowledge (see Figure 5.9). Mitsubishi Plastic maintains vertical integration approximating closed innovation at vertical boundaries and

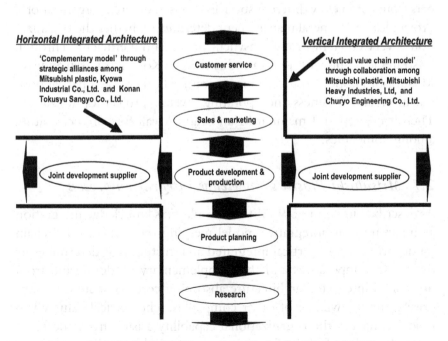

Figure 5.9   Knowledge Integration Model for Mitsubishi Plastic.

adopts the *knowledge integration model* absorbing other companies' knowledge at horizontal boundaries.

One major role of project leaders developing next-generation technologies across companies is to drive projects aimed at realizing new product concepts. The project leaders must commit to developing new technologies, devices, and products in order to realize the product concepts of weight reduction and energy conservation for injection molding machines, and high strength and quality for molding products. The most important factor in realizing product concepts, moreover, is to share those concepts among project members. This is why is it essential that project leaders possess both boundary objects as tools promoting the kind of innovation (see Chapter 4) and the strong shared intent of members rooted in common knowledge and shared values (Kodama, 2001) incorporating common language, meaning, and interest (Carlile, 2002; Cramton, 2001; Star, 1989).

The second role is to efficiently advance a project as a single organization. Inter-company projects are also an assembly of members from completely different specializations in different organizations. Project leaders' general management determines whether the organization is very efficient or else unsynchronized and inefficient. Through its strategic tie-up with Kyowa Industrial and Konan Tokusyu Sangyo, Mitsubishi Plastic considered incorporating both its own partial optimization and business incorporating overall project optimization. Then it created and maintained an original wall-free project culture among companies.

2.7 Mitsubishi Plastic's knowledge integration process

As described in Figure 5.9, Mitsubishi Plastic's knowledge integration architecture is an integrative model merging the vertical value chain model arising from vertical integrated architecture that determines its own core competences and the complementary model arising from horizontal integrated architecture absorbing core competences comprising the knowledge of other companies. The vertical value chain model enhances the organizational capability arising from the accumulation and evolution of its own technological capabilities and goes on to enhance its hard-to-imitate competitive edge. Meanwhile, the complementary model absorbs and integrates the external knowledge to supplement and strengthen a company's own core competences, and goes on to create a new organizational capability.

The strategic emergence and selection domains in the knowledge integration map (see Figure 5.10) correspond to the R&D process for products incorporating next-generation technology development, such as the world's first ultra large-scale — Electric Double Injection Molding Machine with Rotary Platen System (3000 emR). In these domains, development managers must apply both the conventional closed innovation of traditional manufacturers and the concepts of linkage relationship architecture to discover outstanding internal and external partnerships. The manufacturers then build complementary models arising from horizontal integrated architecture with the best partners by seeking out suitable external partners and verifying them technologically, and aspire to a *knowledge integration model* through integrating the knowledge possessed by multiple companies.

Furthermore, in order to develop next-generation technologies, domains I and II require the concept of combining creative and effective new product development aimed at targeted new technologies and products while exploring product development strategies to achieve differentiation from other companies' products. The sustained development of the vertical value chain model from vertical integration of the business activities mentioned in Chapter 4 and the efficient absorption of other companies' core technologies from the complementary model are key processes in the pursuit of the *creativity view* model, and this kind of knowledge architectural thinking enables creativity and efficiency to be combined. Moreover, the knowledge modularity of product architecture comprising the modularization of components produced both internally and by other companies becomes an element in enhancing the efficiency of production systems and customization. Meanwhile, the movement toward integral, internally created products arising from a company's own core competence is also linked to enhancing a company's own Black Box creativity (see Chapter 4). As mentioned earlier hybrid architecture combining earlier modular and integral elements

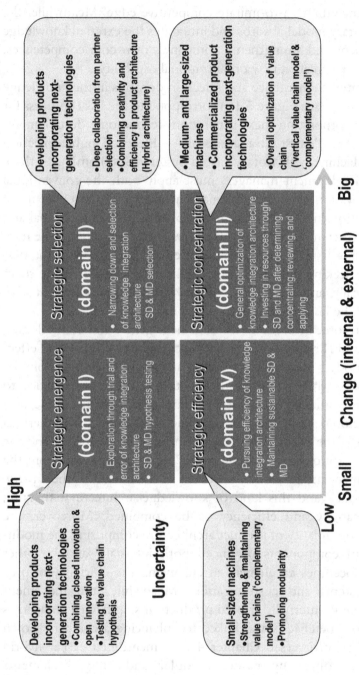

Figure 5.10   Mitsubishi Plastic's Knowledge Integration Map.

Note: Knowledge integration architecture: 'vertical integrated architecture,' 'Horizontal integrated architecture,' 'Linkage relationship architecture'.
SD: Strategy drivers MD: Management drivers.

becomes a robust product development concept combining the manufacturers' creativity and efficiency (see Figure 5.3).

Accordingly, the manufacturers' development managers of the future will have to permit an expanded diversity of knowledge integration architecture as knowledge architectural thinking based on the concept of combining closed (systems promoting technological development contained mainly within the company) and open innovation, and focus on R&D processes of core technologies and products through experiments and trials aimed at the vertical value chain and complementary models building optimized value chains. Regarding the knowledge integration process in these domains, the hypothesis testing and selection process for strategy and management drivers responding to strategic objectives must be pursued further through managers' diverse knowledge architectural thinking.

Meanwhile, Mitsubishi Plastic's existing medium and large-scale machines are leading products selling under fast-changing competitive environments, and these product groups are positioned in the strategic concentration domain. Here, vertical integrated architecture is developmentally reviewed as part of the knowledge integration process; new partnerships are discovered and reviewed on a vertical or horizontal orientation through horizontal integrated and linkage relationship architecture in response to conditions; and a new vertical value chain model is built. Then the knowledge integration process in this domain developmentally reviews the strategy and management drivers in response to strategic objectives.

When a product incorporating next-generation technology development, mentioned above moves from domain II to domain III, the strategy and management drivers are defined and concentrated, and further overall optimization of knowledge integration architecture selected in domain II is implemented.

Moreover, joint branding with other companies and the small-scale OEM-product machines require manufacturers to have still more efficient production systems by developing modularization through established technology. Maintaining of the strategy and management drivers positions this small-scale machine business in domain IV. The manufacturers then cooperate with other companies to promote standardization of knowledge modularity for components, and exploit the complementary model to enhance the efficiency of knowledge integration architecture aimed at maintaining and strengthening the value chain of existing business. Mitsubishi Plastic supports the organizational capability required to strategically realize the targeted product domain and value chain, flexibly applies its own knowledge integration processes, and goes on to build vertical value chains and complementary models.

2.8 *Mitsubishi Plastic's strategic innovation capability*

In Mitsubishi Plastic, the product development process for next-generation technologies as strategic innovation pursuing exploratory activities and small-, medium-, and large-scale machine business as incremental innovation pursuing exploitative activities are implemented simultaneously (see Figure 5.10). The established lineup of this core machine (small-, medium-, and large-scale) business requires the maintenance of a long-term high-profit structure. Response to customer needs must also be strengthened through product MD and MC, and incremental innovation is required by sustained commercialization processes and by reforming supply chains in domains II and III.

Meanwhile, the processes for product development from next-generation technologies in domains I and II require R&D processes arising from new product concepts considering both higher product functionality and environmental needs. This in turn requires Mitsubishi Plastic action to integrate diverse knowledge inside and outside the company. It further requires product development processes to explore new business models aimed at discovering potential client needs.

As Figure 5.10 illustrates, Mitsubishi Plastic requires different knowledge integration processes in these four domains, which also correspond to the management capability of the diverse knowledge integration process (one element of *strategic innovation capability*). The business series of development, sales, and solutions sales for the established product lineup (small-, medium-, and large-sized machines) in domains III and IV is implemented mainly through the Mitsubishi Plastic organizational system promoting the unified management (planning, development and design, production, sales, and support) seen in Figure 5.4, and collaboration with the Nagoya laboratory of parent company Mitsubishi Heavy Industries and group company Churyo Engineering Co., Ltd. (see Figure 5.6).

Here the diverse *Ba* are always present (see Figure 5.7), and dynamic context and knowledge is shared among each organization in response to environmental change and customer needs. *Ba* also comprise SCs as design-built teams of pragmatic boundaries assembling essential personnel (Kodama, 2007a) responding to emergencies and emerging issues. These SCs take on the role of hubs inter connecting organizations building vertical value-chain models, and members' coordination and collaboration developed at these hubs integrates heterogeneous knowledge (see Figure 5.11).

Meanwhile, the operation of new technology and product development (the process of developing products incorporating next-generation technologies) in domains I and II requires knowledge integration merging different core competences as, for instance, the burden of joint development through SC formation arising from strategic alliances with other companies in the same industry grows (see Figure 5.8). The inter-corporate SC (SC-b) becomes an inter-organizational network hub building a complementary model through horizontal integrated architecture (see Figure 5.11). Development team members from Mitsubishi Plastic's Engineering Department participate in the SC through strategic alliances (see Figure 5.4). The development team members participating here always promote information and knowledge sharing with other members of their own company's engineering department while smoothly implementing reciprocal transfers of new technologies and skills. This involves SC-a (concerned with domains III and IV) and SC-b (concerned with domains I and II) forming network links (networked SCs) and continuously implementing the smooth sharing and transfer of information and knowledge.

Thus, developers are inspired by the smooth shift toward commercialization of the products incorporating next-generation

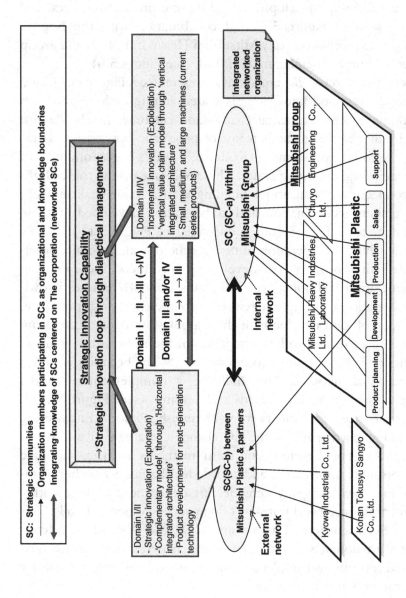

Figure 5.11 Strategic Innovation Capability of Integrated Networked Organization.

technologies from domain II to domain III and emergent action from domains III and/or IV to domain I aimed at meeting the challenge of new customer needs and technology innovations (see Figure 5.11).

These SC formations have the role of promoting management within each domain, while the formation of networked SCs promotes inter-domain management (shifting among domains), which is one of the management capabilities of strategic innovation capability. The sharing of SC and networked SC contexts and the dynamic knowledge integration process drives the strategic innovation loop from domains I through III and/or domain IV to domain I.

In this book, I will use the term "integrated networked organization" for Mitsubishi Plastic's intra- and inter-corporate organizational structure (see Figure 5.11). The deep collaboration among these diverse organizations promotes the dialectical management of incremental and strategic innovation within and among domains, and creates corporate strategic innovation capability. The integrated network organization drives the *strategic innovation loop* while creating a diverse knowledge integration process supporting each domain and building a vertical value chain and complementary model.

3. Summary

In recent years, the most important aspect of the environmental change surrounding manufacturers is the focus on innovating the speedy, agile management practices that can be exhibited by corporate manufacturing features and strengths, even in uncertain times when it is not clear which product lines will sell. The rigorous conditions of market change require, in addition to pricing and quality, reduced development lead times for new products and technologies in alignment with customer needs as well as for manufacturing and sales. Competition is becoming played out on a time axis that makes no concessions to global geography. Focusing on the customer, companies must pursue supply-chain optimization together with economies of scale, scope, and speed. Companies must also pursue overall optimization of various management elements, such as corporate strategy, organization, technology, operation, and leadership, considering the ideal business models for each product and operating as a single aligned function without going into any partial optimization for each function and organization (Kodama, 2009b).

One aspect of new knowledge arising from these case studies is that the elements required for maintaining a competitive manufacturing edge build an integrated networked organization as a *knowledge integration model* required to exhibit a sustained *strategic innovation capability*. Japanese manufacturers currently promote independent development, and at the same time they lead the *knowledge integration-based firm* as a *knowledge integration model* promoting dynamic strategic alliances with outstanding external partners to respond to technological change and diverse customer needs (see Figure 4.4 in Chapter 4). The independent approach through closed innovation enables companies to deliver total solutions to the customer by independently developing all highly specialized technologies and pursuing design and manufacturing consistency. The *creativity view* that comprises one of the management drivers of Japanese corporations promotes unification of development and production, creates new rules for product innovation, and realizes Black-Box creation and all-in-one products. Mastering all of a company's own specialist fields and coordinating and collaborating on internal networks are important elements in realizing this business model.

Meanwhile, as this case study of Mitsubishi Plastic shows, Japanese manufacturers incorporate within their own companies the knowledge and competences of external partners (specialists in the same industry) by building external networks based on the concept of knowledge modularity, and co-establish internal and external networks to promote innovation management as a midway condition between open innovation (distributed knowledge) exploiting external partner specialties and conventionally closed innovation (integrated knowledge). The organizational form promoting these co-established internal and external networks corresponds to the integrated networked organization illustrated in Figure 5.11. As shown in Figure 4.4, Chapter 4, this involves a shift to a semi-structure model with tightly coupled elements within companies having vertically integrated organization and loosely-coupled elements among companies having modular organization.

The second aspect of this knowledge is the concept of product architecture to deliver new value creation to the customer. This customer-focused value creation is multifaceted, but in the industrial equipment field, the combination of creativity and efficiency is a key condition for realizing outstanding, low-cost products and satisfying customer needs. I believe that the hybrid architecture concept integrating modular and integral models is one of the product architecture solutions combining creativity and efficiency. Promoting technological development of the integral architecture model drives the sustainable development and accumulation of core competences as a Black Box, and establishes a hard-to-copy technological competitive edge over rivals. Meanwhile, modular architecture has the potential to evolve solutions supporting customer needs, such as efficient component procurement and customization. Moreover, knowledge integration from merging the core technology processes of one's own and rival companies enables the realization of either the integral or modular models of architecture (especially the closed model of inter-corporate cooperation). The product concept of hybrid architecture is important to realize new product innovation combining the advantages of creative-leaning vertical integration and efficiency-leaning horizontal specialization.

6

A Co-Evolution Model of the Mobile Phone Business: The Case of Study of NTT DoCoMo

1. Combining Strategic and Incremental Innovation

As mentioned in previous chapters, to maintain a continuous competitive edge, companies must combine the practices of incremental innovation and strategic innovation succeed in their core businesses and acquire new strategic positions.

This chapter presents insights gained from the case study analysis firstly, it projects a combination of different innovative processes arising from organizational design (described in this chapter as "emergent" and "traditional" organizations) supporting each strategic and incremental innovation. The emergent organizations form emergent networks from alliances with external strategic partners aimed at exploring new products, services, and business models, and pursue strategic innovation. The emergent networks are networks among SCs (networked SCs) comprising alliance and collaborative networks with external partners to explore and pursue new business.

The traditional organizations are organizations that mostly take on the burden of continuously improving and strengthening existing core businesses including current product enhancement, sales, customer services, and equipment and maintenance. They form deliberate networks arising from external alliance partnerships and pursue incremental innovation. Deliberate networks are networks among SCs (networked SCs). Including collaborative networks formed through strategic outsourcing with external partners to deliberately and reliably implement strategies for existing core businesses.

Secondly, it involves a formation of multi-layered SC networks among these emergent and traditional in-house organizations (see Chapter 1); the merging of marketing and technology orientations; and DoCoMo's demonstration of integrative competences through close linkage, which arises from creative dialogue after forming SCs among diverse specialist organizations. Integrative competences arising from these internal SCs become a creative source for later business models comprising various new services, led by i-mode.

Thirdly, it presents a construction of a business ecosystem exploiting mobile phones (e.g., Moore, 1993). Dynamics of DoCoMo's formation of industry-spanning SCs and networked SCs include dynamic processes achieving the strategic innovations that create future businesses of the i-mode and mobile wallet as well as diverse service development through cooperation across industries.

2. Case Study: DoCoMo's Innovation

Japan's mobile phone market has surpassed the 100-million-unit mark and entered a maturity phase. Now that long-term growth no longer prioritizes acquisition of new customers, DoCoMo has issued a new declaration of a policy to place greater emphasis on customer satisfaction while expanding services for existing customers. DoCoMo's president and CEO, Ryuji Yamada, iterated the following seven-point challenge:

1. Personalize services
2. Develop social support services

3. Develop combined services
4. Develop video services
5. Introduce next-generation networks
6. Develop handsets
7. Develop globally

The leading "i-concier" personalized service has already passed the 1.4-million-contract mark. Speaking of this concierge service, Mr. Yamada stated his ambition of "providing an Aladdin's lamp of a mobile phone". Mr. Yamada also commented: Although the market is already described as mature, significant functional growth potential remains in promoting innovations that exploit mobile phone features. This should contribute to Japan's ICT development and the fullness of its lifestyles". Mobile phones are also taking on the roles of supporting customer behavior while providing means of support for communication, information, and lifestyles. DoCoMo is meeting challenges of evolving all these roles further. Its current innovation strategy comprises *phase four action support centered on personalization* (see Figure 6.1).

Japan's mobile phone services lead the world, and it is no exaggeration to say that DoCoMo is the pioneer in this market. I will discuss these innovation processes below in four chronological phases of support: communication, information, lifestyle, and action (see Figure 6.1).

2.1 *Phase 1: Supporting communication–Cultivating the mobile phone market*

In 1992, the mobile business division of Japan's leading telecommunications company, NTT, was spun off to ensure fair competition in the telecommunications market. This was the birth of DoCoMo. DoCoMo's first president and CEO, Koji Oboshi, cultivated a new sense of unity and values from all employees working as one to break a negative cycle of poor mobile phone sales. DoCoMo then forged a shared intent among all employees to free itself from its deficit and create a new market. Sharing a sense of crisis with all employees heightened the sense of mounting new business challenges.

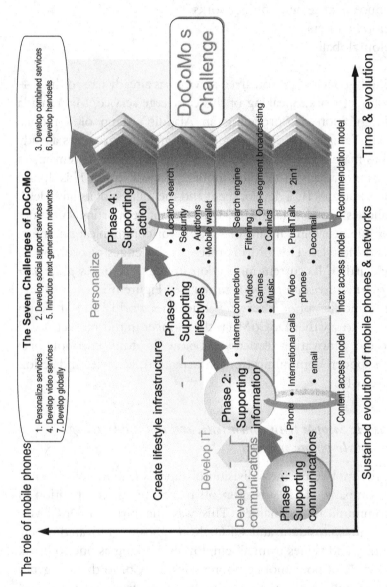

Figure 6.1   DoCoMo's Challenge: Evolving Services.

Source: Materials released by NTT DoCoMo (adjusted)

At the beginning, DoCoMo was a small-scale organization. *Employee work initiatives* constantly shared individually held information and knowledge transcending organizational boundaries, and enabled a climate promoting business operations that channeled shared values and objectives. Employees in individual specialist fields including marketing, sales, development, technology, maintenance, and planning transcended organizational boundaries and form informal project teams in response to urgent issues and spontaneous, independent SCs across the whole company.

SCs formed with the aim of breaking out of the negative lifecycle of mobile phone sales, and dialogue and discussions on individual issues built up. Leaders and managers in development and technology divisions supporting the mobile phone base repeatedly engaged in trial and error during joint development via emergent networks (see Phase 1 in Table 6.1) with mobile phone manufacturers. The aim of the R&D was to surpass the US company Motorola in creating one of the world's lightest high-function mobile phone.

DoCoMo outsourced to sales agents and distributors of existing electrical goods, and built sales networks. This allowed it to expand sales channels in a relatively short time frame and extract new demand while growing market share. In this way, the expansion of sales channels by forming deliberate networks of strategic outsourcing centered on DoCoMo's traditional organizations created new demand widely distributed in the market from conventional business to individual user layers (see Phase 1 in Table 6.1).

The creation of demand enlarged the market pie and led to DoCoMo's dramatic growth. In 1996, at the height of DoCoMo's mobile phone sales, Mr. Oboshi anticipated the next crisis, and considered it risky to become too comfortable with the status quo. He hit on the idea of migrating to a daring strategy aimed at cultivating a new market. In July 1996, he took out corporate newspaper ads to make a public announcement and immediately took decisive action. The ads launched a new vision of converting volume to value. Freshly, DoCoMo had successfully developed wireless packet transmission as network infrastructure, then it delivered services connecting small PCs to mobile phone handsets. Since Internet use was growing at this

Table 6.1   Formation Process for NTT DoCoMo's Strategic Communities (SCs).

→ : Participating in SCs and networked SCs where organizational members transcend organizational and specialist knowledge boundaries.

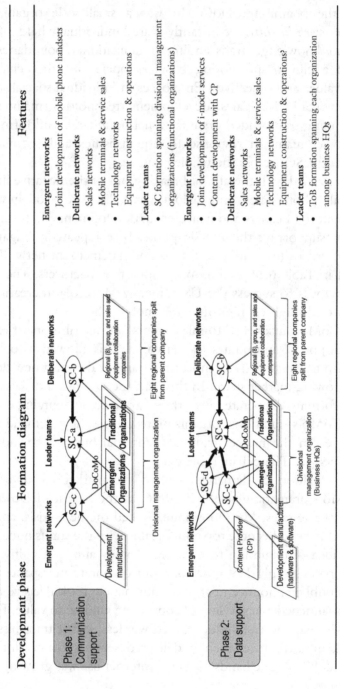

Development phase	Formation diagram	Features
Phase 1: Communication support		**Emergent networks** • Joint development of mobile phone handsets **Deliberate networks** • Sales networks • Mobile terminals & service sales • Technology networks • Equipment construction & operations **Leader teams** • SC formation spanning divisional management organizations (functional organizations)
Phase 2: Data support		**Emergent networks** • Joint development of i-mode services • Content development with CP **Deliberate networks** • Sales networks • Mobile terminals & service sales • Technology networks • Equipment construction & operations? **Leader teams** • ToB formation spanning each organization among business HQs

Table 6.1 (*Continued*) Process for Forming NTT DoCoMo's ToBs (Teams of Boundaries).

Development phase	Formation diagram	Features
Phase 3: Lifestyle support		**Emergent networks** • Joint development of mobile phone peripheral technology domains • Linking settlement and commercial transaction domains • Linking broadcast domains • Linking with global business **Deliberate networks** • Sales networks • Mobile terminals & service sales • Technology networks • Equipment construction & operations **Leader teams** • ToB formation spanning each organization among business HQs
Phase 4: Action support		**Emergent networks** • Cooperation on new business development • Cooperation on social support business **Deliberate networks** • Sales networks • Mobile terminals and service sales • Technology networks • Equipment construction & operations **Leader teams** • ToB formation spanning divisional management organizations (functional organizations) • Integrated organization through a single company structure for the whole country

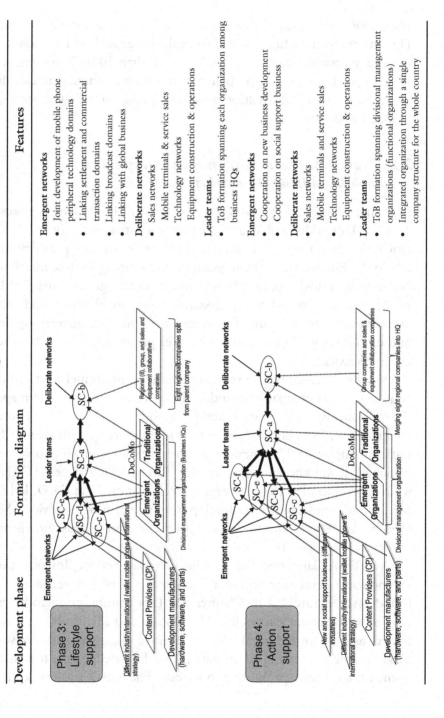

time, DoCoMo launched a handset loaded with a simple browser. This Internet-access function led to explosive growth of DoCoMo. It succeed in creating such demand that more than 20 million users had signed up within two years. It led to the mobile phone multimedia challenge in the "information support" phase. It was the start of i-mode development.

2.2   *Phase 2: Supporting information–exploring mobile multimedia markets*

In January 1997, Mr. Oboshi gave Mr. Keiichi Enoki (former president of DoCoMo Tokai and former executive director of NTT DoCoMo and i-mode divisional director; currently president of DoCoMo Engineering) the mission of "developing mobile multimedia services using mobile phones aimed at the general user". Mr. Enoki was also mandated to assemble personnel and build new organizations by scouting for external talent and advertising in-house. He was given total authority over personnel and funds to set up new services.

Mr. Enoki assembled diverse, outstanding personnel from inside and outside the company (including Mari Matsunaga, a content specialist from Recruit, and Takeshi Natsuno from an IT venture company), and launched a "gateway" project starting with around 10 staff. In August 1997, a new organization of around 70 people was launched. It was known as the Gateway Business Department (GBD), which corresponded to an emergent organization. The GBD, led by Mr. Enoki, undertook to develop the new i-mode service. Mr. Oboshi, Mr. Enoki, and the other GBD staff shared ideas and visions on developing new services.

Mr. Enoki launched the Mobile Gateway Service Introduction Promotion Committee within the company aimed at realizing the i-mode (see Figure 1.4 in Chapter 1). This committee included all DoCoMo divisional leaders like Mr. Oboshi and Mr. Enoki. It functioned as a spatiotemporal SC for creative dialogue and decision making aimed at sharing information and knowledge at a top management level and promoting business. The GBD project leaders formed seven working groups (WGs) from GBD and the middle management of other traditional organizations (see Chapter 1). The promotion committee and the seven WGs were then positioned as DoCoMo's leader teams (networked SCs of layered, hierarchical networks) to develop the i-mode.

The action required to promote i-mode business strategies dynamically promoted emergent networks through strategic cooperation with a range of external partners, and produced concrete results. Regarding DoCoMo's new business strategy proposals, the organizational behavior is the resonating of strategy with external partners and the launch of new projects with individual partner companies. DoCoMo deliberately built emergent networks within its own company and with external partners. These emergent networks always engaged in creative dialogue aimed at forming a new environment (market) to establish and expand mobile-Internet culture. Various problems and issues were dialectically synthesized, and new i-mode business concepts created. The emergent networks formed in the second phase are a key feature in further extending the phase-one structures outside the company (see Phase 2 in Chart 6.1).

i-mode was launched in February 1999; and by August 2000, more than 10 million subscribers had signed up. DoCoMo had created the world's first mobile phone driven Internet market. By then, DoCoMo had embarked on developing new services and businesses of third-generation mobile phones and mobile commerce aimed at the following innovations.

2.3 *Phase 3: Supporting lifestyles–building lifestyle infrastructure exploiting mobile phones*

The issues and challenges faced by DoCoMo as it passed the 40-million-subscriber mark were threefold: one, to expand i-mode sales from domestic to international market; two, to migrate second-generation to third-generation; and three, to realize mobile phone lifestyle tools led by the long-planned mobile commerce (mobile wallets). A major issue in phase three was to combine profitable methods of the time for domestic market growth with new business risks of overseas markets and new-generation systems. A further key issue was to somehow establish new mobile phone services as lifestyle infrastructure.

DoCoMo then formed global emergent networks with external partners to face great challenges of global expansion, to support for new-generation systems, and to create lifestyle tools.

The first task was to form emergent networks with European, Asian, and U.S. communications carriers to develop i-mode and 3G systems overseas. The next task was to form emergent networks across industries as new service strategies to create mobile phone lifestyle tools. It involved forming emergent networks across sectors including banking, credit card, convenience stores, other stores, and railroads in settlement and commercial transaction domains to create mobile commerce services. *To collaboration for* DoCoMo with Sony to achieve the mobile wallet by loading with a non-contact IC card was especially important Sony had already undertaken the development and sales of its FeliCa IC chip, but it was having profitability issues. Sony embraced risks and challenges of exploiting mobile phone to realize mobile commerce, and formed a positive strategic alliance with DoCoMo, which eventually became a joint venture corporation between DoCoMo and Sony named FeliCa Network. DoCoMo delivered full-scale mobile commerce exploiting the mobile commerce platforms jointly developed by DoCoMo and the FeliCa Network. In 2005, it began to offer the iD credit business platform enabling mobile phone credit services through individual credit card companies; and in 2006, it established the DCMX credit card issued by DoCoMo itself.

In the broadcasting domain, DoCoMo formed emergent networks with leading broadcast distributors aimed at merging services for mobile phone communications and terrestrial digital broadcasts. It also established strategic links and joint ventures in the content and Internet domains, and dynamically formed emergent networks with internal and external development partners (such as the U.S. company TI) aimed at joint development of core technologies (hardware and software) for mobile phone handsets. For collaboration with semiconductor companies, development of system LSI, which is at the heart of the mobile phone development requirements of short and high-function lifecycles, was an urgent task. After sharing its handset development roadmap with other handset manufacturers and semiconductor manufacturers and promptly loading the handsets with new functions, DoCoMo entered a mobile phone handset market.

The various issues and problems at these emergent networks were dialectically synthesized, i-mode overseas (including i-mode license contracts with communications carriers in Germany, the Netherlands, Taiwan, Belgium, France, Spain, Italy, and the United States, and launching i-mode services) and roaming services; were realized and mobile wallets were created as leading lifestyle tool services. A major feature of the emergent networks created in phase three was that their global, cross-industry, and expanded technological domains were more extensive than those in phase two. Meanwhile, DoCoMo was establishing new services and businesses around 3.5G and the future 3.9G.

2.4 Phase 4: Supporting action — building social infrastructure using mobile phones

In phase four, the market continued to grow, and the limits to growth from acquiring further new contracts began to appear. DoCoMo reviewed the foundations of its marketing strategy and redefined business domains, customer targets, and market positioning. President Yamada concluded that the strategy's essence should be to built long-term relationships with established customers to achieve sustainable growth, departing from the competitive axis of acquiring new customers, and to deepen the connections with customers' lifestyles.

In April 2008, DoCoMo released a new declaration of intent, which focused its firm decision to reform on the basis of new strategy. The company's focus on brand reform, responding to the changing market environment rather than simply changing the logo, demonstrated DoCoMo's resolution to review the role of business operations from its foundations. The employees working under President Yamada are currently preparing carefully to secure the company's future with the new branding. DoCoMo's new declaration of intent establishes 25 projects based on customer demands (including expansion of the DoCoMo store, network quality, and fee systems), and DoCoMo is now promoting these reforms.

In the mature mobile phone market, the contract lapse rate is a guide to whether existing levels of customer satisfaction can be maintained, and is becoming more important than the net increase. DoCoMo introduced new discount services that lowered the basic charges in return for customers and lengthened subscription periods with two-year contracts. In introducing new sales models, which is achieved by a review of the sales system in which DoCoMo took on some of the handset cost burden, created to encourage new customer acquisition. As a result of introducing these new business models, the DoCoMo customers' lapse rate declined steadily. The rate for the fourth quarter of fiscal 2008 fell to 0.68% and dropped further since April 2008. It demonstrated that the new business model was steadily bearing fruit.

The DoCoMo-launched market for advanced mobile phones came to a major crossroads. With more than 100 million mobile phone subscribers and increasing market maturity in Japan's mobile phone market, the competition for contracts stepped up a level while various growth opportunities arose incorporating people's values and lifestyle diversity. This also gave DoCoMo the potential for new business opportunities.

Meanwhile, as mobile phones have grown increasingly sophisticated and almost all can now satisfy basic customer needs, it is difficult to differentiate one company's product from another on the basis of technology and function alone, and it has become important to respond accurately to diverse values required by customers. Recognizing this, DoCoMo has fixed on a new marketing strategy suited to a business environment, and determined to remake its image as a" relation services company" that deepens links among individuals and puts them in touch with their lifestyles. It expresses DoCoMo's basic policy stance of pursuing hospitality as a service business regardless of conventional mobile phone business domains. It also involves a strategic conversion from, for example, differentiation through mobile phone function to that through services.

Aligning with the evolution of mobile phone handsets, a merging of mobile phones with other objects has led to rise of new services, and it has become more important to commit to innovation to make customer lifestyles more convenient and comfortable.

The first feature of R&D activities implemented today as a new strategy alongside the full realization of DoCoMo's core business of 3G and 3.5G mobile a phone services is development of mobile a broadband through the 3.9G mobile phone system known as "Long Term Evolution," (LTE) to be followed by 4G mobile phone services development. In order to promote advanced and diverse mobile broadband services, DoCoMo is building high-speed, low-delay and high-capacity networks since 2010. The second feature is a commitment to more sophisticated mobile phone terminals. These two features form the content of DoCoMo's continuous technology innovation roadmap so far. The third feature is service personalization (see Figure 6.1), which incorporates personalization of services and functions in line with customer lifestyles and needs, and creates richer customer lifestyles. DoCoMo is targeting the ultimate mobile phone, the "Aladdin's magic lamp", that enhances the selections for the individual from a huge array of services, products, and information, and evolves from a mobile phone that can "do something" to one that can do something *for you*".

One specific initiative is the Ministry of Economy, Trade, and Industry's "Information Grand Voyage" (see Figure 6.2). This project, undertaken as part of DoCoMo's new value creation, is developing a mobile phone with agent functions. Amid the trends toward broadband mobile phone networks, high functioning mobile phones, and mobile phones supporting daily life, DoCoMo is participating in the ministry's project as it targets a move from a "mobile phone that can", to a "mobile phone that works for you". DoCoMo will incorporates agent functions in the mobile phones that deliver information based on individual preferences and action, and endeavors to deliver sophisticated personal services. DoCoMo is implementing substantive experiments linked to such services with the project. The aim is for the service providers to analyze people's behavioral patterns and realize a "mobile phone service that under-

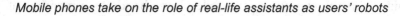

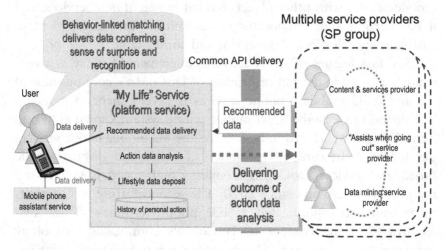

Figure 6.2   The information Grand Voyage Project: Targeting a Mobile Phone that "Understands the Situation".

stands the situation", transmitting optimal information in accordance with time, place, and preferences. Conventional information delivery services were standardized along the lines of "if you come to this place, we will deliver this information", but these services are individually specialized, and the provision of information for features of individual behavior is unprecedented.

The fourth feature is development of new business (social support services) in fields such as environment, ecology, safety, and health management aimed at sustained social growth, and value creation in new domains. Currently, issues on sustained social growth such as the environment and medical treatment are coming to the fore. Meanwhile, DoCoMo is promoting a social-issue approach based on a customer platform numbering about 54 million. By evolving the networks, mobile terminals, and services that are its strengths, DoCoMo is extending the mobile phone applications exploiting mobile, real-time, and personal features, and enhancing its potential to contribute to more efficient individual action and consumption and enhance social productivity.

In this area, DoCoMo's exploitation of social infrastructure building and alliance promotion capabilities, building of social platforms to create more effective information flow in domains where the mobile phone is anticipated to make a major contribution, and promotion of cross-company alliances is of great social significance. Developing these social support services will bring returns by contributing to sustained social growth through linking individuals, companies, and group initiatives via mobile phones to resolve social issues, and by encouraging more effective and active individual activities.

The fifth feature is the provision of integrated services, and convenient, user-friendly services aligned with customer use scenarios through association with mobile phones and various lifestyle tools. Specifically, this includes linking information appliances, vehicles, broadcast equipment, and mobile phone handsets to deliver services aligned with the customers' usage scene and to provide an environment that enables the seamless use of fixed, mobile, broadcast, and home networks.

In phase four, DoCoMo implemented major organizational reforms in parallel with the new declaration. At a time when Japan's mobile phone market was growing rapidly, DoCoMo business management had operated under a nine-company system to develop sales policies supporting the conditions of each region and carry out service area maintenance appropriately. As the Market grew, however, still more complete customer services, faster decision making, and more efficient management were required to respond to customer expectations amid a changing competitive environment. This led DoCoMo to merge its eight regional companies with the HQ in July 2008, thereby simplifying complex decision making processes to cut costs and speed up decisions. Aiming to nullify the various adverse effects (including duplication of resources and inter-HQ barriers) accompanying the enlarged organization of the HQ system during the phase two and three, the hierarchical HQ structure was abandoned in July 2008 to make way for a flatter divisional organization. The result was that DoCoMo achieved faster internal decision making and stronger links among divisions.

Thus, a major feature of the emergent networks formed in phase four, when compared with the emergent networks in phase three, was the further expansion into other industries and new, merged technology domains aimed at new and social support business. As for the traditional organizations, the reform of the HQ internal organization and merging of regional corporations led to flatter, swifter decision making and stronger collaboration. This brought about the formation of DoCoMo's internal leader teams and deliberate networks developing from close linkage (see phase four in Chart 6.1).

3. Consideration and Discussion

In this section, I will consider the formation of networked SCs in the chronological phases 1 to 4 (explained in the case studies above) and the dynamics of corporate boundaries. I will also consider the vertical value chain and co-evolution models that form features of Japan's mobile phone business. Then I will look at *the creativity view* and *the dialectic view* as boundary conceptions creating Japan's characteristic business models (mentioned in Chapter 1). I will analyze the theoretical framework by which the *dialectic view* creates a co-evolution model in the mobile phone business. Finally, I will indicate how dialectical management exploits DoCoMo's *strategic innovation capability* to create the co-evolution model of the mobile phone business.

3.1 *The formation of networked SCs and the dynamics of corporate boundaries*

In phase one, DoCoMo built the value chain for a mobile phone market that had very little penetration. This vertically integrated chain comprised users, DoCoMo itself, communications equipment manufacturers (including manufacturers developing mobile phones), facilities construction and maintenance companies, and sales companies. DoCoMo optimized its own vertical boundaries through the formation of networked SCs. The SC leader teams and others, formed from emergent organizations promoting emergent networks and traditional organizations promoting deliberate networks as the internal organizations, swiftly responded to a number of problems and issues.

In phase two, the new i-mode market was created, diffused, and established out of a sense of crisis at the saturation of the voice communications market. It differs from phase one in that DoCoMo re-defined its vertical boundaries and built new vertically integrated value chains incorporating content providers (CPs) and other new stakeholders. DoCoMo also optimized its vertical boundaries to form mobile Internet markets by rebuilding networked SCs, putting greater emphasis on rebuilding the emergent networks through the inter-corporate networks with external partners than it did in phase one. Key factors for external stakeholders were DoCoMo's demonstration of vision in creating i-mode's new market and building a vertical integrated value chain, and "dialectical leadership" (Kodama, 2007a) in forming win-win business ecosystems[1] among the stakeholders.

In phase three, DoCoMo created and extended new markets to project i-mode's following "S-curve." In this phase, DoCoMo further optimized its own vertical boundaries built in phase two while re-defining its horizontal boundaries to advance into new business domains. The mobile wallet and mobile credit businesses gave DoCoMo a firm foothold in the finance business; and the merged broadcast and communications, vehicle telematics, ubiquitous, and other businesses opened up the prospects for DoCoMo's horizontal boundaries, becoming the trigger in forging new business models. In this way, DoCoMo built a new value chain of horizontal boundaries under a changing competitive environment. The formation of the emergent networks through inter-corporate

---

[1] Data distribution business models in the ICT industry, such as i-mode, are built through co-evolution arising from coordination and collaboration with content and platform providers. For details, see the following publication: "M. Kodama: Innovation Networks in the Knowledge-Based Firm: Developing ICT-Based Integrative Competences," Edward Elgar Publishing (2009).

networks among partners in different industries expanded further from the level seen in phase two. Key factors for external stakeholders were DoCoMo's optimization of the i-mode vertically integrated value chain, demonstration of a mobile commerce vision at horizontal boundaries, and the dialectical leadership to form business ecosystems by building win-win relationships among stakeholders.

In phase four, the further expansion of the emergent networks has been strengthened. These networks aim to build new value chains at horizontal boundaries targeting new business such as personalized and social services. DoCoMo has also hammered out customer-focused sales and equipment strategies to strengthen the vertical-boundary value chains of conventional mobile phone services.

Moreover, DoCoMo has abolished hierarchical structure of regional HQ system and restructured as a flatter divisional organization, thereby eliminating the various adverse effects of organizational enlargement from the regional HQ system existing in phases two and three. On an operational level, the nine-company business operation has reverted to the one-company system of the time of DoCoMo's founding. The flattening of DoCoMo's internal traditional organizations and rebuilding of the accompanying deliberate networks has speeded up decision making and strengthened links among divisions. DoCoMo is currently aiming to optimize vertical and horizontal boundaries by rebuilding emergent and deliberate networked SCs.

As shown above, the SC (SC-a) as leader teams formed within DoCoMo at each phase becomes the hub and node of the network spaces, and later create multiple SC networks outside the company (Kodama, 2007b). The creation of individual SC networks possessing different contexts and knowledge goes on to create further new knowledge. DoCoMo's style of knowledge integration company constantly forms new strategic intent through "boundary vision", optimizes its own vertical and horizontal boundaries through dynamic rebuilding of networked SCs, and create new boundaries innovation as a continuous business ecosystem.

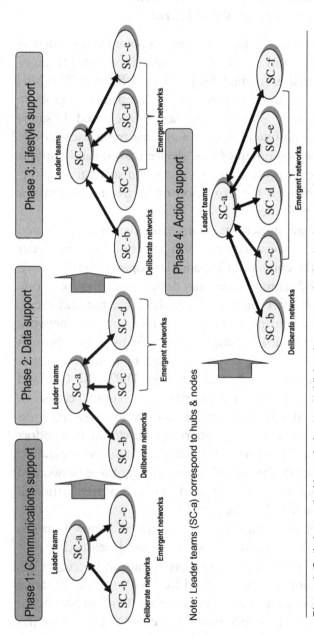

Phase 1: Optimize vertical boundaries to establish voice communication business model
Phase 2: Redefine and optimize vertical boundaries to establish i-mode business model
        (building win-win business ecosystems)
Phase 3: Optimize vertical and horizontal boundaries to establish mobile commerce
        (building new business ecosystems at horizontal boundaries)
Phase 4: Optimize vertical and horizontal boundaries to establish new businesses and services
        (establishing new value chains at vertical and horizontal boundaries)

Figure 6.3 Networked SC Dynamics Centered on DoCoMo's Leader Teams.

3.2 *The vertical value chain and co-evolution models of Japan's mobile phone business*

The main business strategy of Japan's mobile phone carriers such as NTT DoCoMo, KDDI, and SoftBank is to expand the distribution of 3D mobile phone services (named "3G services" below). The production structure of Japanese mobile phone companies is globally distinctive. First by, they possess a vertically integrated business structure, focusing on mobile phone carriers, that transcends mobile phone handset makers, communications device makers, and content providers. Secondly, they possess a new value chain structure exploiting mobile phones through the expansion of horizontal boundaries aimed at creating new business.

i-mode development project members have dynamically formed SCs with traditional, project-centered organizations or emergent organizations within the company, CPs, and development vendors such as mobile phone and communications device manufacturers (see Figure 6.4). Development project members have created and established i-mode service business models enabled by the network externalities of positive feedback (Shapiro and R.Varian, 1998) through consolidating and merging diverse knowledge arising from the integration of these SCs' internal and external networks. DoCoMo, CPs, and development vendors gave birth to a win-win, co-evolution ecosystem.

Then networked SCs formed vertical integration type business structures for vertical boundaries comprising development vendors and CPs, centered on DoCoMo. Management models integrating heterogeneous knowledge through the formation of these networked SCs at vertical boundaries correspond to the aforementioned *knowledge integration model* in Chapter 1.

The expansion of horizontal boundaries aimed at new business is another aspect. With i-mode, DoCoMo has developed a new technology platform aimed at new business expansion to trigger the spread of 3G technology. It has formed SCs with various external partners aimed at expanding the horizontal boundaries of advancing toward the credit card business (see Figure 6.4). DoCoMo has also driven hardware and software platform development aimed at

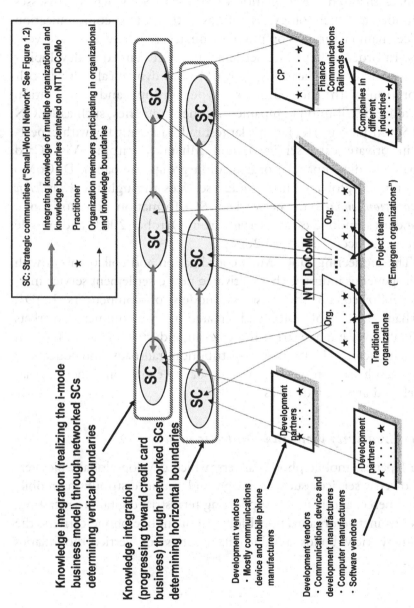

Figure 6.4   NTT DoCoMo's "Knowledge Integration Model."

realizing mobile e-commerce services while promoting strategic alliances through the formation of SCs with Sony, which possesses e-money card technology, as well as with leading communication device manufacturers, computer manufacturers, and software vendors. In order to expand e-settlement services aimed at developing usage structure applications, DoCoMo has dynamically driven collaboration with each industry type, group, and corporation including distribution companies in other industries, such as AEON and Seven Eleven; JR (Japan's largest railroad company with expertise in private card services); and Mitsui Sumitomo Visa Card (Japan's leading financial organization group company). DoCoMo has initiated globally cutting-edge services through the *knowledge integration models* of networked SC formation for horizontal boundaries, mobile e-cash service from October 2004, and mobile e-credit services from April 2006.

The pioneering DoCoMo's coordination and collaboration with heterogeneous industries has cultivated new e-settlement service markets, followed up the business models of competitors KDDI, SoftBank, and DoCoMo, and created new e-commerce markets through diverse usage structures crossing industry boundaries, which in Japan includes ICT, finance, distribution, railroads, and education. As a result, a win-win ecosystem, or co-evolution function, has developed among industries.

3.3 *Creativity view and Dialectic view*

The Japanese mobile phone carriers, which develop globally pioneering diverse services such as image and music distribution, mobile e-commerce, and handsets supporting terrestrial digital broadcasting, have distinctive organizational forms. For mobile phone carriers, the creativity view builds a value chain series for vertical boundaries comprising marketing, services, content planning, development design, device manufacture, sales, and support as a management driver to create new services. Also, the emergent organizations (the project teams mentioned in i-mode development: see Figure 6.4) promote collaboration with external partners aimed at building business models for new services as new organizational models acquired from case-study analysis. These emergent organizations mainly implement planning and development of marketing and business models. As case analysis also shows, collaboration with CPs on i-mode development, collaboration with companies in different industries, and expansion of horizontal boundaries through participating in finance and settlement businesses facilitate knowledge integration activity focused on entrepreneurial organizations. The entrepreneurial organization implements the role of integrating external, heterogeneous knowledge from outside the company with knowledge from inside through external network collaboration with external partners, such as CPs and companies in other industries.

There is also the traditional organization (see Figure 6.4) implementing development design, equipment construction, sales, and after-sales support aimed at realizing new services and the spread of existing services. The traditional organization forms a value chain essential to realizing services based on path-dependent knowledge accumulated over many years, and raises the level of completion for newly integrated knowledge through collaboration with entrepreneurial organizations. Moreover, the long-term partnership between traditional organizations, mobile phone handset makers, communications and increase device manufacturers the quality of path-dependent knowledge. The mobile phone carriers' integration of internal networks among emergent and traditional organizations with external networks that promote the acquisition of new knowledge corresponds to knowledge integration models similar to those of consumer electronics, communications device, and semiconductor manufacturers described in Chapter 4. *The knowledge integration models* with these kinds of vertical and horizontal boundaries are building win-win relationships among partners, including mobile phone carriers and companies in different industries, and the *dialectic view* as a management driver is promoting a co-evolution model with regard to vertical and horizontal boundaries.

3.4 *Framework of the continuous co-evolution process through the dialectic view*

Why is the concept of "co-evolution" connected to that of the *dialectic view*? Moore (1993) explained that business environment is patterned after living ecosystems. A single company is perceived not just as a member of a single industry, but as a part of a business ecosystem spanning diverse industries. With this kind of business ecosystem, organizations and companies correspond to economic communities supported through mutual interaction from various individuals and organizations. This economic community then produces value-laden goods and services for the customer (including vendors, partners, corporate customers, and competitors of the venture), and the customer becomes a member of this community. Then the members (corporate groups) within this community co-evolve their own competences and roles, and develop their own activities in line with the direction indicated by either a single or multiple core companies. Companies displaying leadership within this community may change over time, while their roles as leaders of the business ecosystem continue to be highly evaluated by the community.

Moore (1993) mentioned that the development process of this kind of business ecosystem goes through the following four stages. The first stage is the birth stage, where leader companies seek a new ecosystem. The second stage is the expansion stage, which achieves critical mass enclosing customers. The third stage is the leadership stage of action aimed at the objectives shared by the ecosystem's main members (including vendors and partners), co-evolution through mutual coordination and collaboration, and strengthening one's own competences. The forth stage is a migration to the renewal stage of the existing ecosystem aimed at the new targets of further ideas and innovation.

The leading companies become the core of these four stages, and spiral implementation is significant to achieving continuous innovation (see Figure 6.5). Here, coordination from leading companies and collaboration among community members become important elements in achieving co-evolution. The software business with Microsoft as the leader, the mobile Internet and multimedia businesses with NTT DoCoMo, Sony, Nintendo, and Apple can be mentioned as leading examples of this kind of business ecosystem.

The concept of the business ecosystem according to Moore (1993) is the starting point of social ecology. Social ecologists (see, for example, Bateson, 1979; Norgaard, 1994) introduced analogies of co-evolution to ecology theory, grasped co-evolution as two specific types of evolving patterns, and considered that specific types of heritable characteristics were mutually influenced by other kinds of heritable characteristics (e.g., the relationship between the formation of specific flowers and that of the tongues of specific insects). They also interpreted the social and ecological systems as evolving together (e.g., the relationship with a social system that hypothesizes insecticides and insect drug tolerance) (Norgaard, 1994). With this kind of co-evolution approach to social ecology, the social system is formed according to the ecological system ("second nature"). Rather than opposing the social and ecological systems, dialectical naturalism (Bookchin, 1990) (see Figure 6.5) takes the standpoint of emphasizing the natural and social perspectives dialectically coestablished by society and nature.

With this kind of ecological and social system, the individual subsystems (elements) that comprise these systems are extremely varied, and the relationships are difficult to define. With recent social ecological theories (Norgaard, 1994; Marten, 2001; Levin, 1999), specific ecological and social systems, while content dependent and subjective, are interpreted as "complex adaptive systems", (Morel and Ramanujam, 1999; Stacey, 1996). Social systems comprise mutual interactions as people communicate on a micro-level in countless

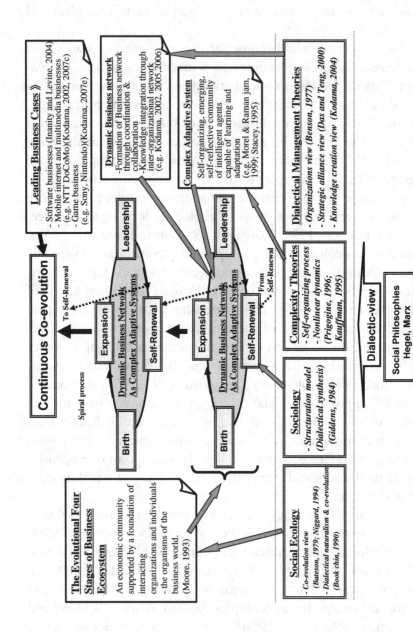

Figure 6.5   Framework of the Continuous Co-Evolution Process Through the Dialectic View.

relationships, and also include complex adaptive systems that co-evolve in response to the environment.

Accordingly, the co-evolution process as it relates to the business ecosystem mentioned above can also be interpreted as corresponding to the complex adaptive system. The complex adaptive system (various social systems including corporations) is self-organizing and forms stable and independent domains. It is the system through which the companies and organizations that comprise it interact with the environment to co-evolve through learning and adapting. Then the individual elements within the system, including people, organizations, companies, and industries, take on a process that dialectically adapts and evolves. The complex adaptive system possesses not only harmonious, parallel, stable features, but also the emerging, nonlinear dynamic aspects of transforming spontaneity and novelty. In recent years, this complex adaptive system has come to be the core concept of complex theories (see Figure 6.5) (Prigogine, 1996, Kauffman, 1993 and others). Management scholars have also attempted to introduce some of these theoretical ideas into administrative science.

Meanwhile, a variety of dynamically formed business networks are realized within the business ecosystem of the complex adaptive system through coordination centred on leading corporations and collaboration (cooperation through strategic alliances, joint ventures, and M&As) among various partners within the business community. Here diverse knowledge is integrated through the formation of inter-organizational networks. However, this knowledge integration process gives rise to various abrasions, conflicts, and contradictions among practitioners and organizations, and the practitioners within the business community must implement management to dialectically synthesize the various paradoxes (see Dialectical Management Theories in Figure 6.5). The dialectical thinking by these practitioners promotes co-evolution among partners through study and application, and becomes the source of the integration of the distributed, heterogeneous knowledge the practitioners should achieve within the complex adaptive system.

As the leading business case in Figure 6 shows, the forth stage — self-renewal is key to achieving the continuous co-evolution of these business ecosystems. Against the background where software, mobile phones, and game businesses continually evolve, the thinking of sociology's duality of structure becomes the starting point (see Sociology in Figure 6.5). In sociology, structuration models (Giddens, 1979 present organizations as continuous feedback systems in which behavior unfolds or emerges from a dialectical process. In other works, structure and action are mutually entwined through a process of reproducing social practice, The action of leading corporations arises from the existing social structure, and at the same time the leading companies and partners introspectively change, renew, and reproduce these structures by means of co-evolution through the leader companies and partners' coordination and collaboration. The formation of business networks for business ecosystems is closely linked to the theory of this duality of structure. The continuous co-evolution process of the business ecosystem thus originates from duality of structure that comprises practitioners' dialectical thinking.

The above concept of co-evolution is based on the four research streams: social ecology, sociology, complex theories and dialectical management theories. These four theories further originate from a leading social philosophy, the *dialectical view* proposed by Hegel and Karl Marx. Practitioners' dialectical thinking and action promote dialectical management and form business ecosystems as complex adaptive systems that embed co-evolution analogy in social ecology.

3.5 Dialectical management through strategic innovation capability

As Figure 6.3 illustrates, the dynamic networked SCs centered on DoCoMo's leading teams combined incremental innovation for the existing core business with strategic innovation for the following new phase (see Chart 6.1). DoCoMo then advanced the knowledge integration process for the company as a whole through integrative competences arising from dialectical thinking and action with regard to various conflicting issues.

Features of DoCoMo's strategic behavior are the simultaneous pursuit of core strategy positions for ongoing business through incremental innovation and exploration of new strategy positions through strategic innovation. This corresponds to the implementation of the spiral strategic innovation loop in Figure 2.3. Chapter 2, In phase one, DoCoMo focused resources on the core 2G mobile phone business while incorporating strategically innovative i-mode development oriented to phase two. In phase two, it focused resources on the core i-mode business while incorporating development of 3G mobile phone and mobile commerce (mobile wallet) services oriented to phase three as strategic innovation. In phase three, it focused resources on the core 3G mobile phone services and mobile commerce while incorporating development of 3.5G mobile phones and new services oriented to phase four as strategic innovation. In phase four (the current phase), it is creating richer mobile phone services for its core 3G and 3.5G systems while developing new services, LTE, and 4G systems oriented to the coming phase five as strategic innovation.

The features of DoCoMo's corporate action demonstrate the *strategic innovation capability* indicated in Figure 2.3, Chapter 2, Figure 2.3, and constantly drive the loops among each domain. This involves the migration of DoCoMo's core business at each of the four phases from strategic innovation implemented in the previous phase to newly created strategic positions. The combined dialectical management of strategic and incremental innovation in each phase requires different organizational capability and knowledge integration processes DoCoMo, however, separates the organizational capability and knowledge integration processes supporting each domain through the skilfull formation of networked SCs at vertical and horizontal boundaries, and combines current and future strategies. The continuous migration (old to new) of strategic positions arising from DoCoMo's *strategic innovation capabilities* in each phase continuously redefines DoCoMo's vertical and horizontal boundaries, builds and maintains win-win relationships among customers and stakeholders (including external partners) focused on DoCoMo, and creates a co-evolution model for the entire industry.

Chapter

7

Strategic Innovation through a Discontinuous Road Map: The Case Study of Nintendo

1. Sense of Crisis in the Game Industry and Nintendo's Surge Forward

Amid the worldwide recession following the Lehman Shock of September 2008, Nintendo stood out as one of a small number of companies that continually recorded increases in sales and stably maintained share prices at a relatively high level. Nintendo had previously maintained a strong competitive edge in its market share of game consoles until that sector of the market was to a great extent usurped by PlayStation products by Sony Computer Entertainment (SCE).[1]

From 1997 to 2004, the software shipment value in the Japanese game market had been trending downwards. This was attributable not only to the effects of the flooding of the secondhand game

---

[1] See Chapter 5, Kodama (2007c) for the story of the development of PlayStation.

209

market, declining birthrates, and the increasing pervasiveness of mobile phones but also to a migration away from games due to the increasing sophistication and complexity in operation of computer games driven by game devotees, or so-called "gamers". Computer games had undergone considerable technological innovations since the days of Family Computer, enhancing their high performance and bringing satisfaction to a large number of game users. However, in recent years, there have been indications that this technology-oriented business model is gradually changing.

Nintendo's President Satoru Iwata asked himself a number of fundamental questions regarding the future direction of Nintendo: What must the game industry do right now to broaden the game population? Can the game market grow if it continues to follow the present technology-oriented business model? What is needed to expand the game market? Reflecting on the past, he commented:

> "I became the president of Nintendo in 2002, the year after GameCube came out. When I took up the position, I realized that I had become the president at a very difficult time. This is because in hindsight I realized that the shipment value of Japan's game software had progressively fallen from 1997 to 2004. If I showed you this on a graph, you would be shocked. The question in my mind was how many years it would take before the business collapsed completely".

Iwata realized that there was no future for the game industry unless it expanded the game population. He also understood that no matter how persistently the industry pushed ahead with progress in hardware technology for game consoles alone, it could not put a halt to the migration away from games. It was essential, he felt, to throw away the past experience of success, return to the drawing board, and think of ways to broaden and deepen the gateway to enjoyable gaming. He then came up with the concept of a game console that any player could pick up and use from the same starting line. Nintendo then set about developing a game console that could be equally enjoyed by experienced players (gamers) as well as novices with no experience in computer games (non-gamers) from the same starting point.

Referring to the DS and Wii, Iwata stated the following:

"If I can speak without fear of being misunderstood, I would like to say that Nintendo is not producing next-generation game consoles. "Next generation" simply means an extension of technological innovations we have seen to date. If we continued along that line as we have, our market will not grow. In fact, there is a good chance that it will shrink. If we want to increase the number of people who enjoy games, we have to promote a novel fascination with games. Games today have become difficult to operate and people who are not used to them find them daunting. When those with no experience at games merely watch someone else playing, they have no desire to try it out themselves. This is a fact. With this understanding, we wanted to create a user interface that everyone would be tempted to try. At the same time, I believe that people in general feel somewhat hesitant when we do away with features that they have grown used to. For example, when we starting producing the DS with two screens, rather than drawing positive reactions from people, it seemed to provoke more expressions of doubt, with people asking: "Why did Nintendo did that?". Ultimately, however, the market did accept the DS. Through this product we were able to demonstrate that by changing the user interface, we could acquire a new market. Because of this precedent, I believe that the number of people who view the Wii controller with curiosity has increased".

Furthermore, through innovation of the user interface (UI), in the operation of these games Nintendo specifically aimed to evoke the reaction: "Even I can do it!" among users who normally do not play games. Based on this product concept, the DS with two touch screens was introduced, enabling simplification in operation and at the same time giving users a wholly new sense of console operation, which has never been experienced before. In the first three years, sales of the DS topped 60 million worldwide and 20 million in Japan alone. With the Wii, on the other hand, they adopted a product architecture different from that of conventional tabletop game consoles and as a result were able to reduce electric power consumption, streamline and reduce the weight of the console, and achieve technical innovation in the controller (Wii remote control) for promoting simpler game operations through a superior UI.

2. The Booby Trap of the Semiconductor Scaling Rule

In the past, progress in video games followed only one direction: the semiconductor scaling rule. According to Moore's Law,[2] semiconductor large-scale integration (LSI) over a number of years results in narrower line widths, improved processing capacity, and the ability to fit more electronic circuits onto a semiconductor chip. With these advances, processing performance increases; screen expression becomes high-speed and high-resolution; and the satisfaction of game users increases accordingly. This was the cycle of progress seen in advances in high functionality of products such as Family Computer (Famicom), Super Famicom, Nintendo 64, PlayStation, PlayStation 2, and Nintendo GameCube.

Sony Computer Entertainment (SCE) outstripped other game console manufacturers in the game market of the previous century with its PlayStation series which have attributes of high performance computers and media players. Sony's product strategy was based on a business model for developing semiconductors that boasted outstanding performance, recovering hardware development costs through a synergy with profits from software sales, and making profits thereafter over the long term. Supporting the foundation of SCE was the hardware which its high-performing semiconductor chip supports and this has been the strength of SCE's product strategy. Following a technology strategy for developing a high-performance

---

[2] President of US Intel Gordon Moore predicted that in three years gate scale and performance would increase four-fold. Even at present that trend is continuing in the semiconductor industry.

semiconductor chip to increase revenues through sales of game consoles, SCE invested heavily in the development of a high-performance processor "cell" for PlayStation 3 (PS3).

Pursuing a semiconductor scaling principle in this way in the game industry was a technology strategy that was considered extremely sound and conventional. However, Nintendo made a clear-cut decision to steer away from this approach and began explaining in detail to the game industry and its game users its new vision of future game consoles. In the development of Wii in particular, one of Nintendo's main goals was to make a clear departure from following the trend in high-function hardware that adhered to the semiconductor scaling principle. To do this, it was necessary for Iwata to explain what was behind the product concept of the Wii inside and outside the company and why Nintendo was steering away from the technology roadmap of game consoles that it had pursued until then.

Referring to the development of software, Iwata stated the following:

"On the one hand, as a result of following the path of development of more elaborate and more complex games, per game software development costs have skyrocketed and the development period has increased significantly. During the Family Computer era, a team of two was capable of bringing a game to completion within a two-month period. Around 1983 we assign this kind of work to freshman just out of university to give them experience. To be able to develop a single game today, however, requires assigning a team of 50 and would require each of the same members three years of work. Not only that, the world of gaming has changed so much that we cannot even get an overall picture of a game (due to the large-scale software). I felt that it was extremely risky for us to simply continue on in the same direction. Clearly what we need in the game industry are players who will fulfill the role of pointing us in a different direction. In new game products, I believe that we have to move in a different direction from the sophisticated and complex".

3. Realization of Destructive Architecture — Lateral Thinking in Dead Technology

Two factors: the contraction of the domestic game market and the cost blowout due to the increase in the scale of development (of both hardware and software) became the two most serious issues of Japan's game industry. To overcome these, the notion of "product architecture using dead technology" was conceived in the development of Wii. In the past, Nintendo actually had a concept of product architecture along those lines. Creator of Game Boy, Gunpei Yokoi (game console developer who was the General Manager of the First Section of the Production Division Headquarters at Nintendo and who was responsible for the development of hit products such as Family Computer and Game Boy who died in 1997 at the age of 56) actually coined the term "lateral thinking in dead technology". Yokoi argued that competing on the basis of ideas spawned from dead technology was one of Nintendo's core competences. Shigeru Miyamoto, the current Senior Managing Director of Nintendo, and world-renown for his development of games such as Donkey Kong for commercial use and Mario for home use, was mentored by Yokoi and has continued to maintain this view.

"Dead technology" is technology that has been already been widely used and its merits and demerits are clearly known. The use of this technology makes it possible to keep development costs down. "Vertical thinking" in this context is the process of thinking of ways to use something in a way that it has not been used before. In the creation of a game, it simply needs to be interesting; hi-tech aspects are not essential. High-cost and hi-tech can also become negative factors in product development. Therefore, the idea is to use common technology or technology that is widely available to create new hit products.

However, both SCE and Microsoft had enhanced performance of their products by following the semiconductor scaling principle (Nintendo's Nintendo 64 and its successor the GameCube, were essentially game consoles of the same nature). Therefore, the difference in performance of a game console developed on the basis of lateral thinking in dead technology would become clearly visible. Getting people to understand the difference on the basis of the idea behind it was difficult. That decision for Nintendo was fraught with substantial risk because the company was setting out on an unproven path which was difficult to get stakeholders and users in the industry to understand. For example, the first time Nintendo decided to use two screens in its games immediately drew the reaction "Why did Nintendo do that?" from a number of people. According to Iwata, when Nintendo came out with the statement: "We are not simply pursuing high performance. Simply increasing the performance of semiconductor chips does not interest us", it drew the reaction: "Has Nintendo withdrawn from competing in the game market?".

However, Nintendo felt it was necessary to show its stakeholders the path to the future by acting on its convictions. Therefore, it adopted its product strategy as a commitment to gaining the understanding of its users by explaining to them what Nintendo was attempting to do and steadily moving forward one step at a time in a way that would make its intentions clear to users. A feature of the Wii product design was the development of a semiconductor chip that was a departure from the previous technology roadmap. Because Nintendo was steering away from the technology roadmap, it decided not to take a rigid stand on that respect. There was also an understanding that they should not renew the platform on the pretext that there had been progress in semiconductor scaling or that the company felt it was time to begin to sell new hardware. Nintendo's goal at this time was purely to surprise its users. Enhancing performance by boosting the processing performance of the game console or enhancing the graphics as SCE did with the PS3 is one product strategy approach but Nintendo's top priority at this time was to determine whether its game console could provide a number of key elements that would offer surprise and delight to its users. Those key factors would not be limited to the hardware. They might include *hardware* or the creation of a completely new UI. Or the source of surprise could be something even more novel. Nintendo gave these key factors considerable thought.

For example, Nintendo's intention was to keep down the scale of the semiconductor chip, even if the processing were miniaturized. This was completely off the beaten track in term of what was considered among game manufacturers common sense regarding semiconductor scaling. Exponentially increasing the scale of the semiconductor chip with each subsequent generation was the iron rule of the semiconductor scaling principle. In term of semiconductor technology, the Wii concept was far off the beaten track, and the most notable feature of the Wii semiconductor chip was its clear departure from the mainstream technology roadmap. The reason for this was Nintendo's fundamental views underlying its strategy goals: to determine how to increase the number of users who would play its games and to determine how to increase the game population itself. It was Nintendo's view that the hardware design for achieving this left it no choice but to steer away from the technology road map. The same applied to the thermal design of the hardware. Making such a choice, however, would enable Nintendo to direct more of its development resources to the UI. On the other hand, if Nintendo increased the surface area of the semiconductor chip, it would be necessary to invest in development costs for that and that would make it impossible in the overall development costs to allocate investment resources to the UI and low power consumption improvement. Therefore, in the development of Wii, development costs were directed to the UI and low power consumption improvement.

3.1 *Challenge to reduce power consumption*

In the 90 nm process, power consumption becomes a critical issue and the developers were confronted with this problem in the semiconductor chip design. To deal with this issue, Wii offered one solution: to improve performance and electric power consumption by keeping the architecture of the semiconductor chip simple. In that sense, the design concept of Wii hardware was extremely clear and unique. In particular, in processes of 90 nm and under, the leak current[3] ratio is extremely high and the developers faced the dilemma that even if the line width were reduced, power consumption would not decrease substantially. As a consequence, the fan in the casing gets extremely loud. Nintendo's technology strategy at that time was to use the same 90 nm semiconductor process but rather than increase the scale of the semiconductor chip in line with the process, they curbed power consumption by producing dead chip architecture using 90 nm. This was so-called lateral thinking in dead technology, which is the part of the technological genetic makeup of Nintendo. It can also be considered "disruptive architecture" to realize "disruptive innovation" (Christensen, 1997).

Nintendo decreased the electric power consumption and reduced the leak current using a silicon-on-insulator (SOI) process.[4] While one approach to innovation is to strive to produce racing cars that run at ultra high speeds like the PS3, another is to create hybrid cars with extremely high fuel efficiency like the Wii, which is also a form of hi-technology and innovation on a different dimension. This analogy may be applied to the Wii design development. One goal of the Wii development was to keep the inside of the unit casing adequately cool even when the casing was kept small by having the fan come to a stop during standby and having it run at a moderate speed even when it was active. This was to keep the noise level down during constant use

---

[3] Leak current is the phenomenon whereby an electric current flows in places where it normally should not flow on electronic circuit. When leak current increases, power consumption also increases and calorific power also increases. Therefore, technology to reduce leak current is essential to continue to increase integration of the semiconductor and to boost performance in the future.

[4] SOI (silicon-on-insulator) is a semiconductor with a single crystal substrate formed on the insulating film, and semiconductor technology developed by IBM. With SOI technology, the stoppage of an electrical charge flowing from the transistor layer above the processor substrate over the insulating layer can be reduced about 45 percent. As a result, the performance of microchips that adopt SOI technology at maximum is 30 percent higher than similar microchips operating on the same clock speed, or the power consumption of such SOI microchip is half of that of the non-SOI chip, theoretically.

of the Wii by players in a household to avoid disturbing other members of the household. The design was also to be based on a machine concept where the power was to be on for 24 hours a day so that contents could be downloaded without bothering other members of the household. To do this, the main challenges were to minimize the noise Wii and make the casing compact.

3.2 *The idea of reverse product architecture — technology orientation from a market perspective*

Iwata instructed the Wii hardware developers to limit the size of the Wii casing to about the size of two to three DVD cases. Normally, the thermal design power consumption is determined by the semiconductor chip design and this, consequently, determines the size of the casing. Therefore, once the thermal aspect is known, a case of a certain size will be needed. If the casing is small, the temperature inside is prone to rising and therefore the thermal budget (the leeway in temperature for keeping the chip cool) is limited. On the other hand, to keep the mechanism quiet, it is necessary to curb the number of revolutions of the fan. Limiting the number of revolutions, however, also limits the air flow within the casing, so it becomes extremely difficult to do this unless the electric power consumption is reduced dramatically. To increase the air flow and have the fan run quietly, the cost of the cooling system will increase. If the air flow is secured by increasing the number of air inlets, keeping electromagnetic interference (EMI) within standards becomes difficult. Taking into consideration the thermal aspect, EMI, and acoustic tradeoffs, producing a slim, quiet Wii at a low cost was an extremely difficult technical challenge for the hardware developers of Nintendo.

Speaking about the Wii controller, Iwata describes it from another perspective as "creative destruction":

"The standard shape of today's controllers was established by Nintendo. Using a controller with both hands and exercising control through the use of a cross-shaped button was first proposed by Nintendo and accepted by users, and has since become the standard of the industry. When we set about destroying a standard that we ourselves set, there was resistance from within the company. A number of people voiced concern and questioned the soundness of such a move. However, 13 months prior to the commencement of sales when the pilot unit was completed and staff had the chance to touch it and actually trial it in a demo game, this time they expressed enthusiastic approval. Buoyed by confidence that came from an understanding after personally using it myself, I announced at the E3 (Electronic Entertainment Expo) that 'innovative human interface would change the games of the future".

The history of game consoles shows that the changeover from Family Computer to Super Famicom and from there the transitions to PS, PS2, PS3 and to Nintendo 64 and the Game Cube were sustainable innovations based on the semiconductor scaling principle (see Figure 7.1). However, from the perspective of the user, the meaning of technological innovation which the game console manufacturers referred to as "next-generation technology based on semiconductor innovation" was becoming increasingly difficult for them to understand. The promise by game manufacturers to create even more fantastic models was having less appeal to users and game manufacturers were finding it more difficult to communicate the virtues of their products to users. In short, for the manufacturers of the game consoles this meant an "innovator's dilemma" (Christensen, 1997) had occurred.

The approaches to product development SCE and Nintendo adopted for products to support the future home game market differed markedly. SCE through its PS series has been promoting the evolution of game consoles to high performance computers for home use through extremely advanced operational performance and image performance technologies that are a dramatic leap forward from the technologies of current units. Nintendo's product strategy, on the other hand, has from beginning to end been centered on the pursuit of enjoyment of games using a console which offers a unique UI that is a distinct departure from the past. In short, Nintendo diverged from the semiconductor technology road map adopted by SCE,

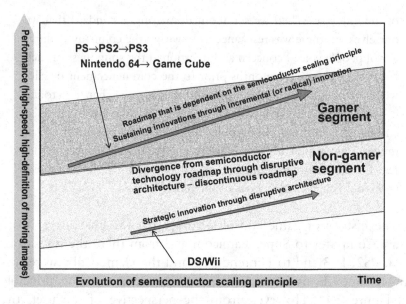

Figure 7.1   Strategic Innovation through Disruptive Architecture.

Notes 1: Wii is the successor model to the GameCube but Nintendo diverged from continuing innovation that relies on the evolution of the semiconductor road map and adopted disruptive architecture.

2: DS is the successor model to Game Boy Advance which adopted disruptive architecture.

adopted a product architecture based on disruptive technology for its proprietary products, and made a decision to allocate its development resources to UI and power consumption improvement. Furthermore, Nintendo set its sights on strategic innovation for realizing product concepts on a discontinuous road map that diverged from the technology roadmap of game console development it had previously followed (see Figure 7.1).

The design concept of the PS series of SCE, which adhered to pursuing high performance and high image resolution, sought to enhance performance with each generation of development, going from two-dimensional to three-dimensional graphics and from CD-ROM to DVD and Blue-ray Disc as a continuum of advances in semiconductor technology, which SCE attempted to improve with each generation. SCE's main target in its strategies has been existing gamers. The game software can also demonstrate to the maximum the console's high performance features (high-speed and high-resolution) for specific titles where drastic movements are required. On the other hand, when Nintendo adopted Wii was a strategy to develop game consoles (realization of a superior UI and low power consumption), instead of adhering to numerical specifications in operational functions adopted a wide variety of game software that could be used by a greater number of users (particularly non-game users who had previously no interest in games). To refer again to the previously mentioned analogy about cars, while there are manufacturers of F1 cars in the market, there should also be manufacturers who create hybrid cars. This perhaps reflects Nintendo's view of the market.

Through this "reverse architecture" approach to utilizing dead technology for new ideas in the DS and Wii, Nintendo achieved overwhelming success in developing new users. After achieving success in strategic innovation through these game consoles, Iwata reflected:

> "I had full confidence that a new market existed out there. To be frank, however, I had no idea how much time it would take to form that market. It was a path nobody had ever taken until then, so I had no idea the kind of time frame we were looking at. You prepare the ground, give it fertilizer and water, and then you plant the seeds, but you have no idea how many of the seedlings will come up and how many will actually blossom. Would we see results right away? Would it take six months? Three years? Or would we have to wait five years or longer? If that were the case, would the shareholders give me the boot? I had no idea what the prospects were. At the same time, however, I had an extremely strong conviction that a new market could definitely be created. So, even before there were any real tangible results, I could go so far as to say, 'This is it'. Because of this strong belief, I think that relatively early on I was able to perceive various signs".

4. Innovation Based on Nintendo's Unique Development Framework

4.1 *Nintendo's strategic innovation loop*

Nintendo's innovation process formed a strategic innovation loop (Domain I to II to III). In Phase 1 (Yamauchi framework) as shown in Figure 7.2, Nintendo was providing Family Computer, Game Boy Advance, Nintendo64 and its successor — the GameCube, which are the existing products in Domain III, in a very severe, competitive environment of change with its rivals (Sony, Sega and Microsoft). On the other hand, in Domain IV, Nintendo was selling traditional products for entertainment that were mature products declining in popularity such as Western playing card games, Japanese playing card games, Japanese chess, and Japanese *go*. Furthermore, aiming for future strategic innovation during Domain I and Domain II, Nintendo simultaneously engaged in its new product plan for the DS (successor console to GameBoy Advance) with its two touch panel screens, and the development of Nintendo proprietary software for the DS as well as product planning and trial experiments of Wii (successor game console to the Game Cube), its proprietary new product with disruptive architecture divergent from the semiconductor scaling principle.

Furthermore, during Phase 2 (Iwata framework), the DS and Wii, which had gone from Domain I to Domain II through product planning, trial manufacture, and evaluation experiments, were merchandised in Domain III. At the same time, DSi, which is a next-phase product, and new software development as well as product planning and trial experiments of various networked services using Wii (Wii Channel, Wii Ware, etc.) were in progress in Domain I and II. Furthermore, paralleling incremental innovation to promote an increase in existing products like those of Nintendo, dialectical management which simultaneously implements and combines strategic innovation, that realizes new product planning, becomes an important element in continually driving the strategic innovation loop in an ongoing manner.

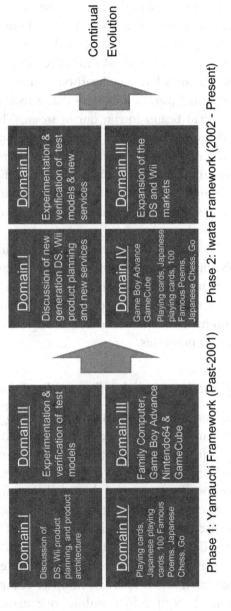

Figure 7.2 Strategic Innovation System in Nintendo.

Iwata commented on this:

"One of the factors in releasing the DSi was the change in circumstances in Japan's DS market, which was different from the overseas market. Overseas the market is also larger and it took a longer time for an increase in users to begin to take full effect. Even now the DS is performing satisfactorily but in comparison with markets in other regions the market in Japan, to the extent that it took off ahead of markets overseas, had begun to run out of steam. Therefore, we launched the DSi as a second rocket for regaining momentum. To sell the DSLite overseas while we launching the second rocket somehow felt like repairing an airplane while we were in flight. In one sense, it's a very rough way of doing things. It's not strategy you can use every time but this time I felt that it worked relatively well".

In this way, the evolution of Nintendo's strategic innovation loop continues to evolve in an uninterrupted manner even now and the present (and future) management system for ongoing strategic innovation, which Iwata referred to as something akin to repairing an airplane while in flight, corresponds to the *strategic innovation capability* which Nintendo possesses.

4.2 *Synthesis of hardware with software development*

Nintendo devoted considerable effort to a project to develop a new UI. After commencing elemental technical research on Wii sales about three years earlier, a task force (TF) for the development team was formed. An organization for developing software and hardware exists at Nintendo's headquarters and the developers frequently share information, have discussions with each other, and hold meetings on a weekly basis to discuss various topics and issues. This interactive, organic, cooperative development concept they practice in the course of software and hardware development is also Nintendo's unique, development edge which sets it apart from other companies.

Iwata reorganized Nintendo's public organization in 2004. Software development was divided into Information Development

Headquarters (led by Miyamoto), which was Nintendo's self-manufacturing software development unit and Planning and Development Headquarters (led by Iwata), which engages in software development through collaboration with external partners. Hardware development was divided into General Development Headquarters (led by Takeda), which develops table top consoles like Wii, and the Development Technology Headquarters, which develops portable games like DS. Under the organizational framework prior to the Iwata framework, there was little interaction within the Hardware Development Division or Software Development Division and there were a number of barriers among organizations. Therefore, synergies failed to form as Nintendo's total integrative competences (Kodama, 2007a) between the Software Self-manufacturing Division and the software development divisions collaborating with external partners, between the table top and portable hardware development divisions, as well as between the software division and hardware division.

However, after organizational reform, collaboration within the company in the Software Development Division and Hardware Development Division progressed at a vigorous pace. Mutual interaction between the Software Development Division and the Hardware Development Division was also encouraged, and an organizational framework for optimizing software development and hardware development was established. As a result, a large number of cross functional teams (CFTs), task forces (TFs), and working groups (WGs) within the Software Development Division and Hardware Development Division and across the Software Division and Hardware Division were formed. For example, various flexible teams consisting of members from various divisions and from all management levels (these CFTs, TFs and WGs equate with strategic communities or SCs) were formed. Another example is the User Segment Expansion PT which is a software development project for DS also involving the Sales Division and the Console Functions Team, which is a new Wii service idea project consisting of 25 elite staff. The formation of these multi-layered SCs involving the software and hardware divisions as well as the sales, management, and manufacturing divisions became for Nintendo the wellhead for forming a knowledge roadmap which will be described in the next section.

4.3 *Nintendo's knowledge roadmap*

Nintendo has continued to create original software-driven integrated hardware and software entertainment products in the area of home entertainment. Its basic strategy is to increase the gaming population and to realize this Nintendo continues to respond on a daily basis to the goal it has set for itself to "have as many people around the world, irrespective of age, sex, language, or culture, and irrespective of whether or not they have game experience, to accept and enjoy video game entertainment". While Nintendo as a company is unique in that it has not articulated a corporate vision, corporate creed, or corporate principles in the conventional sense to date, Iwata on this point refers to Nintendo itself as a "company that creates smiling faces" based on a creative, flexible corporate culture.

Nintendo did, however, articulate its corporate social responsibility (CSR) policy in 2007. According to its CSR, Nintendo is committed to pursuing the wonderful possibilities of entertainment through video games that "bring a smile to the faces of people that come into contact with Nintendo" and to meeting the challenge to develop products in tune with the level of skill of their players. Furthermore, to satisfy all users with a single product, Nintendo declared that in the future it will continue ongoing efforts to "increase the gaming population" by creating games that are literally "everyone's game".

One important point is the repeated questioning on a daily basis the meaning of Nintendo's existence in terms of how it should be as a company in the future by not only top-level management (hereafter Leaders' Team) representing Iwata but also various levels of management. Through this ontological discussion, realizing the vision of "bringing a smile to the faces of people who come into contact with Nintendo" (which has not been explicitly stated by Nintendo) should bring into focus new strategic goals for Nintendo as a company.

Through this questioning of its existence as it looks to the future, the specific goals of "creating a game culture" where users accept and enjoy video game entertainment and "increasing the gaming population" by continuing to pursue this challenge come into being.

In the development of products like the DS and Wii, individual staff of the organization including those from software development and hardware development divisions as well as those from the sales, management and manufacturing divisions question the basic value of the existence of the company and develop a strong will and determination to create a future for achieving concrete strategy goals. As a result, Nintendo reflects on its past as a company and, at the same time, linking the future with the past, Nintendo in the present induces its employees to think about "What should we do?" and connects this to specific and practical activities. At the same time, when Nintendo resolves to realize its strategy goals, there is the underlying basic philosophy of "bringing a smile to the faces of those who come into contact with Nintendo". As a result, it also leads to "sound management".

Furthermore, in the past — present — future axis, to survive in the competitive game market environment and to create a new market for games, Nintendo gives form to its "knowledge roadmap" which is the crystallization of its justification of knowledge for continuing to create new knowledge. The knowledge roadmap is also a strategy map for "creating the future". The question that needs to be asked next is what is the source of Nintendo's energy as an organization for realizing a knowledge roadmap which continually generates new knowledge.

The agglomeration of human beings who have their own visions, convictions, and ideas are themselves the wellhead of knowledge creation, and inherent in the staff at Nintendo is human power which proactively generates new knowledge and human networks for this purpose. These human networks are the organizational platforms for generating new knowledge and they correspond to strategic communities (SCs). The necessary organizational platforms for creating, utilizing and sharing knowledge and creating new value become multi-layered SCs. The next questions then are how do these human beings form SCs and how do they create new business concepts. Herbert A. Simon once indicated that there is a limit to the cognitive faculties of human beings and because of that limitation the hierarchy and differentiation of functions in organizations were established in the world of management.[5]

It goes without saying that business activities are established from various business processes (from basic research, applied research to marketing, product development, production, sales, distribution, after service, etc.) and business contexts are also diverse. In real life, there is no single employee of a company capable of having all basic skills to enable him or her to engage in all activities from the development of new products and services to sales. What became clear from an analysis of Nintendo's development framework was that the formation of multi-layered SCs was essential for the creation and practical application of superior business concepts. SCs transcend organizational boundaries and are a mechanism for creating and sharing dynamic contexts among the staff of core divisions in new product development including the software development and hardware development divisions as well as the sales, management and production divisions, and staff who are not involved directly in game console development but have ideas concerning the game business. The existence of these multi-layered SCs made it possible for Nintendo staff to create and apply new knowledge (new products such as DS and Wii and business concepts such as new services using these).

People have various world views and values but underlying the ways in which people as individuals live are ways of thinking and

---

[5] Cognitive limit, one of the main concepts developed by Herbert Simon, is a concept indicating that human cognitive and information processing capabilities are limited. Simon developed this concept in the area of organizational theory. He asks why humans create organizations and goes on to suggest that they do so because of their need to reduce the complexity of the world because of their own cognitive limitations. The organization is a social mechanism for doing this. By creating an organization with a hierarchical structure, the complexity of decision-making can be broken down to a number of sub-assemblies (similar to modularization). In this way, he argued, high-level decisions that cannot be arrived at by individuals on their own could be achieved.

modes of behavior as paradigms based on past experiences. Individuals from various divisions at Nintendo also have various world views and values. Staff in charge of software development through interaction of their subjective views (viewpoints that attempt to understand latent needs through identification with the user) and objective views (analyses of competitor products and user data) grasp latent user needs by continually creating new understandings through dialectical synthesis: We need to plan products that provide new value to users. How can we grasp user needs and link these to product planning? However, this does not mean that they do not happen to have a technological viewpoint at all. They are continually striving to grasp technical trends inside and outside the company and spare no effort in confirming latent modes of use which users themselves may have not realized: While the concept may be full of uncertainties, if we could achieve this type of technology, or if we could use this kind of existing technology, we could probably provide this kind of function or service.

For example, in the development of Wii, it was the software developers Iwata and Miyamoto who dared to steer away from the conventional semiconductor roadmap to propose a unique concept of product architecture, which adopted new development elements of lower power consumption, reduction in size and weight, and UI. It was because they were familiar with the content of the hardware technology and trends that they were able to propose new disruptive architecture.

Former Nintendo President Hiroshi Yamauchi stated:

"Our business is a business where software and hardware are inseparable. Therefore, if we do not know hardware, we cannot talk about software. Only with a clear understanding of both can we decide where to focus attention. In other words — to give an example — Sony follows a path where hardware comes first, and software is secondary. At Nintendo the situation is the opposite. Software comes first and hardware is secondary. At the same time, however, at Nintendo we understand hardware. That stance, I firmly believe, will not change in the future either".

At the same time, the staff of hardware development division, through a dialectical synthesis resulting from the mutual interaction of their subjective views (the conviction and view that they themselves would like to develop a certain thing) and objective views (concentration and selection based on analyses and evaluations of technological trends), continually create new understandings: We have to develop technology that will satisfy the user. We have to develop core technology that our competitors cannot copy. Furthermore, the hardware developers themselves are not entirely without their view of the market and they themselves may make proposals to the market side based on seed-oriented ideas that can be achieved with certainty. For example, the Wii controller, which is based on a concept of intuitive operation, was the culmination of repeated efforts of trial and error on the part of the Takeda-led development team and proved to be a killer application taking the game culture by storm and at the same time was embraced by all family member users.

Staff of each division then proactively form multi-layered SCs within the company, toss around with their subjective views from software (market) and hardware (technology) contexts and viewpoints, and the clashes of these paradigms generate new energy and form contexts of a higher order. They understand the diversity of their respective world views and values and they create mutual understanding and organizational order through creative and dialectical dialogue among different organizations. However, staff at the same time question the meaning of mutual understanding and the sharing of other's thoughts and feelings, the coexistence of both self-assertiveness and humility, and the creation of new knowledge. Through this process, staff are able to develop concepts and ideas to a higher dimension. Then the market (software) roadmap and technology (hardware) roadmap are synthesized through abduction, and a business concept as a transcendental hypothesis can be created and realized.

At Nintendo, the staff of the hardware and software development division move across divisional boundaries to unite in the formation of SCs and establish a unique organizational culture where they cooperate with each other. In addition, the staff of both development divisions cooperate in hypothesis testing, working together at the same rhythm, and identifing new challenges and issues together in the verification process. The repeated practice of this process through abduction results in the synthesis of the two different paradigms of market (software) and technology (hardware) and brings Nintendo closer to its realization of new creations (new products) it is aiming for on its knowledge roadmap (See Figure 7.3).

Abduction is a concept which makes a quest for the unknown possible. At the base of this methodology is neither deduction nor induction but a practice based on transcendental thinking. Charles Sanders Peirce (1839–1914), the founder of pragmatism, was an advocate of abduction. In short, it is a methodology for arriving at knowledge through attempts at justification and theorization to resolve problems by:

  (i) Systematically grasping latent factors and their mechanisms which bring about new value opportunities through the process of sharing tacit knowledge with the market (environment),
 (ii) Forming predictions about the market that can be shared and explicit knowledge which links to execution,
(iii) Verifying and revising the hypothesis through these. Furthermore, the synthesis of software development and hardware development through this kind of abduction enables the shift to strategic emergence domain I (domain III and/or domain IV → domain I) on the capability map in Figure 7.2 possible.

4.4 *Concept creation in strategic emergence — synthesis of image and entity*

Business concept creation occurs in the transformation domain of tacit knowledge and explicit knowledge. Software developers must perceive and experience social contexts which cannot be expressly known as explicit knowledge such as trends in market structures or latent user needs. Meanwhile, the hardware developers must create a tacit social context (such as images and physical sense of the target product) and a suitable technology context (e.g., engineer's prediction as to

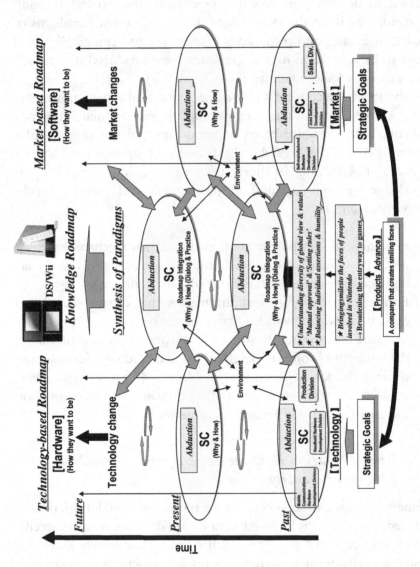

Figure 7.3

whether the product image can be covered within the range assumed from latent needs) through direct experience at the place of use and in-depth dialogue with the software developers. The question "Can a product or service of this nature be realized?" is asked and creative dialectical dialogue between the software developer and the hardware developer ensues through actual experience in abstracted space (the domain of the living world). There a struggle takes place between the convictions and the views of the staff in abstracted image of time and place.

However, a detailed concept or prototype cannot be realized within the confines of abstracted space. Therefore, the image of the software developer and the hardware developer in abstracted space must be given form. This is embodied space (domain of the world of form). This occurs in the area of embodied space (the domain of the world of form) where the image is transformed into explicit knowledge (verbalization of user needs and requirements) by means of metaphors and analogies, and then analyzed and planned. The software developers must render a specific description of a social context arrived at through dialectical dialogue with the engineers in the real world domain as latent user needs and customer demands and conditions. In response to this, the hardware engineers analyze the required specifications from the product planning side including the developers, prepare functional specifications and create a technological context including a system design* for realizing a prototype. Dialectical dialogue between the software developers and hardware developers also takes place in embodied space.

However, the shift from abstracted space to embodied space is not completed in a single move. The actual business activities take place over and over again in a back-and-forth motion as the image and actual form are synthesized through a process of abduction (a hypothesis testing process through improvised learning based on trial and

---

*Various design and analytical methods such as overall system and subsystem designs, functional design and structural design, integrated and modular designs, open and closed designs, hardware and software collaborative designs, overall optimization and component optimization, etc.

error) (Kodama, 2009a). Then a final detailed concept and prototype are completed. How refined the quality of the backward-and-forward activities and the social and technical contexts are will determine the quality of the creation of the concept. The concept platform is the stage where these abstracted spaces and embodied space are synthesized and new knowledge is created through insights regarding latent market demand. The ideas and concepts for the development of new products and services do not suddenly developers' apperar in the minds. The key to success is not the knowledge of experience that comes from practice but the extent to which the developers can accurately tune into market demands through sharing tacit knowledge with the users and absorbing different knowledge as well as trialing ideas and trialing production based on these and confirming results. In the process of realizing product concepts at Nintendo, trial production of products is done repeatedly with the developers going through a process of trial and error over and over again until they are satisfied. As a result, groundbreaking conceptual products like the DS and Wii were created. The integration of software development and hardware development through spiral mutual interaction between abstracted space and embodied space together with repeated discussion of market ideas and technical ideas became the wellhead that realized new hit products (See Figure 7.4).

In the UI world of game consoles in particular, the key point is in how the users feel rather than in the pursuit of technical specifications. Therefore, many aspects of a product cannot be determined without a first trial. At Nintendo, the development team produced many trial products in the development of the Wii controller and repeated abduction over and over again, questioning repeatedly what they needed to do: We have this elemental technology but can it be applied? or We produced one like this but can it be used? It is not easy to demolish an existing idea and develop a new idea. Therefore, in such situation, the dynamic cycle created through a continuous spiral of tacit knowledge and explicit knowledge based on trial and error is necessary.

Renowned neuroscientist Shinsuke Shimojo (lecturer at California Institute of Technology) stated that creative people are

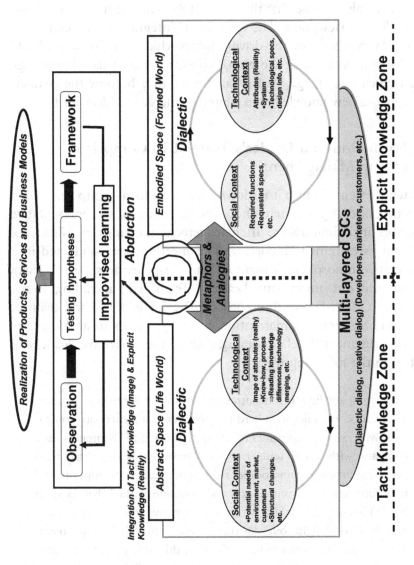

Figure 7.4   Realization of Products, Services and Business Model.

people who can grasp the overall situation by move back and forth
between tacit and manifest knowledge. Manifest knowledge here can
be considered as explicit knowledge and the overall situation the context. It can also be said that this is the global context from a social and
technological viewpoint. The developers' integrative competences of
dialectical synthesis are the driving forces which cause dynamic back-
and-forth movement of the global context between tacit knowledge
and explicit knowledge. At the same time, they become the enablers
for creating new knowledge in strategic emergence (domain I).

5. Formation of a Leader's Team (LT) Comprised of Top Management

Nintendo went from a top-down structure to a group leadership
structure or collegial system under the leadership of six representative
directors including Iwata. In management meetings at Nintendo,
dialogue is extremely important. The meetings are conducted in a
cooperative atmosphere of harmony and outspokenness. Basic policies
are worked out among the Leaders' Team (LT) including Iwata,
Miyamoto, Takeda and three others. The LT is the hybrid team of
managers from every organization and corresponds to an SC at the
top management level. Iwata described the collective leadership
system in the following way:

"The company line to concentrate on software will remain the same.
There are companies with hard temperaments and there are companies with soft temperaments in the world and Nintendo is a
company with a soft temperament. Companies with a hard temperament produce commodities suitable for daily consumption, and
therefore have a common axis and compete within that axis. At
Nintendo, we are dealing with entertainment products and create
products to delight our customers and bring them enjoyment.
There is no common axis in products of this nature, and we recognize that the products we handle are extremely difficult products to
deal with. With the products we develop it is very important for us
always to be thinking if we can delight our customers in a way that

we have not done before. We always have be thinking of something that is different from our competitors. We will continue along this path promoted by Yamauchi and refrain from involvement in the hardware track that the mainstream companies of the industry are following today. In the future we will shift to a collective leadership framework. Therefore, the decisions of the sort previously made by Yamauchi will now be made by six people".

The "soft temperament" mentioned above were used by former President Yamauchi to describe management ideas that do not depend on hardware. A soft temperament, however, refer not only to game software but also to intangible assets such as business mechanisms, rules, system of distribution, concepts and ideas. It also means the overall business systems including, for example, how new value is communicated to users. The view of this soft temperament business system is Nintendo's genes and Nintendo's corporate creed (though not explicitly stated) which must be preserved now and in the future.

Serving under the LT are multi-layered SCs of cross-divisional CFTs, TFs, and WGs of the software development and hardware development divisions where thorough, in-depth discussions take place. Furthermore, within these, SCs includevarious organizations, such as the sales division, production division and the management division. In these SCs, various matters encompassing a wide range of topics including design and product specifications are discussed. The LT as SC fulfills the role of ultimately unifying and integrating knowledge in the software development and hardware development divisions and creating the overall integrative competences of the company (Kodama 2007a). To realize integrative competences, the LT is conscious of implementing an integrative strategy based on "disciplined imagination" (Weick, 1997). The integrative strategy is the integration of a paradoxical strategy which is both creative and emergent and at the same time deliberate and analytical. In addition to the integration of this strategy, the leaders' mission is to execute overall optimization through the balance and linkage of the individual management elements of the organization, technology, operations and leadership in the software division and hardware division (Kodama, 2009b).

Expressing it another way, Iwata referred to this integration of strategies as follows:

> "We have not changed our strategies for reaching our goals for a number of years; however, depending on the circumstances, there will be a need to change tactics, which are the means of reaching our goals. While the company strategies are decided by the management team, we encourage those on the front line of operations who understand the strategies decided by the management team to continually rearrange the tactics in their activities".

The "reaching (3 period) goals" and "strategies decided by the management team" Iwata refers to are deliberate, analytical strategy elements determined by the LT which is the management team of Nintendo. At the same time, when it comes to executing individual, specific strategies, "those on the front line who understand the strategies ...to continually rearrange the tactics in their activities" means executing creative, emergent strategies which the staff flexibly devise on their own according to the circumstances.

In the LT and in the respective SCs serving under management, a thorough understanding of problem areas and issues is promoted through dialectical and creative dialogue between the leaders and the SC members. Furthermore, the leaders and managers recognize the role and value of each other's work through mutual communication and collaboration. As a result, the leaders are able to convert friction and conflict arising between the leaders into constructive content. Compromise is not permitted among the LTs and within the SCs at Nintendo and the individual leaders are held accountable and are responsible for conducting exhaustive discussions.

The following episode retold by Iwata is one example of an exchange which took place at Nintendo.

> "A robust exchange with staff and Miyamoto took place over the inclusion of an SD card slot, one of the new functions of in the

development of the DSi. From the development stage there was within the company a feeling that perhaps it would be preferable to have the SD card slot. However, the addition of a card slot would increase both the cost and the size of the unit. Nevertheless, an ongoing discussion of the value of including the SD card slot continued up to the very last minute. The deciding factor was Miyamoto's enthusiasm for it. Miyamoto actually had very clear ideas regarding the use of the card. The first was for music. The second was for Wii and DSi connection using the SD card slot. After explaining the specific ways of using it, he convinced me that he would be responsible for explaining it to staff in a way that would make them believe that it was good idea to add it".

Iwata also stated: "For a person like Miyamoto who has been at the forefront of forming Nintendo's game market for many years to make his point so emphatically, I felt that if it had value, I would go along with it". Even when the other person is a leader like "world-renowned Miyamoto" known for his development of Super Mario and other series, Iwata, as head of the LT, required him to show his accountability like others in the company, and this is the strength of Nintendo as an organization. As this episode demonstrates, each of the leaders and managers are required to engage in a thought-and-action process for achieving the mission they are aiming for in the Leaders' Team and each of the SCs by asking: If it were me, what action would I take in terms of strategy and tactics? and What can I contribute for the growth of the company and for innovation?

To develop superior products that can satisfy the users, the developers give exhaustive, deep consideration to various issues through productive discussions up until a very last minute before production. This persistence along with the passionate drive of the developers to push themselves to the limit is also the creative routine of Nintendo. The "return tea table" (named by Miyamoto) thinking and actions of Miyamoto is creative routine in software development at Nintendo. This is also the attitude of Miyamoto who, stubbornly honest almost to a fault, pursues the ideals of truth, virtue and beauty to create the best software and breaks the rules he himself sets down in efforts to repeatedly test his hypotheses during self-abnegation. In this way, the dialectical process of practicing "denial of denial" sublimated the product concept and enabled the realization of topnotch products.

In this regard, Iwata refers to the importance of "thoroughly considering cause and effect of things" and "thinking about one thing persistently for a long time":

> "Shouldn't an organization thoroughly consider the cause and effect of things over a long period? If there are a lot of people in the front line who routinely think about the cause and effect of things, I believe that we would be able to respond to change rapidly. I myself am the kind of person who becomes more concerned with processes than with results. If products don't sell, it's only natural that we ask the reason why, and even when products sell better than expected, I personally ask quite persistently why that is the case (Iwata)".

The practice of this kind of pattern of strategic thinking instills in the organizational members' creative routine based on a hypothetical testing process of trial and error where the developers themselves consider exhaustively and persistently "What can we do to realize the best products?". Furthermore, the habit of considering cause and effect also lead to the development of an organizational culture which can respond readily to social changes and be able to deal with them flexibly.

President Iwata, demonstrates top-down leadership and at the same time strengthen collaboration linkages between the president and the leaders to create opportunities for discussion and dialogue within the LT. To maximize leadership coherence among the respective leaders, he also demonstrates Nintendo's total integrative competences through strategy integration created by the multi-layered SCs interdivisionally across their divisions.

5.1 *Nintendo as a dialogue-type company*

Coexistence of the strength of the individual and the organization and knowledge integration from multiple viewpoints

Nintendo is a dialogue-oriented company. Iwata holds discussions not only with executive officers in the LT but also with development staff and together they decide how a game should be. The shared values resulting from thorough, deep dialogue intersects and develops across various organizations from the development division to the sales division until all staff recognize one common goal. The ideals, values, and strategy goals of the LT at the top level of management permeate down through to middle management and below and create innovative products through mutual top-down and bottom-up processes. Iwata emphasizes that in sharing such a vision or a sense of crisis, repetition is important. Iwata also indicates that what unites diverse, brilliant personnel from various divisions from software development to hardware development in a company like Nintendo is not the top-down leadership but "the ability to engage in discussions thoroughly".

After assuming the position of president, Iwata shared his vision through presentations and direct dialogue with staff from various organizations over a number of years. Recently the company website is carrying stories about product development through interviews with company staff. In addition to providing customers the views and thoughts of the developers, the site also provides a venue for actively promoting direct dialogue between the President and the staff of Nintendo.

Iwata also stresses the importance of "the coexistence of the strength of the individual and the organization". Nintendo encourages the free movement of the individuals in the organization and the development based on free-thinking. The concept of "disciplined imagination" at Nintendo promotes the autonomy and creativity of the individual and at the same time leads to the realization of "coexistence of the strength of the individual and the organization" by

guaranteeing control and effectiveness of Nintendo as an organization. On this subject Iwata notes:

> "Only a very few people with a special sensitivity can perceive what
> will delight others and give them a sense of enjoyment, so in this
> respect, the contribution of the individual is quite significant. In that
> respect, Nintendo is to some extent different from general manu-
> facturing businesses. However, in the creation of programs and
> turning them into products, having a lot of people engage in the
> very ordinary work of troubleshooting and resolving every problem
> one at a time is very important. Therefore the strength of the indi-
> vidual and the strength of the organization are both important.
> Without both the skills and know-how of the individual and the
> organization, we will not be able to develop interesting games.
> Furthermore, one of the more notable aspects of Nintendo is the
> respect all staff have for the talent of outstanding individuals irre-
> spective of their age or history with the company and the concerted
> wholehearted supported Nintendo provides as an organization".

Furthermore, in addition to the concept and spirit of "return tea
table" mentioned earlier, another practice of Miyamoto's, which
emphasizes activities that break away from company rules and for-
malities, is what Miyamoto refers to as the "view over the shoulder".
This involves staff in various capacities and encourages them to think
deeply about issues by and restructure them through "exhaustive dialogue" from various perspectives. This "view over the shoulder"
becomes an important process in generating new concepts and ideas,
and together with the spirit of "return tea table" through denial of
denial, as mentioned earlier, is equivalent to the concept of knowledge integration from multiple viewpoints.

To realize such coexistence of strength of the individual and the
organization and knowledge integration from multiple viewpoints,
exhaustive dialogue among staff is necessary. For this reason the ability of the organization to create close mutual interaction among staff
is an important element, and at the base of this is the existence
of multi-layered SCs which promote the deep sharing of tacit

knowledge. At the background of the realization of the coexistence of individual and organizational strength and knowledge integration from multiple viewpoints through exhaustive dialogue among company staff in a dialogue-centered company is Nintendo's unique networked collaborative organization based on multi-layered SCs, which will be explained in the following section.

6. Nintendo as a Network Collaborative Organization

In Nintendo, the organizational bodies which have properties of SCs such as the LT are formed not only at the top management layer but also interdivisionally across various divisions at the management level. In the development of DS and Wii, SCs were formed in which attempts were made to integrate the software development division and hardware development division. Furthermore, various SCs are continually being formed in Nintendo not only for new product development but also for undertaking product upgrades and promoting new network business using Wii. In this way, various SCs are continually being formed at Nintendo through organic collaboration among official organizations and have a single network organization configuration. In this chapter, Nintendo's distinguishing organizational configuration is referred to as a "networked collaborative organization".

The fundamental form of the structural elements of the networked collaboration organization is a multi-layered SC made of the formal organization which has a flat organizational structure and the actors of the formal organization (See Figure 7.4). Individual SCs enable mutual interaction through dialogue and practice between individual people and realize the coexistence of individual and organizational strength and knowledge integration from multiple viewpoints. It is also an organizational platform which creates new knowledge.

Knowledge is deeply connected to conditions, locale and space, in other words, to context. To acquire, share and create knowledge, the context must be dynamically shared among the actors. In addition, there are certain times and spaces when contexts cannot be shared unless the actors are participating in certain SCs. Furthermore, through a shared context, the linking of the community knowledge creating cycle (Kodama, 2007b) of knowledge sharing, inspiring, creation and accumulation becomes possible. At this time, exhaustive dialogue creates the actors' context architecture capability (Kodama, 2009a), and through this capability, hidden contexts become manifest and are shared among actors, and these, new contexts are formed.

To create new, high-quality knowledge, the actors participate in a number of different SCs and circulate contexts and knowledge among these different SCs. As a result, this knowledge is shared among the actors and the actors take part in activities that inspire the knowledge. The coexistence of individual and organizational strength and knowledge integration from multiple viewpoints create the ability to consolidate boundaries intersecting the organizations of actors (Kodama, 2009a). Furthermore, the networking of various different SCs (equivalent to multi-layered SCs) by the actors according to circumstances creates new contexts, further enhancing the context architecture capability.

These SCs and formal organizations are not direct opposites. Rather, SCs embrace SC management methods where issue-resolution and new product development are the main tasks and the management of routine and every day tasks in formal organizations. The actors not only comply with decision-making processes based on fundamental discipline as well as planning and rationality as a formal organization but also manage challenging organizational activities in the SCs that are creative and autonomous. At the same time, they coordinate the multi-layered SCs and further expand and develop them. This is the organizational behavior of actors based on the concept of disciplined imagination mentioned earlier. By thinking of organizational management from the perspective of the SCs, the actors are liberated from the constraints of formal organization management model and a wholly new management model becomes visible. In other words, the actors in the formal organization create multi-layered SCs that intersect the formal organization to suite the context and environment, and flexibly change (restructure the SCs) in line with the strategy goals.

The formal organization in the networked collaborative organization does not mean a business-as-usual, bureaucratic organization with a stratified, hierarchical structure (the image of a mechanical organization). The networking collaborative organization has the formal organization with the flat organizational structure where the transfer of authority and speed in decision-making are well-established (See Figure 7.5). The flat, formal organization at Nintendo consists of a number of business units (Information Development Headquarters, Planning and Development Headquarters, General Development Headquarters, Development Technology Headquarters, Sales Headquarters, Management Division, and Production Division), and the leaders and managers of the business units form autonomous, decentralized SCs and networked SCs as they collaborate with leaders and managers of other business units depending on the context. Furthermore, the greater the level of complexity of the business model or the level of difficulty of the issues or

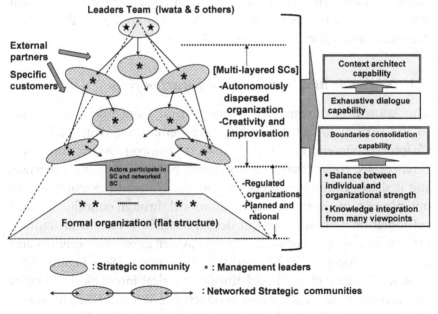

Figure 7.5   Networked Collaborative Organization.

problem areas is, the more necessary the decentralization of the SCs and their integration become.

In other words, the formation of networked SCs by actors makes possible the integration of knowledge created by different decentralized SCs inside and outside the company (Kodama, 2007a, 2007b). SCs are the organizational forms which have goal-oriented, issue-resolution type missions, and embrace concepts of organizational forms such as projects and cross functional teams (CFTs). A number of projects establish a project network (Kodama, 2007c) and organizational behavior whereby members of different projects establish new business models as they collaborate correspond to networked SCs. The more sophisticated the form of these SCs and their networking, the more sophisticated their level as networked collaborative organizations will be. Furthermore, SCs bring in external partners and certain customers as required.

Networked collaborative organizations of this nature create a coexistence of the strength of the individual and the organization and integrated knowledge from multiple-viewpoints through exhaustive dialogue. Furthermore, in the networked collaborative organization structure a new management style will be required as in the case of Nintendo under the Iwata framework.

6.1 *Nintendo as a knowledge integration firm*

The knowledge integration architecture at Nintendo corresponds to the vertical integrated architecture demonstrated in Table 1.1, Chapter 1. Nintendo is a typical "fabless" company whose core competences are concentrated in R&D and product planning expertise, and it shares common aspects with Apple. Nintendo executes overall optimization of a vertical value chain model through coordination and collaboration with development design manufacturers, manufacturing makers, and component manufacturers as well as software vendors and contents holders with Nintendo at the center (See Figure 7.6). Nintendo's value chain model through vertical integration facilitates the creation of new competitive products like Wii and DS. This is one of the features of Japanese companies as mentioned in Chapter 1.

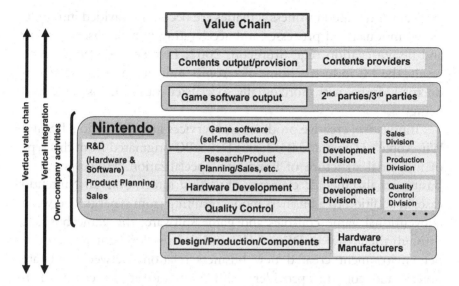

Figure 7.6   Nintendo Business Model-Vertical Value Chain Model.

As mentioned in Chapter 4, in the computer and electronics industries, vertical integration of business activities which worked advantageously in the 20th century shifted to disintegration due to changes in the business environment, namely changes in technology and the market (changes in technology through the standardization of technical interfaces and modularization as well as advances in ICT tools, etc.). Such changes in the environment significantly lowered transaction costs between companies and the market and enabled finished product manufacturers to effectively procure components externally. For finished product manufacturers, the optimal vertical boundaries also changed with the times (Christensen, Raynor and Verlinden, 2001).

In recent years, companies that owned brands (for example, Apple in the US and Nokia and Nintendo in Japan) concentrated on product R&D and product planning, while in an increasing number of cases, production is outsourced to electronic manufacturing service (EMS) companies which have factories throughout the world and accept production consignments from large companies. As a result, vertically integrated business activities are becoming divided into individual modularized processes and accelerating vertical disintegration and disaggregation (e.g. Sturgeon, 2002; Lichtenberg, 1992). As a result, the PC industry, home electronics industry, and the semiconductor industry with horizontally specialized value chains came into being.

Innovative, creative products and services like Nintendo's DS and Wii, Apple's iTunes and iPod, and Dell's PC originated from this type of industrial structure of horizontal specialization. However, these businesses also include elements of vertical integration. In Nintendo case, in addition to a business model resulting from synergies between conventional game consoles and game software, the game business through the arrival of DS and Wii and the development of an internet environment created new business relations between software houses and contents providers with Nintendo at the center. This means that in the current business environment, DS and Wii, like mobile telephones, is becoming a platform for promoting diverse contents and information distribution and is developing into a business model similar to NTT DoCoMo's i-mode in Chapter 6.

Due to such changes in company relations, Nintendo is creating a vertical value chain so that all stakeholders establish win-win relations from contents (contents providers) to game software (software houses: third parties) to Nintendo (overall value chain coordination, decisions on DS & Wii product planning and product architecture, quality control of finished products, partial self-manufacture of game software and joint production of game software with a second party) to hardware vendors (DS & Wii design, component development, production and support). This corresponds to the co-evolution model for constructing a business ecosystem, which is also a feature of Japanese companies mentioned in Chapter 1.

Although Nintendo is a fabless company that outsources its hardware design and production to external manufacturers, it does not leave all the decision-making to its agents. To realize a product concept, Nintendo engages in intense dialogue and collaboration with its external manufacturers (design, production, and component manufacturers) from the design, trial production, testing, and verification stages to achieve optimal product architecture design. Its relationship with software vendors (second and third partners), which are external partners, is the same as with hardware vendors. The establishment of close, virtually integrated corporate relations among software vendors, Nintendo, and hardware vendors promotes the transfer and sharing of deep knowledge through the formation of SCs and networked SCs and these becomes organizational platforms which create new knowledge.

The knowledge integration process through Nintendo's vertical value chain model has also been an ongoing, consistent business model since Nintendo entered into the game business. This kind of *knowledge integration model* which skilfully integrates superior core knowledge inside and outside the company is also a feature of Nintendo business model.

Apple's music delivery business model is also virtually vertically integrated and the respective stakeholders maintain a win-win relationship in a vertical value chain consisting of contents (music labels), Apple (coordinator of the overall value chain and decision-maker for iPod product planning and product architecture), and vendors (iPod design, production, and support). In addition, Dell engages in online sales of PCs for consumers but is to a great extent dependent on external companies for PC components manufacturing. However, it must procure optimal components to answer individual consumer needs and produce PCs at a low cost. Therefore, Dell pursues both the merits of efficiency through vertical disintegration by outsourcing business activities and the merits of close coordination activities through vertical integration (Kodama, 2009a).

Generally, the vertical integration of the development and production of parts and finished products enables close coordination between organizations. At the same time, in combination with strategic outsourcing (including the use of ICT) as in the cases of Apple and Dell, it can also promote the sharing and integration processes of information and knowledge among different companies and at the same time reduce governance costs while maintaining the quality of coordination tasks. Coordination and collaboration processes in strategic outsourcing determine the boundaries of companies and organizations and enhance the potential for establishing vertical boundaries as optimal value chains for companies.

Meanwhile, the knowledge integration structure inside Nintendo is a multi-layer model as shown in Table 1.1 in Chapter I. The knowledge integration process in the multi-layer model through the formation of multi-layered SCs can also be applied to in a networking collaborative organization mentioned earlier. The multi-layer model, as mentioned in Chapter 1, is not just for large-scale product development or large-scale projects; there are also cases where multi-layered SCs are regularly formed within organizations such as the promotion of TQM at Toyota Motor (Kodama, 2009a). Like Toyota, in Nintendo, multi-layered, interdivisional SCs which intersect the software and hardware divisions are regularly formed, and each of the SCs which have individual project goals collaborate and are integrated with each other, creating a single, coherent knowledge (realization of new product concepts, test production and completion of the final product).

Finally, Nintendo from top to bottom consistently defines its own business model as "game business specialization" and in recent years has hardly entered into any related or new business. In other words, Nintendo has not been proactive in pursuing a knowledge integration process in a horizontal direction through vertically integrated architecture. Nintendo sees its corporate role as providing users with entertainment services as "a company that puts smiles on the faces of people". Furthermore, the ideas of former President Yamauchi, who in the past promoted a management policy based on thorough concentration and selection are today being honestly continued by a management team of six.

Chapter

8

The Global Innovations of Japanese General Trading Companies: The Case of Mitsubishi Corporation

1. The Modern General Trading Companies

A Japanese general trading companies today operate in a wide range of business fields and functions, and deliver products and services to the world across the entire spectrum from foodstuffs to energy. The companies are concerned with all business functions, whether upstream or downstream in the value chain, and contribute to value-added enhancement processes ranging from materials development and procurement to final product and service sales. Mitsubishi Corporation is one of the largest general trading companies with more than 200 bases in Japan and around 80 countries overseas. It is currently developing its business by collaborating with partners throughout the world, working with more than 500 companies targeted as affiliates. Its business domains span a wide range of industries under a six-group system representing the industrial finance

251

development, energy, metal, machinery, chemicals, and living essentials businesses.

In the past, trading companies were seen as intermediaries focusing on trading business; but modern trading companies exploit a wealth of data to obtain at the forefront of business, and deliver high value-added goods and services while integrating distribution, finance, investment, marketing, IT, and other functions in addition to conventional trading transactions. They design value chains to integrate and freely exploit these multiple functions while undertaking major strategy conversions to corporate structures comprising new business investment, all kinds of management support, and solutions businesses as the new business model for the 21st century. It means that the general trading companies have also aligned with the times to anticipate trends, flexibly change and enlarge business models. When participating in business as partners, the general trading companies take risks and enhance business value by exploiting their organizational capabilities and global networks to acquire necessary management resources. Another key role for the general trading companies is to offer to the user optimal solutions proposals concerning business models generally, ranging from development through procurement, production, and distribution to sales and to support this undertaking, and to coordinate links among users by combining with other businesses. Thus, Mitsubishi as the general trading company could be termed the "company that creates new business models."

The essence of Mitsubishi's business is to gain the attention of "needs and seeds" embracing users and society, conceive business mechanisms, and steadily deliver the functions and services required to achieve and promote them. Furthermore, Mitsubishi promptly grasps social change and market trends, and actively develops business as an actor. In Japan, the general trading companies established around were the high-growth era following World War II. Their activities changed over time, and the companies explored developments in new fields in response to changes in the environment. Entered the 21st century, the general trading companies aimed to evolve further amid the structural transformation of Japanese economy, and undertook to create new markets while proceeding with their own structural reform by, for example, enhancing capital efficiency, profitability, and risk management capabilities. In this way, either leading from the front or responding to environmental change, the general trading companies came to transform their own functions. This flexibility, planning capability, and creativity in responding to the environment core competences of are Japanese trading companies.[1]

In recent years, global business environment has been rapidly transforming in speed and scope with the appearance of "resource nationalism" and industrial reorganization on a global level, fund incomes, and other phenomena. Untested issues have also arisen for people combining global environmental protection with sustainable economic growth. In an era of major change, for companies, governments, and any form of organization, it is always essential to move in the direction of innovation for new industries, business, and

---

[1] In the post-war reconstruction period, meeting people's lifestyle needs adequately was a matter of utmost priority. In this context, the trading company's activity domain started up with the focus on light manufacturing, such as textiles and food products. When Japan entered a high growth phase, activities expanded into fields such as iron and steel, shipbuilding, heavy machinery, transport machinery, electronics, and chemicals together with the development of the heavy chemical industry. The traders developed a worldwide network, becoming the advance party of Japan as a trading nation. In the 1970s, Japan economy experienced an oil crisis, and a stable supply of resources became an important issue. Initiatives for large-scale projects to develop and import resources or develop alternative energy sources began to increase around this time. The urban development and housing supply businesses also expanded as the living standards of the Japanese people rose. As the yen rose following the Plaza Agreement in the second half of the 1980s, direct foreign investment and the shift to overseas manufacturing bases grew popular. Trading companies intensified activities, especially in Asian and other emerging economic networks. At the same time, initiatives to promote imports and ODA business also expanded. Within Japan, the aim to expand internal demand and take on the challenge of new, non-trading business areas also grew popular, and the new domains of satellite business and program delivery were developed. Trading companies from the 1990s on entered the IT industry, expanded LT (logistics and technology) functions, increased the sophistication of FT (finance and technology) functions, and took on the challenge of cultivating the trading sphere in advanced technology, healthcare and lifecare, environment-related, and other areas.

technologies. Mitsubishi formulated and implemented a four-year, mid-term plan named "Innovation 2007" to run from fiscal 2004 to fiscal 2007.[2] CEO Yorihiko Kojima put it this way:

> "You can't put off today's thoughts and methods until tomorrow; but creating innovation in everyday life is no easy matter. What is most important of all is free, varied ideas and creating an environment in which to blend them. It is especially difficult to create innovation at entrenched organizations. It is always necessary to reform the organization and create fluidity with regard to personnel. In Silicon Valley in the U.S., brand-new businesses arise because outstanding personnel always pour in across ethnic and national borders, and new innovations can only arise from communication accompanying friendly competition."

Then in April 2007, Mitsubishi established a new "Innovation Business Group" and an "Industrial Finance, Logistics and Development Group" as additions to its five existing business groups, and assembled diverse personnel in-house. These personnel came from different organizations, and aimed to create new innovation through communication and interaction among the various personnel with accumulated experience in various industries. Externally, Mitsubishi undertook technology innovation while implementing R&D and incubation through coordinating not just with other

---

[2] Innovation 2007 is a new medium-term business plan launched in 2004. Within this, Mitsubishi Corporation is communicating its vision of a new industry innovator that creates the future, and grows together with society. There are three key issues: to energize and educate people, establish footholds, and grasp change to open up the future. The systematic reinforcement of core business and support for future strategic areas are mentioned as medium-term growth strategies. Innovating at each group's business worksite is fundamental to Mitsubishi Corporation's innovations. The corporation is also restructuring the whole company and incorporating an R&D focus while carrying out the following six future-oriented initiatives: changing the structure of the general trading company; developing functions to restructure business models; strengthening customer approach capabilities; developing regional strategies; developing business models; and developing new fields.

companies, but also with universities and research laboratories. According to Mr. Kojima, Mitsubishi is positioning itself for "a time of consolidating new mechanisms and footholds targeting the next era" as a highly uncertain era approaches, and it has become an urgent task to create pillars of growth for the coming era while promoting still more sophisticated selection and concentration, and enhancing business quality.

After that Mitsubishi formulated "Innovation 2009," a new, two-year mid-term business plan for fiscal 2008 and 2009. The plan inherits the basic thinking of Mitsubishi's "Innovation 2007," enhancing corporate value on a consolidated base while achieving sustainable growth as a global, integrated general business company, and aims to contribute to sustainable social development. However, the seismic shift in the external environment arising from the global economic crisis, which stemmed from the U.S. financial predicament in September 2008, led Mitsubishi to partially revise its plan, emphasizing corporate soundness for the immediate future while maintaining its corporate vision, basic concepts, and initiatives for the environment and CSR.

In December 2008, those responsible for each of the global regions and corporate groups gathered and immediately took the necessary measures to respond to the crisis on the basis of information gained at each site. In April 2009, Mitsubishi once more convened its executive team, and systematically debated issues that required a new response. The basic policy of "Innovation 2009" is to balance growth, efficiency, and soundness while achieving sustainable growth and maximizing corporate value.

2. Mitsubishi Corporation's Core Competences and Business Model

As mentioned above, general trading companies of the past adapted to environmental change and changed their business models. Their traditional business model has evolved from that of simple product-trading go-between. It has become important to acquire profit from various domains in the value chain by participating as concerned parties to supply required portions of customer needs within the upstream-downstream value chain for industries and business.

Mitsubishi's business model implements trading support, financial services, and strategic investment across the whole value chain from resource development and materials trading to final product manufacturing and wholesale and retail sales. Acquiring profits through building win-win relationships with partners across the entire optimized value chain is a key challenge. To achieve this, Mitsubishi is identifying business process bottlenecks and waste through hypothesis testing of optimal, targeted value chains based on its own specialist knowledge and expertise (products and industry sector × region × function), selecting optimal partners in Japan and overseas aimed at resolving the issue, and collaborating with partners to provide business solutions. Enhancing customer or partner satisfaction as a total coordinator of business models is becoming one of Mitsubishi's great strategic aims (see Figure 8.1).

To take the liquid natural gas (LNG) business as an example, Mitsubishi first negotiated as a buyer for major Japanese corporation Tokyo Gas, and concluded a 15-year contract with Alaska LNG. Next, it actively participated with Brunei LNG, not simply as a buyer but also through 50% funding and financing for liquefaction plants. Later, Mitsubishi actively developed LNG (including upstream mining development and investment in production) through a partnership with Royal Dutch Shell of the US. Mitsubishi has also set out to maintain the logistics systems for LNG imports incorporating Japan's shipping companies while investing in sales companies and gas liquefaction companies, thereby taking risk. It also imports LNG for electricity and gas corporations, especially in Japan. In recent years, Mitsubishi has committed to a business establishing bases for the receipt of LNG from harbors on the west coast of the U.S.

Thus, Mitsubishi merges and integrates the basic functions of transactions, investment, and finance within the upstream-downstream value chain comprising exploration development and production, liquefaction plants (LNG production), distribution (LNG shipping transport), and reception bases and sales; participates in various phases of the value chain; and acquires profits (see Figure 8.2).

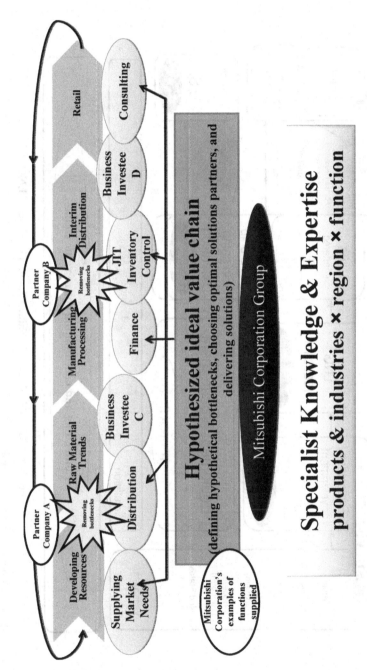

Figure 8.1   Mitsubishi Corporation's Business Model.

Source: Mitsubishi Corp.'s publicly released materilas.

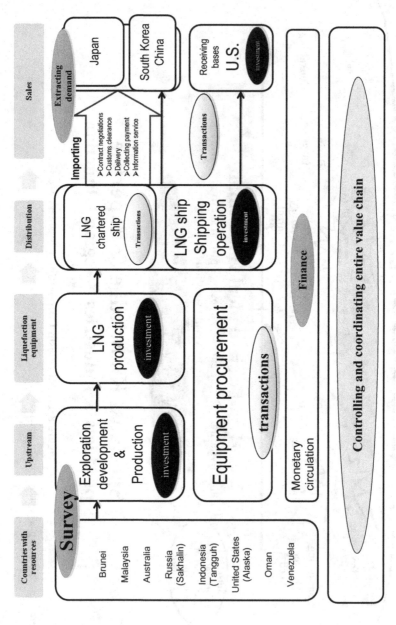

Figure 8.2   Mitsubishi Corp.'s Value Chain: The Case of LNG.

Source: Mitsubishi Corp.'s publicly released materilas.

Accordingly, general trading companies' total coordination competences become important in realizing such unique business models. These are the integrative competences of the fine-tuning coordination capability that are the specialty of Japanese companies. The architectural thinking of the overall value chain is important for general trading companies to demonstrate these competences. It could be termed the thinking of optimal knowledge integration processes for building optimal value chains of strategic targets.

For Mitsubishi, the existence of diverse, wide-ranging partners, customers, and regional networks is significant to the overall design of the value chain. These chains include alliance networks with domestic and international partners (including manufacturing and service industries, funds, major corporations, venture companies, governments, local authorities, and NPOs), and global business networks with bases around the world (including Mitsubishi Corporation's oversea bases, group companies, and affiliates) and business investors. Mitsubishi sets up joint ventures with numerous partners inside and outside Japan, and the choice of partners to form business networks with has a great impact on business performance. Therefore Mitsubishi's core competences, or integrative competences, are also the capabilities to build these networks.

As mentioned above, Mitsubishi as the general trading company clearly differs from other business structures. Mitsubishi itself is transmitting the features of its own past business formations externally. The differences between Mitsubishi and, for example, consulting firms or investment funds are as follows (see Figure 8.3). Mitsubishi emphasizes thinking and action to grasp new needs of markets and potential technologies. It focuses on business value chains, conducts a range of activities in response to customer demands, dispatches specialists in the relevant technologies, finance, and law as conditions require, and commits to actual business over the long term while holding equity and accepting risk. In these areas, Mitsubishi business model clearly differs from the business model of consulting firms that sell knowledge and expertise piecemeal in response to customers' special needs and acquire short-term, no-risk profit, and investment funds that collect short-term investment returns by exploring

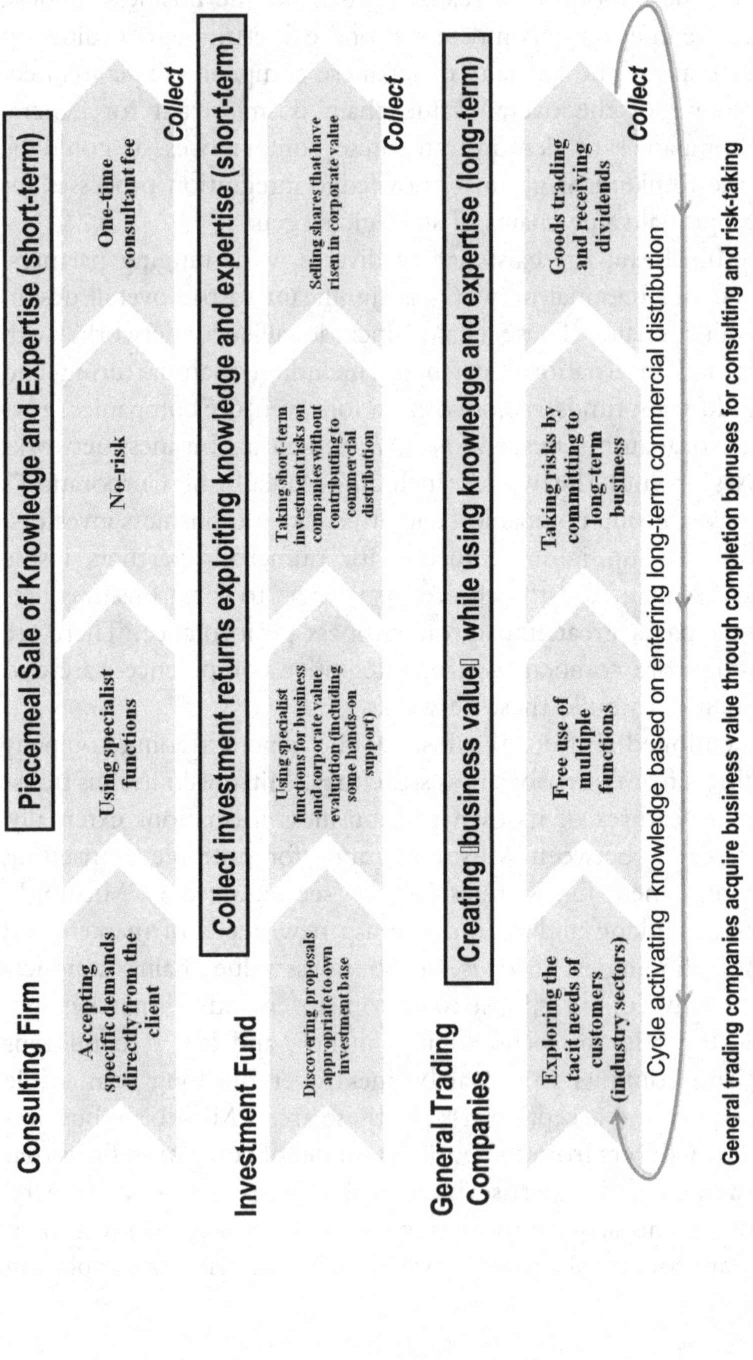

Consulting Firm | Piecemeal Sale of Knowledge and Expertise (short-term)

Accepting specific demands directly from the client → Using specialist functions → No-risk → One-time consultant fee → **Collect**

Investment Fund | Collect investment returns exploiting knowledge and expertise (short-term)

Discovering proposals appropriate to own investment base → Using specialist functions for business and corporate value evaluation (including some hands-on support) → Taking short-term investment risks on companies without contributing to commercial distribution → Selling shares that have risen in corporate value → **Collect**

General Trading Companies | Creating [business value] while using knowledge and expertise (long-term)

Exploring the tacit needs of customers (industry sectors) → Free use of multiple functions → Taking risks by committing to long-term business → Goods trading and receiving dividends → **Collect**

Cycle activating knowledge based on entering long-term commercial distribution

General trading companies acquire business value through completion bonuses for consulting and risk-taking

Figure 8.3   Mitsubishi Corporation's Business Model: Comparison with Other Business Structures.

Source: Mitsubishi Corp.'s publicly released materials.

investment proposals without contributing in detail to specific business models.

Mitsubishi has demonstrated investment fund capabilities since the latter half of the 1980s, and consulting capabilities in-house and through subsidiaries.[3] In this way, business processes that explore customer needs, freely exploit its own multiple functions (including finance, investment, marketing, distribution, and IT), and acquire profits by committing to business long-term while taking risks could be termed the business model of Mitsubishi.

3. Mitsubishi Corporation's Business Domain and Value Chain

Mitsubishi is defining classified strategy maps for its own business using business domain and value chain matrices (see Figure 8.4). Firstly, the "existing business model" is the existing business grouping of business domains together with value chains, with the aim of expanding existing core business by extending management corps and expanding channels. These might be traditional core businesses. Natural gas (maintenance and expansion of existing LNG project and progressing with the Sakhalin and Tengguh LNG projects), metal resources (raw steel material, MDP [Mitsubishi Development Pty], and non-ferrous metals), vehicle businesses (existing overseas MMC [Mitsubishi Motor Corporation] business and Isuzu Thailand business), overseas IPP business (Mexico, North America, Asia, and Australia), resource model chemical products (including SPDC of Saudi Arabia), and foodstuffs (strengthening the value chain through increased capitalization from existing business investors) belong to the existing business model.

---

[3] In recent years, a trend can be seen toward investment banks and consulting companies becoming general trading companies. It has been noted, for example, that investment banks are entering the procurement business for aircraft fuel from derivatives trading, and consulting companies and investment funds are linking up and merging.

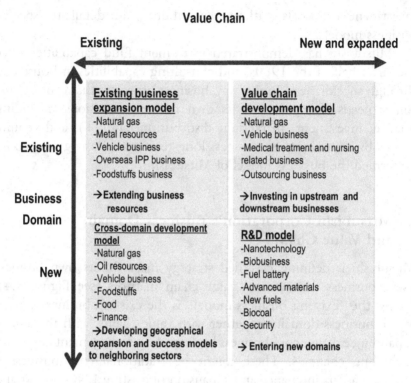

Figure 8.4   Mitsubishi Corporation's Business Model by Category.

Source: Created from Mitsubishi Corp.'s publicly released materials.

Secondly, the cross-development model keeps the existing value chain, changing the business domain alone, and aims to develop toward the neighboring existing-business sectors of geographical expansion and success models. These correspond, for example, to natural gas (Venezuela LNG and others), oil resources (exploring, developing, and producing petroleum gas in West Africa, the US Gulf of Mexico, and elsewhere), vehicle business (European sales financing business, and developing in China, Russia, and Eastern Europe), foodstuffs (business investment expansion in China and Southeast Asia), food products (strengthening the nationwide distribution system full-line, and building the Chinese SCM system), and finance (including support for corporate restructuring and asset financing).

Thirdly, the value chain development model changes the existing value chain alone, and aims to invest in upstream or downstream business. Natural gas (LNG bases on the West coast of the US. vehicle business (creating export bases for Thai business), medical treatment and care-related business (developing toward general health-care business), and outsourcing business would correspond to this value chain development model.

Forthly, the R&D model changes the existing business domain and value chain together, and creates business models in new business domains. Fields such as nanotech, biobusiness, fuel cells (hydrogen generation technologies), advanced materials, new fuels (GTL), bio-coal, and security would correspond to this.

The business created from these four models differs in context and requires different capabilities for practitioners to plan and implement strategies. Adjusting these four models from the capability map relationship (mentioned in Chapter 2) leads to the situation in Figure 8.5. The "existing business expansion" model of businesses are stable core businesses positioned in domain IV (strategic efficiency), and clear corporate boundaries and established value chains exist. They require efficient, sustained business expansion through incremental innovation comprising enhanced activities for existing business through dynamic capability in slow-moving markets. Businesses under this existing business expansion model undergo a shift from domain I to domain II, and then to domain III. The traditional core businesses then create value-chain development and cross-domain development model businesses, and develop and establish themselves in environments with the changing markets of domain III.

Businesses under the value chain and cross-domain development models are growth businesses positioned in domain III (strategic concentration), requiring developmental transformation and application of corporate boundaries and value chains. Here, the requirement is for business expansion from strategic investment through dynamic, incremental innovation comprising further development and application activities of existing business responding to the dynamic changes of customers and competitive environments. This response occurs through dynamic capability cultivated via higher learning.

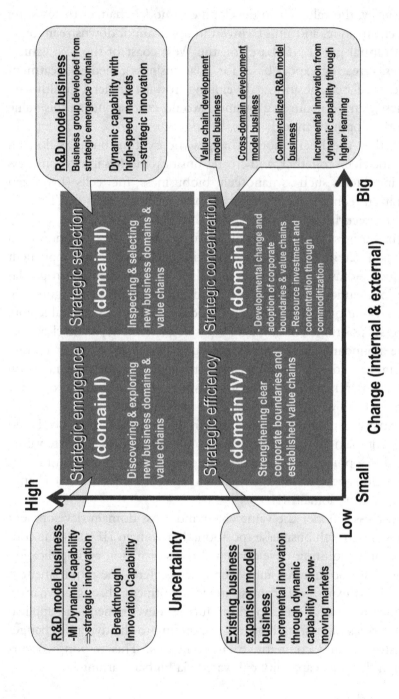

Figure 8.5   Mitsubishi Corporation's Capability Map.

R&D model businesses are positioned in the strategic emergence and selection domains (I and II), and the exploration, discovery, verification, and selection processes of the new business domains and value chain are dynamically implemented on a time axis. The organizational capabilities required in these two domains differ from conventional dynamic capabilities, and require MI dynamic capability (strategic innovation) and breakthrough innovation capability to respond to uncertainty and environmental change. Meanwhile, these R&D model businesses enter competitive markets as the level of uncertainty falls, and shift to domain III (strategic concentration), where resource input is focused on full-scale commercialization. This R&D model business differs from the core business of the existing business expansion model, the value chain development model, and the cross-domain development model, and corresponds to newly created value chains and business domains arising from strategic innovation.

In Mitsubishi, the business groupings that created these four models are progressing simultaneously within the company, and performance evaluations and risk management models have also been established and adopted in-house to support each created model. Mitsubishi possesses four different capabilities supporting each domain, and implements dialectical management combining strategic and incremental innovation. The organizational structure within Mitsubishi was also created by specialist organizations supporting each domain, and these different organizations go on to implement management within and between domains.

Mitsubishi expresses the creation of multiple tiers for basic and new functions with its own business model, and presents these concepts externally (see Figure 8.6). Business arising from basic functions corresponds to the three business models of existing business expansion, value chain development, and cross-domain development. It promotes core business strength and businesses that develop and apply them. Business arising from basic functions strengthens and establishes value chains that match customer needs through long-term business commitments based on medium risk and return.

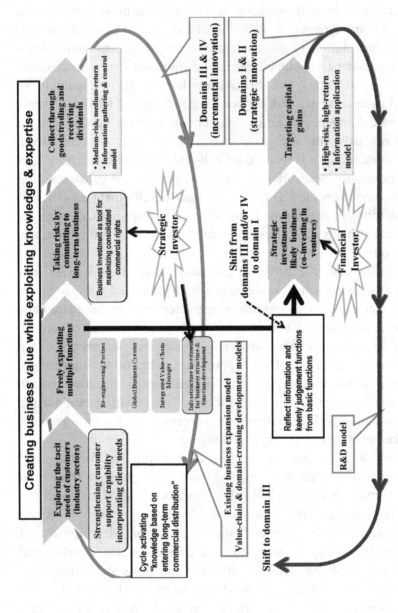

Figure 8.6   Mitsubishi Corporation's Multilayered Functions (Basic and New).

Source: Created from Mitsubishi Corp.'s publicly released materials.

Businesses arising from the basic functions iterated by Mitsubishi correspond to domains III and IV on the capability map.

Meanwhile, the new functions correspond to the R&D model business of strategic innovation. They hypothesize and test business models that should acquire capital gains through strategic investment in likely businesses on a high-risk, high-return basis. These new functions are induced from information gathering and keen judgment (including recognition and inspiration of new knowledge) arising from the basic functions of the core competences of existing business. The trigger for inspiring new from basic functions corresponds to the shift from domain III and/or IV to domain I in strategic innovation loop (see Figure 8.7). The business arising from the new functions iterated by Mitsubishi corresponds to the shift to domains I, II, and III in the capability map.

Mitsubishi's global network shoulders much of the knowledge inspiration process for the domain shifts (domains III and/or IV to domain I) arising from the recognition and inspiration of new knowledge. Mitsubishi differs from companies (such as manufacturers and distributors) which are always internally embedded in the existing value chain in that it inspires and induces new knowledge based on a new focus from outside the existing value chain, and creates buds of innovation in the building of new value chains and business models. In this way, Mitsubishi's globally distributed bases can also be called the knowledge discovery and transmission center promoting emergent and entrepreneur strategies (Mintzberg, 1978). Such concept of Mitsubishi creating multitiered basic and new functions can be interpreted as corresponding to the implementation of dialectical management arising from the strategic innovation loop combining the above-mentioned strategic and incremental innovation.

Nowadays, Mitsubishi is promoting incremental innovation business in domain III and IV (see Figure 8.5) while focusing on full-scale commercialization through a period of business incubation and start-ups R&D model business of strategic innovation in domain I and II. The key to Mitsubishi's sustainable growth lies in whether or not this new strategic innovation business succeeds. In this sense, Mitsubishi is both growing its core business in diverse industry sectors and

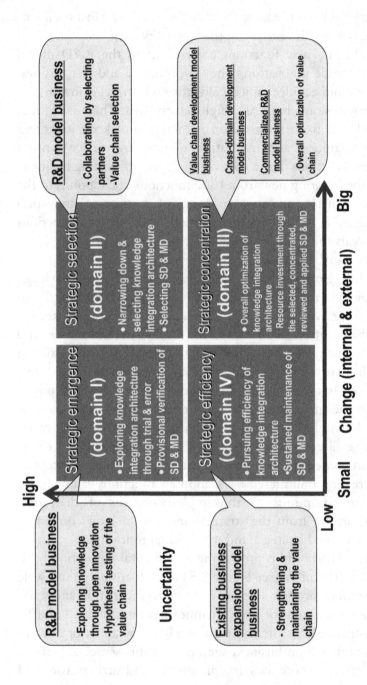

Figure 8.7   Mitsubishi Corporation's Knowledge Integration Map.

Note: Knowledge integration architecture: 'Vertical integrated architecture,' 'Horizontal integrated architecture,' and 'Linkage relationship architecture'

SD: Strategy drivers MD: Managements drivers

conditions while creating *strategic innovation capability* to cultivate new business. The following segment considers Mitsubishi's knowledge integration process supporting each domain.

4. Mitsubishi Corporation's Knowledge Integration Process

Mitsubishi's knowledge integration process forms and closely connects with its own value chain. As with the LGN business, Mitsubishi freely exploits its own multiple functions (such as finance, investment, consulting, and distribution) from upstream to downstream on the value chain, and optimizes the vertical value chain from internal and external collaboration with outstanding partners while promoting the co-evolution model to build a win-win relationship among partners.

The presence of wide-ranging and diverse knowledge networks throughout the world becomes the basis of the architecture to create value chains. The existence of personnel and personnel networks capable of applying recognition, merging, and integration of diverse knowledge on a global scale is at the source of creating these knowledge networks. The dynamic building of SCs and SC networks became important elements for Mitsubishi. The specialties of the kind of personnel required for Mitsubishi to innovate are indicated in the three-axis matrix of industry sector, region, and function, and enterprising people with the ideal trinity of product, region, and function integrate knowledge on a global scale.

The strategic emergence and selection domains shown in the capability map are a commercialization process for R&D business, which differs from the closed innovation of traditional manufacturers. The domains mainly adopt the knowledge integration process from open innovation (Chesbrough, 2003) to explore outstanding internal and external partnerships, and the *knowledge integration model* (see Figure 8.7) comes to dominate through the integration of various knowledge.

In domain I and II, general trading companies must consider how to search for business models and value chains in order to cultivate new business. The questions might include:

- How to build the vertical value chain and co-evolution models committed with upstream/midstream/downstream structures through vertical integrated architecture.
- How to focus one's own management resources in specific value chain functions within the industrial structure of the horizontal specialization business model (as in the IT industry), and collaborate with other companies with the aim of building the entire targeted value chain (vertical value chain and co-evolution models).
- How one's company should focus resources in specific specialist domains alone through horizontal integrated and linkage relationship architecture, and go on to maximize profits.
- How to compensate for one's own weaknesses while searching for strong or weak ties with other companies, and build new value chains by collaborating across industry sectors to integrate one's own and other companies' strengths.

Accordingly, general company managers must permit the expansion of diversity of knowledge integration architecture (vertical integrated, horizontal integrated, and linkage relationship architecture; see Chapter 1) as knowledge architectural thinking based on open innovation thinking, and focus on the core business selection process through experiments and trials aimed at building optimal value chains (vertical value chain and co-evolution models). In the knowledge integration process of these domains, moreover, the hypothesis verification and selection process of strategy and management drivers responding to strategic aims must be pursued through the managers' diverse knowledge architectural thinking (see Figure 8.7).

Meanwhile, business under the value chain development model is positioned in the strategic concentration domain. Here, the knowledge integration process involves developmentally reviewing vertical integrated architecture, discovering or reviewing horizontally oriented new partners from horizontally integrated or linkage relationship architecture in response to conditions, and building new vertical value chain models. The process then developmentally reviews the strategy and management drivers in response to strategy aims.

Cross-domain development model business is also positioned in the strategic concentration domain. Here, existing vertical integrated architecture is adopted as a knowledge application model. Strategy and management drivers remain almost unchanged, and partners are selected depending on the geographical situation. Alternatively, regarding application of the success model to the neighboring domains, the horizontal boundaries for the strategy drivers are extended, and the existing vertical value chain model applied for horizontal boundaries. Meanwhile, regarding the shift from the R&D model business domai]n II (strategic selection) to domain III (strategic concentration), strategy and management drivers are defined and focused on, and knowledge integration architecture chosen in domain II (strategic selection) is further optimized.

Business in the existing business model is positioned in domain IV (strategic efficiency) through sustained maintenance of strategy and management drivers. Then knowledge integration architecture is efficiently pursued aimed at maintaining and strengthening the existing business value chain. As shown above, Mitsubishi flexibly separates its own knowledge integration processes and builds vertical value chain and co-evolution models. These support the capability to respond to the strategic realization of targeted business domains and value chains.

5. Mitsubishi Corporation's Strategic Innovation Capability

As mentioned above, the elements that created Mitsubishi's four models are divided into the R&D model business as strategic innovation pursuing exploratory activities; value chain development model business as incremental innovation pursuing exploitative activities; cross-domain development business; and the existing business expansion model business (see Figure 8.8). The existing business expansion model for core business requires maintenance of a long-term, high-profit structure, and

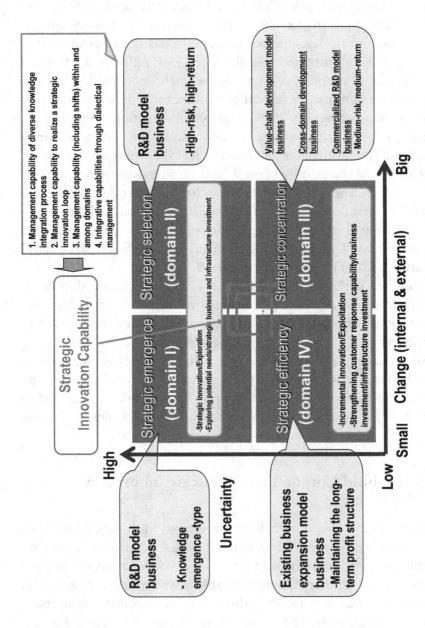

Figure 8.8   Mitsubishi's Strategic Innovation System.

the value chain development model and cross-domain development model businesses require medium-risk, medium-return performance. In both these domains (see domain III and IV in Figure 8.8), it is necessary to strengthen customer response capabilities while investing in sustained business investment and infrastructure.

Meanwhile, the R&D model businesses in domain I and II target high-risk, high-return through strategic business and infrastructure investment (including venture investment). They require development processes to explore new business models that arise from emergent activities aimed at exploring potential customer needs. The organizational capability required at Mitsubishi activates the knowledge and expertise of various multiple functions (including distribution, credit, finance, marketing, and IT), collects through goods transaction and dividend receipts while taking risks arising from long-term business commitments, and targets capital gains.

As shown in Figure 8.7, Mitsubishi requires different knowledge integration processes in these four domains. They correspond to the management capability of the diverse knowledge integration process, which is one element of the *strategic innovation capability*. Moreover, major internal organizational reform can set the trigger for acquiring the management capability to build the *strategic innovation capability*.

Mitsubishi implemented new organizational reforms to build the *strategic innovation capability*. In April 2007, it established the three key R&D model business areas of credit, new forms of energy and the environment, and medical peripherals as new profit mainstays that the entire company should study with urgency. It then founded the Business Innovation Group and the Industrial Finance, Logistics and Development Group to add to the existing five business groups (energy, metal, machinery, chemicals, and living essentials) aimed at creating full-scale business from these R&D models. These two new business groups then assembled the divisions connected to the new business from existing business groups (including the HQ corporate division) as new organizations. Management resources were effectively deployed, and new organizations built (see Figure 8.9). This organizational reform was implemented from the top-down through the attention of the CEO.

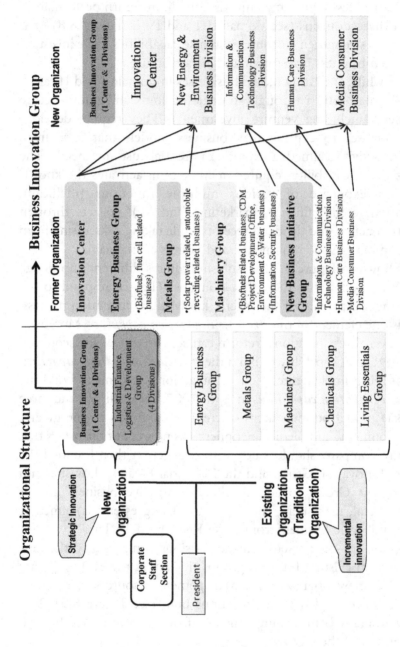

Figure 8.9   Mitsubishi Corporation's Organizational Reform (April 2007).

Source: Created from Mistubishi Corp's publicly released materials.

Figure 8.9 indicates the separation of the strategic innovation of exploratory activities and the incremental innovation of exploitative activities in terms of organizational structure. Authority was given to the top management (mainly senior executives) of each organization, and the CEO took responsibility for final deployment of key business resources and other decisions. The structure resembled an "ambidextrous organization." Many examples of innovative success through ambidextrous organizations have been reported in American companies (O'Reilly and Tushman 2004). The key to innovative success is effective resource allocation from top management and collaboration among senior executives.

The new organizations of the Business Innovation Group and Industrial Finance, Logistics, and Development Group promoted R&D model business and took on a series of missions from R&D through to commercialization. Rapid results were required of these two business groups (see Figure 8.9). The Business Innovation Group, for example, included five individual business units, and these units required intra- and inter-domain management from development to commercialization activities (the shift from domain I to II and then III in Figure 8.8).[4]

Meanwhile, the expansion and upgrade of existing business had long been a major mission for the existing five core business groups (energy, metal, machinery, chemicals, and living essentials). They were promoted by businesses from value chain development, cross-domain development, and expansion of existing business models. Thus, various businesses were simultaneously implemented and promoted through the seven business groups (five existing and two new) at the four domains shown in Figure 8.8, and Mitsubishi acquired the management capability to realize the strategic innovation loop, which is the second element of *strategic innovation capability*.

Showing the fruits of organizational reform, the Industrial Finance, Logistics and Development Group, added knowledge from real estate, construction, commodity distribution, IT, and other areas

---

[4] The "Innovation Center" of Figure 8.9 was more precisely a cost center, and its business mission was mostly R&D.

to that of finance, implementing trials and incubation while collaborating with other business groups. It successfully migrated from domain I to II, and executed trial product launches in domain II, which features high uncertainty, while reaping some success as a new business in domain III. This involved acquiring management capability within and among domains that form the third element of *strategic innovation capability.*

Meanwhile, the Business Innovation Group, undertaking new businesses such as new energy, the environment, ICT, and healthcare, was finding it difficult to create sufficient success both in domain II, which features high uncertainty fast-changing external environment and high-risk, and in the commercialization stage of domain III, despite cooperating with other business groups and aiming to rapidly achieve a high-profit commercial business. This indicates that the Business Innovation Group was unable to sufficiently demonstrate management capability within and among domains. To summarize the fruits of Mitsubishi's business activities over the two years of fiscal 2007 and 2008, while Mitsubishi was generally able to implement the dialectical management of new and existing business, a part of the new business arising from the Business Innovation Group was unable to sufficiently achieve this.

In April 2009, Mitsubishi established a greater organizational reform aimed at issue resolution. On April 1st, it reformed the Business Innovation Group to strengthen corporate development initiatives, and established the Corporate Development Section under the direct control of the CEO. Mitsubishi established the Business Innovation Group through the policies of Innovation 2007, and promoted new business development of future groups and HQs. While selecting and concentrating still more systematically under a dramatically changing corporate environment, Mitsubishi restructured the group and strengthened its corporate development function from the viewpoint of promptly grasping new business opportunities from the standpoint of the entire company.

The essential features were, firstly, to strengthen the company-wide development promotion system to undertake new energy, environmental and other businesses, which will become the pillars of the next generation, and IT business development, which will have a major impact on the functional strength of the entire company. The company also strengthened initiatives toward regional development, such as infrastructure projects in globally promising business sectors. Secondly, since the human care and media consumer businesses within the Business Innovation Group are closely connected with retail business, was to transfer control to the Lifestyle Industry Group (the existing business group), and pursue business-wide synergies for consumer market strategies and consumer-related business aiming for further growth in response to the changing times. Another aspect was to divide the corporate sections into corporate staff and corporate development, and for the Corporate Development Section (under the direct control of the CEO), executives in each section were appointed to assist the CEO.

The Corporate Development Section played a major role in drafting and implementing medium- and long-term growth strategies promoted company-wide in the four regions of functional, business sector, customer relationship, and regional development, grasping advanced technology trends and supporting development operations for the sales division. The organizational structure of the Corporate Development Section comprises the IT Service Development Division, New Energy Development Division, Environmental & Water Business Development Division, Innovation Center, and the IT Planning Department (see Figure 8.10). A committee was set up to draft, plan, and coordinate company-wide strategies and policies in each domain. Recently, the IT Management Committee has been established in addition to the Energy & Natural Resources Committee, Food & Agricultural Resources Committee, and the Consumer Market Strategies Committee (see Figure 8.10).

The appointment of managers and a clear division of roles and authority are essential to building a new organizational structure. In Mitsubishi, executives were charged with the mission of assisting the CEO with regard to IT service development as functional development, and resources and energy strategies, food and agricultural resource strategies, and consumer market strategies as business sector development; and also with regard to customer relationship development and

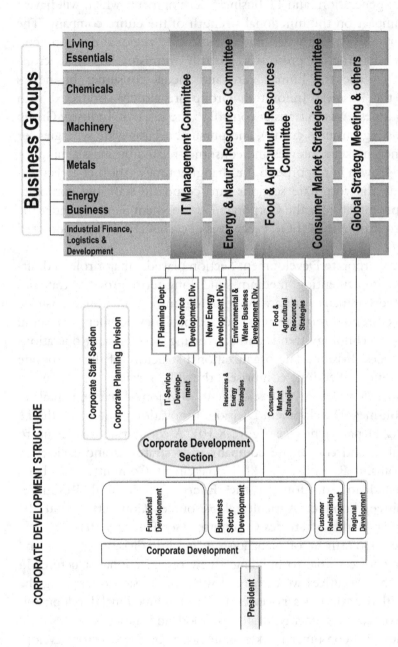

Figure 8.10   Mitsubishi Corporation's Organizational Reform (April 2009).

Source: Mitsubishi Corp.'s publicly released materials.

regional development. Each of these executives acted as one through close mutual ties to assist the CEO's corporate functions while planning and promoting company-wide strategies pertaining to functional, business sector, customer relationship, and regional development by collaborating with existing business groups. It is also an important mission to actively take up newly emerged themes in each domain, and productively debate and implement them.

The organizational structures in Figure 8.10 differ from those of the conventional ambidextrous organization, and have stronger relationships with functions corresponding to the Business Innovation Group (Corporate Development Section) and other business groups. Thus, the weak relationships (the degree of sharing and collaboration over information and knowledge) among the conventional new-old organizations transform into strong relationships at all management levels (top, middle, and low), and form organizational structures that raise the integrity of the old-new organizations through the business performances of each committee, led by the responsibility and strong commitment of top management. I name these forms "integrated organizations" (Kodama, 2009b). Integrated organizations are also structures that create the management capability for the dialectical management that implements strategic innovation (exploratory activities) and incremental innovation (exploitative activities) simultaneously.

The organizational formation of these integrated organizations realizes both autonomous, independent new organizations implementing new products, services, and business development in-house and existing organizations implementing core business through deep interaction. The integrated organization is adopted by a large number of major corporations to achieve innovation. The key to successful innovation lies in clearly dividing duties among new and existing organizations, and strengthening linkage from collaboration among practitioners at every management level of new-old organizations. For large corporations like Mitsubishi, creating and optimizing business processes through deep collaboration arising from the formation of leadership teams (Kodama, 2007c) at each management level across heterogeneous organizations are important. Each committee, driven by the responsibility and firm commitment of the top management at each of Mitsubishi's organizations, corresponds to these leadership teams.

An important aspect of the ideal organization required by the integrated organization is to integrate multiple, heterogeneous organizations possessing different qualities. Innovative companies create well-balanced integration of functions for organizational platforms having emergent, entrepreneurial elements with heterogeneous new knowledge assets (at Mitsubishi, these correspond to the Corporate Development Section and Industrial Finance, Logistics, and Development Group in Figure 8.10) and those with traditional elements possessing long years of experience and a track record (in Mitsubishi, these are the existing five business groups in Figure 8.10). The deep collaboration of old-new organizations at this kind of integrated organization promotes intra- and inter-domain management and the dialectical management of incremental and strategic innovations, and goes on to create corporate *strategic innovation capability*. This creates diverse knowledge integration processes supporting each domain, and returns to build the vertical value chain and co-evolution models.

Mitsubishi is currently in the midst of determining and implementing sustainable growth strategies by combining innovative and existing business through this integrated organization. While judging the performance of these new organizational structures will take a little more time (as of the time of this writing), the fruits of integrated organization are observed in innovation case studies of major Japanese corporations, such as those in Chapters 3 to 6 above.

6. Summing up: Organizations and Human Resources Creating New Knowledge

In the future, general trading companies must demolish the walls between organizations and companies and prepare an environment that facilitates innovation in order to sustain an international competitive edge. The creation of new knowledge through global-level collaboration has become a major topic, especially among Japanese companies, which have a strong vertical awareness. The source of innovation from new value chains lies in how to detect, integrate, and actualize at an operational level the information and knowledge distributed throughout the world. It becomes important to refine and renew the strategy drivers of vertical and horizontal boundaries; flexibly build up global-level collaborations and alliances; and build a vertical value-chain and co-evolution model from the strongest business networks to optimize the value chain. This is also the true shape of the *knowledge integration firm* (*knowledge integration model*) mentioned in the Preface and Introduction and Chapter 1.

Now that business models are growing increasingly complex and sophisticated, Mitsubishi and other global companies must discover knowledge on a global scale as industry innovators and drive the knowledge creation cycle (Kodama, 2007b) that shares, inspires, creates, and accumulates this knowledge, with the aim of educating personnel globally. Moreover, it is important to build shared value and resonance of value at a personal, organizational, and global level and to create human resources and organizations. The aim is to build new value chains from linking and integrating with different industries, and sustainably reform core business. Then the building of relationships (especially building values and trust) (see Kodama, 2007b) with stakeholders from different cultural backgrounds from around the world will surely become an urgent issue.

9

Knowledge Integration Dynamics and Strategic Innovation Capability

I have analyzed the following four features of Japanese management through the multiple case studies in Part 2.

1. The value chain model of Japanese companies arising from vertical integration encourages the creation of competitive new products and services and innovative business models. This is called the vertical value chain model.
2. Coordination and collaboration across industries among Japanese companies encourages the creation of win-win business models. This is called the co-evolution model.
3. The dynamic knowledge integration process crossing knowledge boundaries inside and outside the company is a core competence of the Japanese company.
4. The knowledge integration process of the Japanese company enables the acquisition of *strategic innovation capability*.

The *strategic innovation capability* driven by the knowledge integration process (feature 4) strategically generates a continuous stream of new products, services, and business models enabling companies to acquire long-term, sustainable competitive excellence. As mentioned in Chapter 2, *strategic innovation capability* is a concept that embraces the following four competences:

- The management capability to implement a range of innovative knowledge integration processes in response to target and situational strategies;
- The management capability to implement the spiral strategic innovation loop;
- The management capability within and among domains, including shifts; and
- The integrative competences to achieve the coexistence of two different archetypes through dialectic management.

This *strategic innovation capability* drives the dialectical management of exploitation and exploration and synthesizes incremental innovation by improving the existing core business with strategic innovation of new product and business development. The knowledge integration firm then constantly generates new product and business concepts from the creation of new knowledge. This concluding chapter demonstrates the relationship of dialectical synthesis among concepts and knowledge, and considers the *knowledge integration dynamics* framework from the viewpoints of conceptualization, dynamic practical knowledge, *strategic innovation capability*, the knowledge integration process, and the new theory of knowledge difference.

1. The Dialectical Synthesis of Conceptualization and Dynamic Practical Knowledge

Companies renew their own organizational capability in response to changes in the environment (markets and technologies). The companies in the digital consumer electronics sector (Panasonic, Canon,

Sharp, Sony, and other corporations making large-screen liquid crystal and plasma TVs, DVD recorders, and digital cameras, considered in Chapter 4) and the machine tools sector (Mitsubishi Plastic in Chapter 5) renew their capabilities and continuously expand product lineup while upgrading existing products, thereby maintaining dominance in the global markets. In this way, Japanese companies update R&D technological capability and process capability (building supply chains incorporating a global sales, production, and support system) as organizational capability, and maintain a competitive edge in the markets against a background of diversifying customer needs with regards to new products (emphasizing such aspects as quality, price, and function), technological progress (especially miniaturization, higher functionality, energy saving, and environmentally friendly products), and changes in the competitive environment (cost-war offensives from South Korean, Taiwanese, and Chinese companies).

Moreover, as considered in Chapter 6, in the broadband service sector arising from fixed communications carriers such as NTT and the mobile phone service sector including NTT DOCOMO, KDDI, and SoftBank, these companies always renew their own technologies and process capabilities in response to environmental changes such as the development of customer needs and technologies, and continue to invest in the markets — broadband services using new fiber optics and new product developments and services for high-functioning mobile phones. It is important for high-tech companies involved in consumer electronics, machine tools, fiber-optic communications services, and mobile phone services to take strategic action to adapt to the environment by adjusting to change and constantly and dynamically transforming their own capabilities. This corresponds to the dynamic capability to adapt to environmental change in domain III (strategic concentration) shown in Figure 2.1, Chapter 2. It also drives incremental innovation for the strategic innovation system in Figure 2.3, Chapter 2.

Nevertheless, strategic action with regard to environment creation, by which a company spontaneously generates its own new markets and technologies, is also important. This corresponds to companies deliberately generating their own new markets and technologies, for example, the i-mode mobile Internet services from NTT DoCoMo (see Chapter 6), J-PHONE's (currently through SoftBank) camera-loaded cell phones (Kodama, 2007c), and mobile-phone e-money services through a strategic tie-up between NTT DoCoMo and Sony rather than triggered by customer needs and technology developments. Moreover, communications carriers such as NTT in the broadband business sector (see Chapter 3) and electronics manufacturers, such as Panasonic and Sharp, amid the increasingly fierce competition of the digital consumer electronics sector (see Chapter 4) are deliberately generating new markets and technologies through their own product development capabilities spanning technological fields and industries. Leading cases include ubiquitous markets merging consumer electronics, broadband, and mobile multimedia; telematics markets merging electronics, IT, and automobile technology; and home electronics businesses merging electronics, energy, and housing. Moreover, Japan's general trading company Mitsubishi Corporation (mentioned in Chapter 8) is taking strategic innovation initiatives toward new industry sectors including new energy, medical treatment and welfare, and biotechnology.

An important point is that companies not only take strategic action to deliver updated or improved versions of products and services to adapt to environmental change, but that the environment creation process of deliberately forming the market positions of new products and services from new concepts will become a key theme in achieving future innovation. The former (environmental adaptation) process corresponds to incremental innovation, and the latter (environment creation) to strategic innovation in the strategic innovation system (Figure 2.3). In the high-tech sector, especially, where environmental change is dramatic and the markets for new products and services must be invested in continually, companies must adapt to environmental change while developing a dynamic view of strategy (Markides, 1999) to acquire and manage positions that generate their own environmental change and confer a new competitive edge.

The positioning view (Porter, 1980), which was hitherto a leading strategy theory, becomes a framework for discovering appealing positions through market structure analysis (including analysis of competitive and transaction structures among companies). It is also a thought process from external (market) to internal (company) that determines new products and business concepts of targeted market positions, and initiates studies of the capability to bring them about. Meanwhile, the resource-based view (Barney, 1994) framework emphasizes that the difference between competitive capacities and profitability among companies is an inherent resource (competence and capability) possessed by companies. The resource-based view defines the rare capabilities of the company that other companies find difficult to copy, and discovers the market position to support this. It can also be the internal (company) to external (market) thought processes to realize new product and business concepts. These two theories also comprise theoretical frameworks that can be fully applied in the situations that the market structures can be ascertained or predicted with relatively stable environments under conditions that enable market and organizational analysis.[1]

Nevertheless, current market activities also involve companies forming and executing strategies while dynamically complementing and strengthening each other's ideally targeted market position and capability. In other words, the essence of a company's strategy behavior is not to grasp the dichotomous relationship of markets (external) and organizations (internal), but to demonstrate the strategy view to dynamically synthesize this dichotomy.

In particular, the strategy formation process that transcends a company's core capability knowledge to spontaneously and deliberately form new conceptual positions for new products, services, and business models endlessly in a fast-changing, uncertain environment

---

[1] The dynamic capability approach, which is considered to be a theoretical framework with a still more dynamic strategy view, is a concept that dynamically changes its own core capabilities in line with environmental change (Teece *et al.*, 1997). However, the dynamic capability approach is a concept that considers path dependency and market positioning are given. It moves from an internal (organization) to an external (market) view, strengthening market position from the practitioner's thoughts and actions redefining the company's capabilities. Dynamic capability corresponds to path A described in the main text.

is a key issue for practitioners on a daily basis. Because of this, companies must establish the targeted concepts (market positions) to create new environments deliberately, and continuously endeavor to create new knowledge (capability) required by the company. To do this, it is important for a company to establish a competitive position for a targeted new concept through trial and error and act strategically to continuously maintain existing positions of competitive superiority. In other words, a dynamic thinking and action framework that synthesizes practice processes from external (market company) to internal with those from internal to external (market company) is required from the practical viewpoint of corporate strategy.[2] Thus, corporate strategy activity is a dialectical synthesis relationship of the realization of new concepts from the acquisition of new knowledge (internal [corporate] to external [market] thinking-path A) and the acquisition of new knowledge to realize new concepts (external [market] to internal [corporate] thinking-path B).

Path A is a strategic action process of realizing new products and business concepts (conceptualization) through (dynamic) practical knowledge acquired through practitioners' daily dynamic dialogue and practice. Meanwhile, path B is a strategic action process whereby practitioners acquire new practical knowledge (dynamic practical knowledge) from dynamic dialogue and practice to realize targeted new products and businesses (conceptualization).

---

[2] Drawing on some 20 years of business experience in fields such as product and service development, sales and customer support, and establishing corporate ventures in the IT and telecommunications sector, I consider that the foundation of the analytical framework to ascertain dynamic strategy formation lies in the dynamic practical knowledge possessed by individuals, groups, and organizations inside and outside the company. The leading research results up to now including the knowledge-based view of the firm (e.g., Grant, 1996a, 1996b), organizational knowledge creation (Nonaka, 1994), wellsprings of knowledge (Leonard-Barton, 1995), intellectual capital (Stewart, 1997), working knowledge (Davenport and Prusak, 1998), and a community of practice (Brown and Duguid, 1991) focus on grasping corporate activity from the creative process of the intangible asset of knowledge. The essence of strategy lies in how a company strategically creates new practical knowledge while forming targeted market positions (conceptualization).

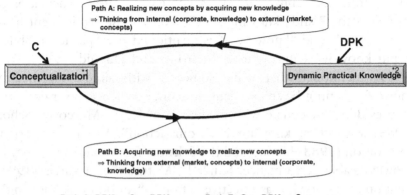

Path A: DPK → C → DPK →   Path B: C → DPK → C →

1 Conceptualization refers to the realization of new products and businesses arising through new ideas and other means.
2 Dynamic practical knowledge refers to the acquisition of practical knowledge possessed by people, groups, and organizations to embody concepts.

Figure 9.1 **The Dialectical Synthesis of Conceptualization and Dynamic Practical Knowledge.**

To indicate the importance of practitioners' dynamic practice process on a daily basis, the term "conceptualization" is used to mean the realization of new products and services arising from new ideas. The term "dynamic practical knowledge" is used to refer to the acquisition of new practical knowledge through the dynamic practice of daily routines and strategic action (see Figure 9.1).

I would like to mention the relationship between knowledge and "dynamic practical knowledge". Knowledge is the source of a company's competitive capability. In actual business activity, however, the dynamic knowing process, or knowledge of the actual process, becomes more important for practitioners than static knowledge. The dynamic acquisition and practice of practitioners' practical knowledge, especially, become key elements from the viewpoint of the practice-based view of strategic management (Kodama, 2007b).

Up to now, numerous scholars have perceived knowledge from the following viewpoint. Knowledge is taken to be acquired through practitioners' deliberate activity based on their previous experiences in various contexts (Schutz, 1932). As with Ryle's (1949) articulation of "knowing that" and "knowing how", "know-how" is different from "know-what", and "know-how" is mentioned as a "particular ability to put know-what into practice" (Brown and Duguid, 1998). Ryle (1949) mentioned that while someone with almost no medical knowledge cannot be an excellent surgeon, excellence in surgical procedures does not equate with medical knowledge. Moreover, Schon (1983) said: "Our knowing is in our action". Schon's important observation (1983) highlighted the essential role of human agency in knowledgeable performance. Similarly, Maturana and Varela (1998) mentioned: "Knowing as effective action", "All doing is knowing", and "Knowing is doing".

Meanwhile, when grasping knowledge from the viewpoint of social structure and individuals, actors are understood to act knowledgeably as a routine part of their everyday activity. Actors are always purposive and reflexive, and routinely execute practical activities of monitoring and coordinating thinking and action of themselves and others (actors inside and outside the organization, including customers and partners) while constantly executing practical activities of forming human networks. Regarding the actions of these actors within the social and physical contexts, Giddens (1984) defines human knowledgeability as "inherent within the ability to 'go on' within the routines of social life". Moreover, Giddens and Pierson (1998) add the meaning of "immense knowledgeability involved in the conduct of everyday life". Furthermore, Orlikowski (2002) mentions that "Such ability to 'go on' is inseparable from human agency, where agency is the capacity of humans to 'choose to do otherwise'. Knowledgeability or knowing-in-practice is continually enacted through people's everyday activity; it does not exist 'out there' (incorporated in external objects, routines, or systems) or 'in here' (inscribed in human brains, bodies, or communities)".

In this way, the acquisition of dynamic practical knowledge as everyday practical capability meaning knowledgeability, or knowing in practice, becomes vitally important for practitioners' strategy action. The origin of the dynamic thinking and action drivers synthesizing path A practice processes from internal (organizational view) to external (market view) with path B practice processes from external (market view) to internal (organizational view) is, in essence, that of practitioners realizing the conceptualization of new products and businesses and acquiring dynamic practical knowledge.[3]

Next, I will consider the relationship between these two paths (A and B), the capability map (see Figure 2.1) and strategic innovation system (see Figure 2.3) mentioned in Chapter 2, and demonstrate how the synthesis of these two paths becomes an element creating *strategic innovation capability*.

2. Different Practice Processes and Strategic Innovation Capability

The dialectical synthesis of companies and organizations realizing conceptualization while acquiring dynamic practical knowledge becomes a framework to continuously create new products and businesses. I would like to consider the relationship between this way of thinking and the strategic innovation system discussed in Chapter 2.

The practice process (path A) from internal (organization) to external (market) includes a major element that realizes new products

---

[3] The source of "practical knowledge" is the "*Nichomachean Ethics*" (Aristotle, 1980) written by the ancient Greek philosopher Aristotle. The concept of human activity as practice first arose in ancient Greece. Aristotle's practical knowledge confers important and valuable insights regarding leadership vis-à-vis practitioners in the current business society.

According to Aristotle, there are three intellectual virtues, the possession of which (along with the possession of moral virtue), will enable an individual to achieve *eudaimonia* (well being). One virtue is scientific knowledge (*episteme*), which consists of deduction from basic principles. Scientific knowledge corresponds to universal objective knowledge through logical analysis. Another virtue is craft knowledge (*techne*), which is about how to make things. "Craft knowledge" is the skills and expertise to create something through the application of practical knowledge and skills, including technology. A third is practical wisdom (*phronesis*), which deals with both universals and particulars.

Phronesis is knowing what is good for human beings in general and having the ability to apply such knowledge to particular situations. Practical wisdom (*phronesis*)

and businesses based on existing core competences, and with regard to actual corporate activity, corresponds to activities that improve existing core businesses (including upgrading existing products). Path A strategic action corresponds to practitioners' activities in the strategy concentration and strategic efficiency domains (see Figures 2.1 and 2.3). In the strategy concentration domain, companies sustainably and strategically upgrade technologies and review business models to enhance product and business values with the aim of rapidly adapting to the competitive environment. Because of this, companies must improve and continuously upgrade new products and businesses that have shifted from the strategic selection domain. This strategic concentration domain also incorporates the concept of essential dynamic capability that promotes incremental innovation (exploitation processes), and has the capability to evolve operating routines through high-order learning and realize high-performance through diversification to adapt to internal and external change and create profit. Incremental innovation requires the dynamic refinement of existing practical knowledge through path A practice processes.

---

can be thought of as the practical knowledge by which actors can make optimum decision and action in response to these occasional contexts. *Phronesis* is a methodology that incorporates the merit of ethical excellence in targeting correct strategic objectives, and achieves strategy objectives in response to circumstances on this basis. People with practical wisdom are defined as people that are outstanding in their careful consideration, either wholly or in part. According to Aristotle, *phronesis* is neither scholarly nor technical. Put another way, with regard to several good and bad aspects of humanity, it is the intellectual attitude and action that enables practice with the discernment not to abandon the truth. *Phronesis* is the practice process whereby people perceive the essence of everything, and accomplish the skilful, correct, adaptation of things to circumstances. With actual business activity, practitioners need to address individual specific problem areas, issues, and strategic objectives amid the various temporally changing contexts, and act not only by prioritizing rigorous theoretical thought employing logical analysis, but also by optimizing and accurately judging the situation at such times, and correctly accomplishing the strategic objectives. The concept of *phronesis* refers to the best practice process in response to the situation. With this process, even if unforeseen issues and interorganizational problems arise, practitioners discover the best methods and deal with them appropriately through improvisation (Weick, 1995). For details, see Kodama (2007b).

In the strategic efficiency domain, the incremental improvement of existing practical knowledge through path A practice processes is demonstrated, and incremental innovation driven with the aim of systematically increasing business efficiency through the exploitation process of activities to enhance existing business. The advance of process management in this domain goes on to accelerate the organizational response and achieve incremental innovation (Benner and Tushman, 2003).

Meanwhile, another path B practice process from external (market) to internal (organization) has a major element of freshly created products and businesses based on completely new competences, and actual corporate activities also correspond to R&D, new business, and internal corporate ventures. Path B strategic action corresponds to the strategic emergence and strategic selection domains, which are the creation and selection stages of new technologies and business arising from new ideas, business concepts, discoveries and inventions (see Figures 2.1 and 2.3). These domains are mainly driven by strategic innovation (the exploration process). The new core technologies and business concepts arising from the concepts of new market creation from practitioners' path B practice in the strategic emergence domain rapidly transform the acquisition of personnel resources and organizational maintenance and innovation from inside (and sometimes outside) the company aimed at incubating to create concrete business, and migrate to an environment of great change (strategic selection domain) while maintaining uncertainty. Here, uncertainty and risk in markets and technologies are reduced and the chances of business success rise through "learning by doing" setting hypotheses, trial production, experimentation, and evaluation aimed at realizing new business from practitioners' path B practice processes (exploratory process through strategic innovation).

Accordingly, the relationship between these practice processes (path A and B) and the four-domain strategic innovation system is shown in Figure 9.2. Among these, the shift to the strategic concentration domain's exploitation process to rapidly establish new product, service, and business model markets that pass through the exploration processes of the strategic emergence and selection

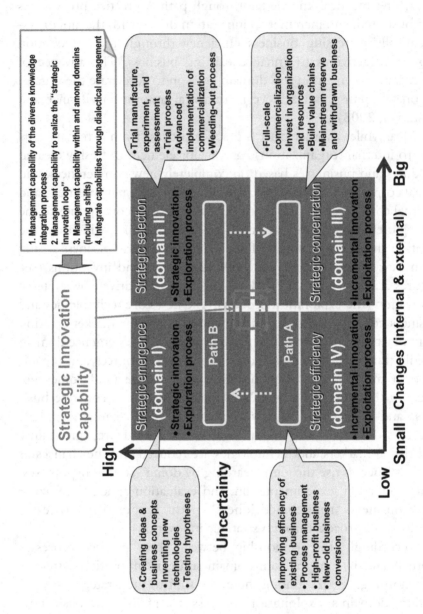

Figure 9.2   Strategic Innovation System.

domains signifies the movement of practice processes from path A to path B. Moreover, the shift from the strategic concentration or efficiency domains resulting from the absorption and acquisition of new knowledge (heterogeneous knowledge including, for example, the new mobile phone services in Chapter 6 and game businesses based on new concepts, such as DS/Wii in Chapter 7) signifies a shift of practice processes from path A to path B. Thus, the synthesis of these two paths drives the strategic innovation loop (see Chapter 2, Figure 2.3), creates a corporate *strategic innovation capability*, and enables the simultaneous promotion of incremental and strategic innovation.

Next, I will describe the relationship between these two synthesized paths arising from the dialectical synthesis of conceptualization and dynamic practical knowledge based on the new concept of knowledge difference. I would like to derive a framework (termed "knowledge integration dynamics" in this book) whereby companies create strategic innovation capability through the knowledge integration process, and continually create new products and businesses.

3. The Framework of Knowledge Difference

I would like to take up the absorption capability of knowledge difference required in practitioners' strategic thinking in order to speedily develop new products through the continuous knowledge integration process and realize (conceptualize) new concepts.

Practice processes to realize the concepts of brand new products and businesses generally exist as the two paths. The first path (A) is the process to create new concepts from path-dependent knowledge accumulated within the company. The second path (B) is the process that creates new concepts from coupling and merging heterogeneous knowledge that does not greatly rely on path-dependent knowledge. Many of the actual commercializations are path A practice processes based on the thinking of moving from internal (corporate, knowledge) to external (market, concepts), and correspond to incremental innovation (exploitation) responding to environment adaption in

Chapter 2, Figure 2.3. Path B's practice processes correspond to strategic innovation (exploration) responding to environment creation based on thinking that shifts from external (market, concepts) to internal (corporate, knowledge). These two paths are both important, and *strategic innovation capability* is created from a synthesis of these two paths. Next, I will consider these two paths individually.

The first path (A) does not generally involve the kind of thinking that suddenly produces new products and services; rather, the greater part comprises incremental growth and development based on knowledge assets accumulated within the organization over many years. Being considered from a technology viewpoint, path A is also a technological history specifically realized as goods and services. DVD recorders, digital TVs, digital cameras, mobile phones, and other leading digital consumer electronic products incorporate a major element of accumulated core technologies. Many of the technology elements that go to make up these product groups have achieved incremental technological evolution despite the historical change from analog to digital technologies.

In this regard, an executive responsible for Panasonic's semiconductor division said the following about DVD product development.

"First, once marketing has finished, the products should sell. It might be a good idea to sell as a set product. Right, next we'll manufacture LSI, but the discussion whether Panasonic can actually complete a number of goods in a short time frame and succeed or fail must first address whether all the parts can fit in the palm of one's hand. DVD recorders have a long development history, and around 1992 Panasonic took the decision to make optical disks the core business for the entire company. At that time, the concept of building the kind of DVD recorder we have today did not exist, but since then Panasonic's research lab and semiconductor divisions have incorporated all essential technology elements. Around 2000, the marketing and set-making divisions entered the scene, and specific product development began. The accumulated element technology was the key to speed. DVD recorder platforms based on these elemental technologies were finished and promptly supported by adding new technology elements, including the extension of existing platforms or the design of new dedicated circuits, in line with required specifications from the set making divisions. Accordingly, the technology is already in hand for existing IP (intellectual property)in 70 or 80 percent of system LSI. What is important is how to develop and accumulate elemental technologies by looking into the future".

Every digital product, including DVD recorders, has been developed and become a finished product through incrementally accrued path-dependent knowledge arising from the path A practice process; it is a new product and business development based on thinking that moves from internal (corporate, knowledge) to external (market, concept) (see Figure 9.1). In order to explain this kind of incremental technology evolution, I will first describe the concept of knowledge difference. Figure 9.3 shows how the evolution of technology (ideas) relates to their degree of novelty (see Figure 9.3), and not necessarily to the increasing sophistication of that technology. This diagram clarifies the gradual accumulation of new knowledge based on existing knowledge assets.

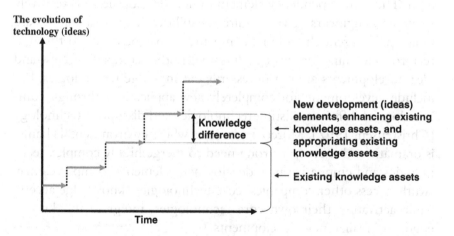

Path A (incremental innovation): Few elements of knowledge difference among new developments (ideas)
Path B (strategic innovation): Great element of knowledge difference among new developments (ideas)

Figure 9.3   Knowledge Difference.

Logically, knowledge differences can be broken down into a flow of existing knowledge assets, an improvement of existing knowledge assets, and new development (idea) elements. Engineers require the capability to disassemble, analyze, and rebuild targeted product development (idea) elements, based on existing tacit (the experience and expertise of engineers and engineer groups) and formal knowledge, into new elements (including improvements of existing knowledge) and existing elements (knowledge). Thus, knowledge difference is one capability by which engineers recognize the three general categories of existing technology flow, existing technology improvements, and new development (idea) elements through thoroughgoing debate to create new concept.

A key aspect for engineers is the need for the capability to promptly and accurately discern the degree of new development (idea) elements (including degree of difficulty, development scale, and operability), which also becomes an important factor in determining development costs and timescales. The appropriation and improvement of existing technologies is strongly influenced by the accumulation of technology. In other words, the path dependency is high. The path dependency element in new developments is relatively small, and engineers newly acquire capabilities. These capabilities are built up from scratch within a company, or may be acquired through reciprocal learning via strategic links with other companies. New and idea developments are not necessarily cutting-edge technologies, but include developments for completely new applications through combinations of different existing technologies and disruptive technology (Christensen, 1997). Moreover, in cases where environmental change is dramatic and there is a strong need to merge highly complex technologies and emphasize new development elements, companies may swiftly access other companies' core technologies (knowledge access) while activating their own core technologies, integrate this knowledge, and realize new developments.

The knowledge difference capacity to recognize and accurately discern new development and idea elements relates to the common knowledge of engineers (e.g., example Carlile, 2002; Cramton, 2001; Star, 1989). The presence of common knowledge is also necessary to acquire inherent domain knowledge required for the new product development targeted by engineers (e.g., Carlile, 2002; Cramton, 2001; Star, 1989). SCs are formed in digital consumer electronics companies such as Panasonic and Cannon (see Chapter 4). In these individual SCs, the engineers of the various organizations transcend organizational boundaries to share and understand contexts, and discover new development elements based on the engineers' common knowledge. In Chapter 4's case study of digital consumer electronics, this included specialist terminology, experience and expertise handed on from previous individuals, and the capacity to mutually perceive and grasp this explicit and tacit knowledge among engineers, including architecture, video and voice, semiconductor, and software technologies related to digital technology. They answer such questions as "What architecture is best to achieve the new product concept", and "What component technologies and software developments are required to realize this?". In the SC, the dynamic context of common knowledge is shared among engineers to create new contexts.

For example, various black box technologies such as Panasonic's and Canon's system LSI development, optical pickup, lens, video processing, and high-density packaging are accumulated knowledge assets; and it is important to discover new knowledge differences on this foundation and absorb them rapidly and accurately though a process of abduction. Panasonic and Canon are able to accurately achieve core technologies to reflect various customer needs in new product functions based on previous knowledge assets. In other words, they have a high capacity for knowledge difference, and this is also a reason why they can speedily develop and achieve continuous product lineups.

In this way, engineers accurately ascertain knowledge difference, and develop new products. Next, they repeatedly undertake trial and error and test hypotheses through business model experimentation in actual fields (including experiments with specific customers and trial services through consortiums) with the aim of confirming whether targeted concepts can be realized. Another key issue is to build business processes in order to introduce new products and services to the market. This requires knowledge of product development and production together with a diverse, heterogeneous range of knowledge (including the establishment of sales structures and channels inside and outside the company, and system and employee training for technical support and aftercare services) in such areas as sales and support. In order to achieve this, practitioners must understand and share the differing contexts of specializations, integrate heterogeneous knowledge (development, production, sales and support) through the formation of networked SCs; establish business models that can reliably bring new products to market; and build and consolidate value chains. Then the practitioners must maneuver towards thinking and action to shift from an internal (acquiring the dynamic practical knowledge of new organizational knowledge) to an external (conceptualization to realize market positions through new concepts arising from introducing new products and services to the market) focus. This corresponds to "Path C from DPK: hypothesis testing and KI from KD" in Figure 9.4.

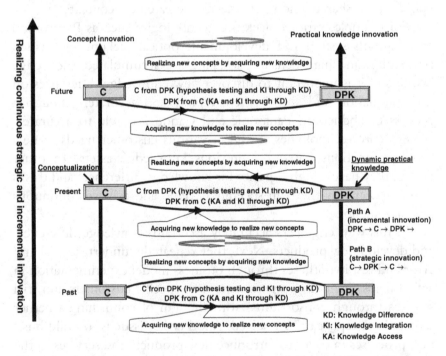

Figure 9.4   Knowledge Integration Process Through Dynamic View of Strategy.

Meanwhile, the market response is received through sales of the realized product concepts and feedback from a range of customers is considered, and further upgraded product concepts are created in the minds of the marketers. Here, the consideration of knowledge difference between accumulated knowledge and new concepts takes place through creative dialogue with engineers, aimed at realizing new concepts for the next round of product planning. Practitioners access knowledge inside and outside the company while appropriating existing technology assets in incremental innovation, including product upgrades. In the case of incremental innovation, the degree of knowledge difference is relatively small. Thus the practitioners shift the orientation of their thinking and action from outside (realizing market positions from new concepts arising from the introduction of new products and services to the market) to inside (acquiring new organizational knowledge) aimed at the next product upgrades (see the "DPK path from C: KA and KI from KD" in Figure 9.4).

The second path (B) concerns practitioners deliberately establishing new concepts relating to new products and businesses as new market positions from a dynamic view of strategy. It also includes strategy action to create new markets from blue ocean strategy (Kim and Mauborgne, 2005) and disruptive technology. The essential focus of new product and business concepts is not the individual black box technologies of architecture and components, but a market orientation asking such questions as "what value can we deliver to the customer?" and "what business concepts will create new markets?". New services including NTT DoCoMo's i-mode and mobile phone credit (see Chapter 6), and new product and service concepts such as Nintendo's DS/Wii game business (see Chapter 7) were created from practitioners acting on the firm belief in delivering unprecedented new value to the customer to create new markets with product and service concepts aimed at future society and new lifestyle proposals, rather than arising from the acquisition of facts supported by detailed marketing data for new product and service concepts with the sense that "customers definitely have this kind of potential need" (Hamel and Prahalad, 1989).

To achieve this, organizations need to innovate existing mental models, and discard the precedent-based model in order to nurture radical ideas (also incorporating external knowledge) (Hamel, 1996, 2000). Then practitioners must take the stance of setting high targets to realize the new concepts of strategic market positions and explore challenging new business while shouldering the risk of development investment. From the viewpoint of creating new markets, especially, developing new products from a path-dependent technology base alone makes it easy to fall into competency traps (Levitt and March, 1988; Martines and Kambil, 1999), core rigidities (Leonard-Barton, 1995), and innovator's dilemmas (Christensen, 1997), and so it is essential to develop products and services from a conceptual base focusing on market creation and customer view. Insight arising from "intersectional innovation" (Johansson, 2004), including new concepts with different fields and the merging of different technologies, increases the possibility of creating new concepts.

Marketing or engineering practitioners form concepts while testing them through trial and error against their own thoughts and beliefs via productive, creative dialogue in the product and technology planning SCs. After determining the product and service concepts, the engineers undertake the technology issues (the realization of functions to achieve the concepts, including basic product design, detailed design, prototypes, verification experiments, production, and testing). In this area, too, knowledge difference can be considered a key focal area.

Knowledge difference and common knowledge creatively promote knowledge access and the knowledge integration process, both internally and externally, through the efforts of marketers and engineers. This makes the practitioners acquire practical knowledge to actualizing prototypes reflecting the new product concepts and specific new products and businesses. Practitioners confirm the knowledge difference aimed at establishing market positions for the new concepts (conceptualization), access internal and external knowledge through networked SCs (knowledge access, or KA) aimed at acquiring the newly essential organizational knowledge (dynamic practical knowledge), integrate this knowledge (knowledge integration, or KI), and dynamically acquire the new practical knowledge necessary to realize new concepts.

In this way, the product development process to recognize knowledge difference and the desired concept lead the practitioner's thinking and action from an external (realizing market positions from new concepts, or conceptualization) to an internal (acquiring new organizational knowledge, or dynamic practical knowledge) focus (see "DPK path from C: KA and KI from KD" in Figure 9.4).

Meanwhile, in order to test and verify whether the new product development and targeted concepts can be achieved, practitioners must repeatedly experiment through trial and error and test hypotheses with business models (including products and services) in actual fields, and go on to build business processes. Then practitioners must turn to thinking and action that shifts the focus from internal (acquiring new organizational knowledge, or dynamic practical knowledge) to external (realizing new market position concepts by introducing new products or services to the market, or conceptualization) to establish business models that can reliably bring new products to market and build and consolidate value chains (see "C from DPK path: hypothesis testing and KI from KD" in Figure 9.4).

In this way, practitioners must form networked SCs to access, share and integrate a range of knowledge inside and outside the company, which are required not only in product development but also in various business processes by implementing a series of practical knowledge integration processes. Practitioners then go on to build the new value chains required to introduce new products and services to the markets. As a result, the realization (conceptualization) of new concepts (market position) and the acquisition of new practical knowledge (dynamic practical knowledge) can be achieved simultaneously.

As seen above, the knowledge integration firm holds a dynamic view of strategy. It implements the knowledge integration process through interactive thinking and action that synthesizes the path A practice process moving from internal (organization) to external (market) and the path B practice process moving in the opposite direction arising from the ability to recognize knowledge difference.

Practitioners implement the dynamic strategy-practice process to deliberately acquire new concepts (market position) and knowledge through spiral development of an dual-path (A and B) knowledge integration process on a time axis (past through present to future) (see Figure 9.4 for a dynamic view of strategy arising from the spiral knowledge integration process). As a result, continuous strategic and incremental innovation are achieved simultaneously.

4. Knowledge Integration Dynamics

The practitioners' interactive thinking and action (internal and external) synthesizing the path A and B practice processes moving from external (market) to internal (organization) and vice versa through the recognition capability of a range of knowledge differences are linked to the synthesizing of continuous strategic and incremental innovation. This thinking and action is the practice process that promotes both concept and knowledge creation. The productive, creative dialogue and practice processes are embedded among practitioners within the company (organization) to continually create new conceptualization and dynamic practical knowledge. This creative dialogue and practice process enhances practitioners' ability to recognize knowledge difference and promotes the interactive process of conceptualization and dynamic practical knowledge. At the same time, the ability to recognize knowledge difference accelerates the knowledge integration process of dynamic access and integration toward the company's internal knowledge and the external knowledge of partners, including customers. Then the company goes on to realize the desired concepts and continually acquire new knowledge aimed at corporate vision and strategic goals.

In this book, the interactive process of conceptualization and dynamic practical knowledge through practitioners' creative dialogue and practice process is called *knowledge integration dynamics*. *Knowledge integration dynamics*, the dialectical motive force behind conceptualization and dynamic practical knowledge, simultaneously and continuously enhances strategic actions that constantly create new products and services from new concepts while enhancing a company's own organizational capability as practical knowledge.

Furthermore, this *knowledge integration dynamics* achieves a synthesis of incremental innovation (exploitation, path A) supporting environment adaption with strategic innovation (exploration, path B) supporting environment creation, and goes on to create corporate (organizational) *strategic innovation capability*. The framework of the knowledge integration firm that continually realizes this kind of new concept and knowledge creation, and promotes sustainable corporate growth, is shown in Figure 9.5.

This *knowledge integration dynamics* framework becomes the driving force behind corporate activity to create and apply new products and businesses in an unending spiral through interaction between the distinctive conceptualization and dynamic practical knowledge possessed by the *knowledge integration firm*. Companies must create

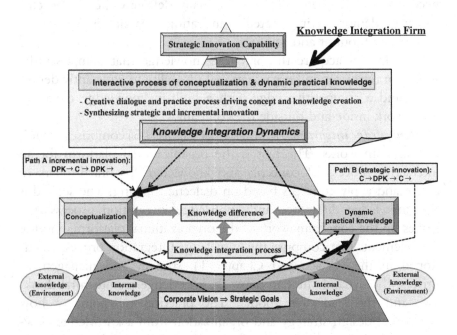

Figure 9.5 **Knowledge Integration Dynamics in the Knowledge Integration Firm.**

streams of new knowledge to constantly achieve strategic and incremental innovations.

The theory of the *knowledge integration firm*, which has a different focus from that of conventional corporate or strategy theory, takes as its starting point the question of how to continuously pursue new corporate value in the age of knowledge. The *knowledge integration firm* requires not only conventional incremental innovation, but also an organized practical framework to realize products and business concepts with unprecedented absolute value through strategic innovation. *Knowledge integration dynamics* lie at the core of this new systematized theory. By acquiring *strategic innovation capability*, companies create and implement new products and businesses through the interactive processes of conceptualization and dynamic practical knowledge through the knowledge integration process inside and outside the company (including customers). With the *knowledge integration firm*, the acquisition of practical knowledge necessary for the company to continually deliver value to the customer by demonstrating strategic innovation capability is the essence of dialectic thought and action.

Companies acquire the practical knowledge that comprises the source of resources and organizational capability to constantly deliver value and a competitive edge with a built-in knowledge dynamics framework inside and outside the company.

Knowledge integration dynamics (see Figure 9.5) comprises the following frameworks. The first is the organizational platform for an interactive process of concepts and knowledge for practitioners to create and apply concepts based on dialectic thinking. The second is the knowledge difference and knowledge integration process that makes up the core framework of the organizational platform, and the four elements that comprise the knowledge integration process (mentioned in the Preface and Chapter 1): strategy and management drivers, the dynamic human network, knowledge architectural thinking, and the leadership model. The practical viewpoint of how companies design strategy and organization from a knowledge viewpoint and then create and apply new knowledge under a dynamic environment has become important in the knowledge integration firm.

5. The Knowledge Integration Process

As mentioned in Chapter 1, the knowledge integration model is a corporate model that integrates diverse knowledge inside and outside the company resulting from dynamic changes in corporate (vertical and horizontal) boundaries. This knowledge integration model delivers two new insights to realize new product, services, and business models through the Japanese corporation's distinctive vertical value chain model and new win-win business models from the co-evolution model.

The knowledge integration process through the formation of networks inside and outside the company is at the heart of the knowledge integration model. Specifically, it integrates internal knowledge through in-house internal networks and external knowledge through a company's external networks (see Figure 9.5). With the knowledge integration model, corporate boundaries are transcended and new knowledge created through the formation of these networks inside and outside the company. In this book, innovation resulting from such knowledge integration processes is called "boundaries innovation". At the heart of the two features of boundaries innovation mentioned previously (the vertical value chain and co-evolution models) are the two new boundary conceptions of the creativity view and dialectic view (see Chapter 1).

5.1 *Innovation through the creativity and dialectic view*

The *creativity view* is a key factor in promoting a company's vertical integration. Japanese companies exploit this view to upgrade their path-dependent knowledge through vertical integration while absorbing new knowledge through coordination and collaboration arising from the external networks built with external partner companies and accelerating integration of the new knowledge and their own knowledge. The business models of Japan's electronics and communications equipment (Chapter 4), machine tools (Chapter 5) and mobile phone service (Chapter 6) sectors are prominent cases.

The lessons learned from Canon and Panasonic mentioned in Chapter 4, especially, are that since cutting-edge digital products require transfer and sharing of high-level tacit knowledge, the entire value chain should be unified (vertical integration) and creativity and efficiency should be synthesized by collaborating with the simultaneous progression of each of the R&D, production technology, manufacturing, and sales and marketing functions (boundaries "linkage and synchronization" in Figure 4.6). As mentioned in Chapter 4, vertical integration promotes the transfer and sharing of tacit knowledge and inspires employee creativity. Moreover, the concurrent operation and collaboration of each function is linked to the efficiency of speed to deliver solutions whenever issues arise and the optimization of product function and cost through the unification of design and production.

Meanwhile, we need to ask whether creativity can occur without the element of vertical integration. In exceptional cases, the answer is yes. The music distribution business of Apple's iTunes and iPod, and the Dell's PC were born out of a horizontally specialized industry structure. Nintendo's business model also resembles that of Apple (see Chapter 7), and Nintendo is a "fables" company specializing in research development, product planning, and sales and marketing activities.

Nevertheless, these businesses also include vertical integration elements. The business model for Apple's music distribution resembles that of DoCoMo's i-mode, and each stakeholder within a vertical value chain comprising content (music labels), Apple (coordinator of entire value chain and determiner of iPod product planning and architecture), and vendors (iPod design, manufacturing, and support) sustains a win-win relationship with loose vertical integration (conversely, the vertical value chain of Japan's mobile phone business is tightly integrated). Moreover, Dell simultaneously pursues the merits of efficiency through the vertical disintegration of business activity outsourcing and tightly knit coordination activities through virtual vertical integration utilizing ICT. Accordingly, the delivery of high quality business models such as Apple, Dell, and other requires the elements of tight coordination and collaboration among players in each business layer through virtual vertical integration, even in a horizontally specialized business structure.

One more new boundary conception, the *dialectic view*, promotes the building of a win-win co-evolution model among the stakeholders that comprise the vertical boundaries. i-mode, for example, built a win-win business model structure for vertical boundaries marked by content providers, communications carriers, and equipment vendors, creating a network externality effect (see Chapter 6), and Nintendo's game business also built a win-win business model for vertical boundaries comprising game software manufacturers, game machine manufacturers, and equipment vendors (see Chapter 7). The *dialectic view*, moreover, creates new products, services, and business models from industry-spanning co-evolution models and enables the expansion of horizontal boundaries. Examples include Japan's mobile phone carriers mentioned in Chapter 6, the DS/Wii-driven game business of Chapter 7, and the general trading company business model distinctive to Japanese companies, mentioned in Chapter 8. The case studies of co-evolution arising from the *dialectic view* are reported outside the Japanese mobile phone and game businesses in the US-focused IT sector including Microsoft, Cisco Systems, and Intel; the semiconductor sector including Taiwan's TSMC; and the retail sector including Wallmart (e.g., Gawer and Cusumano, 2002; Iansiti and Levien, 2004).

The creation of new business models through the co-existence and co-prosperity co-evolution models among stakeholders are arising from strategic action resulting from the corporate *dialectic view*. The *dialectic view* determines the corporate boundaries, and the co-evolution model spanning various industries becomes the core concept for creating the win-win business model.

The knowledge integration model does not simply involve producing differentiable technologies and services in-house, and outsourcing the rest. As observed in these cases, the characteristics of the knowledge integration model are to integrate the optimal knowledge to realize new strategies from dynamic collaboration transcending corporate boundaries, and create new product, service, and business models. The outstanding Japanese manufacturing sector promotes continuous operation management unifying R&D, production technology, production and sales within the company while proactively absorbing and integrating other companies' knowledge and investing in new products through joint development and strategic alliances. Moreover, the companies are building co-evolution models and win-win new business models through reciprocal core knowledge synergies arising from collaboration in various industries including mobile phones, games, and general trading. The knowledge integration model implements the best knowledge integration process from the viewpoint of innovation, or new knowledge creation. Here the foundation is the idea of synthesis considering the strategy views (creativity and dialectic) rather than prioritizing the efficiency view arising from the disintegration of the value chain.

Considered from the above viewpoint, the fundamental difference between the business models of Japanese and Western firms can be interpreted as a difference in strategy action priority based on the *creativity view* and *dialectic view* of nonefficiency conceptions. Meanwhile, Western firms that prioritize considerations of short-term profit and shareholder preference are seen to have a strong tendency to promote a horizontally specialized business model (this tendency is especially striking in the IT and digital industries) based mainly on the efficiency view. The advanced IT companies of Apple, Dell, Amazon, and Google, however, feature the simultaneous promotion of short-term profit acquisition and innovative activities through building virtual integration models activating coordinative and collaborative capabilities based on the creativity and dialectic views within the horizontally specialized industry structure.

5.2 *Open innovation versus closed innovation; vertical integration versus horizontal specialization*

In recent years, consultants, journalists, and others in the mass media have pointed out that the management of the vertical integration model based on closed innovation has been a key factor in the competitive decline of Japan's manufacturing industry. Although Japan's manufacturing industry is not proactively adopting the horizontally specialized business model in the same way as Taiwanese or U.S. companies, in recent years, it has been developing low cost and model products through commission to appropriate Electronic Manufacturing Services (EMS), and delivering them to newly developing countries as part of a global strategy. High-value-added merchandize requiring great technological expertise, however, goes through the commercialization process in part through vertical integration. In other words, business models that cause the *creative view* to function lead toward vertical integration of the business model. Meanwhile, if the efficiency view functions, there is a tendency to outsource. This kind of consistent vertical integration model for the Japanese manufacturing industry is building business models similar to those of South Korea's Samsung Electronics (mentioned later).

Management personnel at Japan's major electronics manufacturers have said the following about the vertical integration and horizontal specialization models.

Vertical integration is a means of focusing wholly on profit, and horizontal specialization is a means of earning reasonable profit. Horizontal specialization applies to product selection. In the future, it will also apply to ODM (Original Design Manufacturing from companies commissioned with the design and manufacture of other companies' brands) to outsource TV assembly. (Panasonic executive).[4]

Vertical integration is the foundation of the Japanese manufacturing industry. Japan's factories are mostly located within the same locations, with the buildings and offices of the manufacturing, design, research, and management divisions adjacent to one another. This is necessary to deal with all kinds of issues and problems. In recent years, however, EMS has been used to partially support the development of product features. (General Manager, Sharp).[5]

In product development, a number of cases exist of joint ventures with overseas manufacturers (including ODM and EMS) supporting

---

[4] See "In Sony and Panasonic versus Samsung, Why Aren't Sony and Panasonic Winning?"

[5] According to interviews by the author.

situations such as product features and price setting. There is a marked tendency for vertical integration to develop when new development elements have great business merits of scale, product outsourcing when new development elements are few but the market risk is great, and joint development with external vendors when new development elements are great but potential demand is uncertain. (Senior manager, NEC).[6]

This means that Japan's electronics companies are also active in flexible outsourcing flexible design and manufacture in response to conditions, and proactively absorb outstanding technologies from other companies while partially incorporating open innovation elements from closed innovation to promote integration with their own technologies (Shift to Knowledge Integration Model described in Figures 4.1 and 4.4 in Chapter 4).

Meanwhile, Taiwanese and other EMS manufacturers had been promoting cost leadership through mass production based on economies of scale and acquiring profits. In recent years, however, market changes have expanded and tastes in consumer goods shown a tendency toward diversification. The business model of mass production through EMS requires a rethink about the future. One of the objectives of strategy conversion for EMS businesses to enhance a product's value-added on the "smile curve" is as a method of shifting toward stronger R&D and enhancing a company's brand value. While grasping the importance of this strategy conversion, however, many of the current Taiwanese EMS companies devote themselves to manufacturing. The reason is that new product and technology developments actually carry risks.

Nevertheless, as mentioned in Chapter 4, the U.S. and Taiwanese EMS companies and the semiconductor foundry companies that have promoted horizontally specialized business models are all in the process of shifting from manufacturing to R&D in order to respond to technological changes and diversity of customer needs in recent years. At the same time, they are embedding elements of the

---

[6] Op, cit., 5

self-sufficiency principle from management to emphasize coordination with the modular organizations of external partners with individually separated functions. Taiwan's TSMC and other foundry companies not only target improved cost competitiveness in the same way as the EMS, but also drive support for enlarging interdependence with semiconductor designs and manufacturing processes alongside the micronization of LSI. Specifically, it comprises a change of foundry companies' strategy action to contribute proactively to design businesses. Moreover, the post-processing of manufacturing (including LSI packaging) that had previously been outsourced is being carried out beforehand, and the entire value chain, from semiconductor design to manufacturing, is capable of delivering full turnkey services to the customer. This involves embedding self-sufficiency elements similar to those of the EMS from the modular organizational form used up to that time.

The EMS and foundry companies, which are always subject to cost competitive pressure, have to enter high-value-added business domains that demand the *creativity view*, and bring about change in their own vertical boundaries in order to respond to market and technology changes. EMS and foundry companies have to coordinate more closely with external partners, and hone new knowledge and competence internally (full turnkey services including design skills and expertise) while promoting knowledge integration of their own and other companies' technologies. This thinking is also a stance of embedding within the company closed innovation self-sufficiency elements from previous open innovation thinking. Meanwhile, the organizational form involves embedding vertical integration elements within the corporate organization aimed at uniting design and manufacturing. This indicates the gradual tendency towards vertical change through the merging of design and manufacturing in the horizontally specialized business model (see Figure 4.4 in Chapter 4).

At the time of its founding, for example, the Taiwanese HTC (High Tech Computer Corporation) mainly undertook commissioned production of PDA products. Later, however, HTC shifted away from PDA manufacturing technology to focus on R&D

activities for PDA-related applied technologies. HTC needed large sums of investment to promote its R&D activities, but by investing profits obtained through commissioned production from brand manufacturers all over the world in R&D into new products and technologies, it has become a good example of success in expanding the value chain from manufacturing to R&D business. As a result, HTC now maintains a competitive edge in the smartphone market through joint development with Google and association with communications carriers.

The basic concept of the *knowledge integration firm* is also as a business entity that demonstrates the benefits of both closed and open innovation, and where a company's internal networks promote closed innovation while inter-corporate external networks (including customers) promote open innovation. U.S. and Taiwanese manufacturers are also targeting the knowledge integration-based firms, but as a point of departure, Japanese manufacturers are shifting from the vertical integration model, while U.S. and Taiwanese manufacturers are also shifting from the horizontal specialization model (see Figure 4.4 in Chapter 4).

6. Elements that Asian Companies Have Learned from Japanese Management

This section looks at how the *creativity view* and *dialectic view*, which form distinctive elements of the Japanese company's *knowledge integration model*, have been able to influence leading companies in Asian countries including South Korea and Taiwan. Drawing on numerous interviews and case studies, I would like to describe the kind of management elements that South Korean and Taiwanese companies, especially, have learned (and are still learning) from doing business with Japanese companies. The study elements that become clear from this survey analysis have two aspects: the *creativity view* of vertical integration, teamwork, and collaboration on the one hand, and the *dialectic view* of co-creation and co-evolution on the other.

9.6.1 *The creativity view, vertical integration, teamwork, and collaboration*

Japan's major consumer electronics and telecommunications device manufacturers have had extensive relationships with South Korean and Taiwanese companies for some time (See Table 9.1). South Korean company Samsung Electronics, which is now a leading global brand, is one example. Samsung absorbed vertical integration strategy expertise from Japanese companies through self-sufficiency encompassing development, production, and sales resulting from tie-ups with Japan's Sanyo Electric and NEC from the 1970s.[7] It strengthened the R&D system in line with Japanese-style original, competitive product development while studying Japan's quality control techniques (which result in the high quality of Japanese products) and teamwork through mall-group activities-problem-solving methods using task teams and cross-functional teams (CFTs). By studying the management techniques of Japanese companies, Samsung has promoted "creativity strengthening" technology strategies aimed at developing its own original products. Then Samsung built a global brand encompassing not only core technology such as DRAM semiconductors and liquid crystal displays, but also completed digital consumer electronics products (set products), especially mobile

---

[7] Recently, a Japanese business magazine special noted the following with regard to Samsung's technology development in an article entitled "In Sony and Panasonic versus Samsung, Why Aren't Sony and Panasonic Winning?": "Japanese products from the likes of Panasonic and Sony are taken to the laboratories and the design and development departments of Samsung Electronics and dismantled, screw by screw and clasp by clasp. Engineers understand the features, deficiencies, and merits of each product and their components as if they were their own. Taking the optimized designs of the Japanese manufacturers as its starting point, Samsung reverse-engineers mechanisms and functions from the product's architecture, and designs and completes its products. If it were simple imitation, this would be the end of it, but here Samsung is different. Samsung's feature is that after analyzing the functional elements, it divides the functions for regionally localized product development. The reporter on this magazine dubbed this "Reverse-flow design originating in imitation; in other words, reverse engineering."

phones. The basis of this kind of Samsung technology strategy is the pursuit of product concepts and technology creativity through consistent vertical integration, ranging from development and production of elemental technology and parts to that of products (sets). This concept shares numerous aspects with the technology strategies of Japanese companies such as Matsushita Electric, Sharp, and Canon.

The recent case of LG Electronics promoting a vertical integration-type business model similar to that of Samsung involved a mobile phone joint development project with NTT DoCoMo. DoCoMo (in charge of mobile phone marketing, product planning, technology specifications, and quality management) and LG Electronics (in charge of mobile phone design and manufacturing) studied intensely. LG Electronics recognized the importance of building a value chain from a series of vertical integrations comprising product planning, development, production, testing, and quality management through joint development with other companies, while studying the level of completion of DoCoMo's mobile phone technology specifications and the rigor of quality control (see Table 9.1).

Meanwhile, Samsung and LG Electronics have gone beyond self-sufficiency through total vertical integration to promote the building of the *knowledge integration model* through collaboration with competitors and companies in related areas. They have achieved this by means of a complementary model of horizontal integrated architecture (mentioned above) responding to requirements.

As in South Korea, the Taiwanese companies (IT and telecommunications equipment vendors) that have built up experience of jointly developing new products with Japan's major consumer electronics and telecommunications equipment manufacturers are learning a great deal from the challenge of realizing the originality and differentiation of Japanese product functions together with their high quality and degree of completion (see Table 9.1). Japan's outstanding high-tech companies believe that high performance, high quality, and high functionality should co-exist with the contradictory elements of miniaturization and low weight and cost. The high functionality and quality corresponds, for example, to the incremental innovations formed through improvements to individual modules in the product interior, while low cost involves incremental innovation resulting from improvements to production technology. Meanwhile, high function, miniaturization, and low weight are elements of product differentiation through original technologies. Architectural innovation realizing these three elements can come about, for example, by merging new and existing modules with original interfaces among individual modules (Henderson and Clark, 1990). The mobile handsets and single lens reflex digital cameras comprised of the most advanced technologies involve a large element of this architectural innovation.

Meanwhile, Chunghwa Telecom Corp., a leading company in Taiwan's telecom field, was privatized in 1996 as the fixed telecommunications business was liberalized. Chunghwa Telecom learned from the cases of NTT, which preceded it on the road to privatization (Japan liberalized its fixed telecommunications business in 1985), and other communications carriers' experience in several developed countries while adhering to the four principles:

1. Structural reform targeting true customer satisfaction,
2. A switch toward network collaboration business,
3. Internationalization including technology cooperation, sales cooperation, and franchises,
4. Promotion of corporate social responsibility under the slogan "change yourself before change is anticipated."

Network collaboration management, especially, maintains vertically integrated business activities within the company while promoting the building of mixed, cross-functional teams inside and outside the company and implementing the *knowledge integration model* of management that aims to integrate knowledge distributed inside and outside the company. This management system shares numerous aspects of its techniques with Japan's NTT, NTT DoCoMo, and KDDI (see Table 9.1).

Chunghwa Telecom is dynamically promoting mixed teams and small-group activities within the company, aiming for high revenue and profit arising from originality, product quality, and high functionality combined with a shift from volume to quality. It is also establishing in-house systems forming teams responding to project requirements while flexibly implementing members' job rotation. Chunghwa Telecom is, moreover, dynamically promoting collaboration through strategic alliances with Japanese companies pioneering fiber-optic communications technology. The recent introduction of Fiber To The Home (FTTH) devices from Japan's Sumitomo Electronic Network Inc. is an example of this.

As shown above, South Korean and Taiwanese companies in the consumer electronics, telecommunications device, and telecom fields are studying features of Japanese companies, aiming to acquire *creativity view* thinking, build value chains through vertical integration, and build flexible teamwork, and putting them into practice with the aim of collaborating inside and outside the company.

9.6.2 *The dialectic view, co-creation, and co-evolution*

The archetypal example of building a win-win model through co-evolution is that of a mobile phone business. Mobile phone carriers such as Chunghwa Telecom and Far Eastone (merged with KG Telecom) are endeavoring to disseminate and promote the 3G service. The key to accomplishing this is a content service. Taiwan's communications carriers are seeking to build win-win relationships with mobile phone carriers, content providers (CPs), mobile handset manufacturers and others by learning from services such as Japan's i-mode. Currently, i-mode's international branch is providing services through nine communications carriers throughout the world. In Asia, Taiwan's FarEasTone, Hong Kong's Hutchison Telephone Company Ltd., and the Philippines' Smart Communications Inc. are providing news, finance, sports, music, entertainment, games, and other content through i-mode licenses contracted with DoCoMo. These communications carriers are aiming to build win-win business models in their own countries that resemble those in Japan.

The content providers in Asian countries, moreover, are beginning to cooperate with Japanese content providers, absorb mobile phone content creation and distribution expertise, and take initiatives toward success in the new content business. For example, Taiwan's JoyMaster and Japan's g-mode CPs have begun to cooperate and distribute game software to Chunghwa Telecom. On the mobile phone handset procurement side, moreover, DoCoMo and KT Freetel (KTF) are undertaking initiatives for joint procurement of LG Electronics' 3G mobile phone. Both DoCoMo and KTF mainly target customers who choose handsets from the viewpoint of ease of use and refined design in the Japanese and South Korean markets. They selected LG's 3G "Wine Phone" handset. The joint procurement was implemented as part of a joint handset procurement project of the Business & Technology Cooperation Committee, established between DoCoMo and KTF. Conexus Mobile Alliance, which promotes international roaming and cooperation in the corporate services field (related to the above-mentioned horizontal integrated architecture in Asia) is also contributing to the co-creation and co-evolution of the mobile phone business in various Asian countries.

In the above manner, Asian communications carriers are learning from DoCoMo's win-win i-mode business model through licensing contracts and strategic alliances (see Table 9.1). This win-win business concept is promoting the building of dialectical growth models (the above-mentioned business ecosystems) through co-creation and co-evolution among partners. The *dialectic view* aimed at the success of business models that transcend industries (communications carriers, content providers, and mobile phone manufacturers) and national borders is the starting point of the mobile phone business' success. The business concept of Taiwan's semiconductor foundry TSMC, mentioned in the case analysis above, also has the building of a business ecosystem for growth through collaboration with customers and partners as a strategic objective, giving it many points in common with Japan's mobile phone businesses. Again, Samsung's and Sony's recent joint development of liquid crystal panels through a strategy of "competitive cooperation" is promoting the co-creation and co-evolution of new markets through collaboration with partners.

Thus, one of the elements that Asian companies have learned from Japanese management is to challenge issues aimed at creativity and originality to realize new technologies and product concepts. The vertically integrated organizational system comprising the intellectual capital to achieve their aims and the *knowledge integration model* arising from teamwork and collaboration spanning the company internally and externally are important lessons. The second aspect is developing management to realize win-win business ecosystems. This is a lesson in industry co-evolution arising from corporate dialectic thought and action through co-creation with partners and customers.

7. Implications and Conclusions

Japanese companies are globally competitive in specific high-tech fields. They are building original *knowledge integration models,* and producing the vertical value chain model and co-evolution model. These models differ from those of Western management, which emphasize specific core competences and horizontally specialized business models. The Japanese models are also creating the *strategic innovation capability,* which can synthesize strategic innovation (exploration) and incremental innovation (exploitation), as *knowledge integration firms* that dialectically integrate knowledge within and outside the company based on value chains and vertical integration of the industrial structure. This can happen because of the background of the knowledge integration process existing through the formation of dynamic and networked SCs based on Japan's corporate tacit knowledge.

In contrast to the management styles of European and American companies, Japanese companies stand out for an emphasis on tacit over explicit knowledge. The Western management style prioritizing the re-use of explicit knowledge focusing on short-term profit differs from the Japanese style that emphasizes taking the time to create and share tacit knowledge from a long-term viewpoint. Effective sharing of tacit knowledge is promoted through a shared corporate organizational culture and sense of values. In companies where these elements are widely shared within the organization, employees become able to share tacit knowledge effectively, and this effective sharing in turn promotes the creation of organizational knowledge in Japanese companies. In fact, high-performing Japanese companies have devoted a significant amount of energy to spreading their own corporate culture and values based on the philosophy of their founders. The *creativity view* and *dialectic view* rooted in Japanese companies' distinctive culture and shared values create and accumulate tacit knowledge through vertical integration, promote teamwork, collaboration, and co-creation and co-evolution, and influence the management of Asian companies in South Korea, Taiwan, and elsewhere.

This book has demonstrated the *knowledge integration dynamics* framework for companies to constantly build new-concept market positions (realizing new products and businesses) aimed at achieving strategic innovation for the future, and acquire the dynamic practical knowledge to realize this. *Knowledge integration dynamics* becomes a key issue that synthesizes the aspect of incremental innovation for a company to adapt to environmental change with the achievement of business creation for the future (strategic innovation) by forming deliberate new market-position concepts.

Companies must adapt to environmental changes while taking a dynamic view of strategy arising from *strategic innovation capability*, or constantly acquire new, competitively dominant positions generating their own environmental change, especially in high-tech fields where environmental change is intense and new products and services must be continually introduced to the market. To achieve this, the corporate activities must mutually augment and strengthen the companies' targeted market position and own dynamic practical knowledge, while forming and executing strategy. The essence of strategy is to have a strategic view of dynamically synthesizing markets (external) and organizations (internal), rather than a dichotomous relationship.

Recently, the development of new products and services in the high-tech sector has necessitated the integration of different technologies. Previously, technological innovation closely followed and developed from specialist knowledge, but with the new product development from unprecedented new ideas, numerous cases have arisen where the technology of one sector merges with that of another. A key issue for practitioners is how to integrate diverse, heterogeneous knowledge (how to integrate knowledge of different technology sectors perceived from a technological viewpoint). As mentioned in Chapter 1, moreover, distributed knowledge is embedded in spatiotemporally distributed strategic communities (SCs). To integrate, individually held knowledge must transcend SC boundaries to accumulate in networks. Put another way, it is necessary to link distributed SCs in networks, and deeply embed the knowledge distributed in each SC in those networks. In terms of social network theory, SCs can be seen as practitioner cliques (assembling closely linked actors) and the ties are linking SCs to one another on a network.

An important aspect here is practitioners' knowledge architectural thinking mentioned in Chapter 1. Practitioners must build network relationships while maintaining an awareness of knowledge architecture (vertical integrated, horizontal integrated, see Tables 1.1 and 1.2, and linkage relationship, see Figure 1.7, architecture).

Practitioners who commit to multiple SCs play a central role oriented to knowledge integration linking SC to SC. To integrate heterogeneous knowledge, practitioners must deeply grasp and share this knowledge (knowledge sharing), tacitly and explicitly, in each SC, and the shared knowledge must then transcend the SC boundaries to deeply embed in a network. This deep embedding factor is essential. The sharing of tacit knowledge, especially, requires sharing contexts deeply on a network and linking SCs through strong ties. The cases of new product and business development in this book are created by businesspeople inside and outside the company, including customers, linking SCs with strong ties (tightly coupled networks), sharing by deeply embedding heterogeneous knowledge, and creating new knowledge by forming knowledge and technological integration of new products and services. This building of strong-tied SC networks is key to the integration of heterogeneous knowledge, and practitioners must consciously and deliberately consider the relationships of such ties. This is the thinking of linkage relationship architecture building deep embedded networks.

According to social network theory, meanwhile, weak ties have the potential to form a bridge to new, heterogeneous information (Granovetter, 1973). Moreover, Burt's "structural hole" (1992) indicates that weak ties with structural holes make it highly likely that actors can access new information and acquire new business opportunities. The practitioners in these case studies in this book sense the core knowledge of numerous external partners through weak-tie SC formation (loosely-coupled networks), and seek out the best partners to integrate core technology aimed at product and business development.

For optimal organizational design, companies require the advance of new business development through the thinking of linkage relationship architecture. This combines the building of both strong-tied, tightly coupled and weak-tied, loosely coupled SC networks. Practitioners must then promote paradoxical management by continuously synthesizing (consciously and deliberately) the relationships between these two kinds of ties. While maintaining strong ties, they also form weak-tied networks, and absorb and integrate heterogeneous knowledge by bridging the structural hole in a timely fashion. According to Watts and Strogatz (1998), the small world network also confers practical insights into how the organizational design for accessing value-laded knowledge distributed throughout the world and creating SC networks aimed at knowledge integration (new business) can swiftly and efficiently become architecture.

Moreover, the design ideas of vertical and horizontal integrated architecture knowledge are essential elements of strategy concepts for a company deciding whether to build a vertically integrated or horizontally specialized business model and value chain, or to go with a hybrid type knowledge integration model. Recently, the emergence of smart phones and e-books (such as Kindle and the iPad) from Apple, Google, and Amazon and the development of Nintendo's game machines have led the drive to build virtual vertical integration value chains and business models from vertical integrated architecture comprising a company's own core competence plus those of the ODM or EMS. Moreover, joint development through open innovation with other companies in the same industry and knowledge integration through the horizontal integrated architecture of strategic alliances across industries aimed at expanding new business have also become important.

These kinds of knowledge architecture, comprising vertical integrated, horizontal integrated, and linkage relationship architecture, must be appropriately built and rebuilt depending on the situation with regard to strategic measures targeted by the company and implementation processes. Recently, selection and concentration of one's own core competences and the use of EMS and ODM have become mainstream in the IT and electronics industries centered on Euro-American and Taiwanese companies. Every cost-oriented "volume strategy" (low-price product strategy) in Chinese market exists against this backdrop. A successful volume strategy is one that raises brand power at a stroke.

Nevertheless, Japan's manufacturing sector and South Korea's Samsung Electronics are positioned around the axis of vertical integration type business models, and outsourcing to EMS or ODMs is implemented as appropriate. Japanese companies and Samsung Electronics exist against a backdrop of the *creativity view* and strategy view, which emphasize high-function, high-quality products with distinctive qualities. The thinking of the *creativity view* drives the formation of business models through vertical integration (including that of Nintendo and Apple), while that of the efficiency view has come to accelerate business models based on the vertical disintegration that is horizontal specialization. Accordingly, companies must plan whether to optimize strategy by specializing or synthesizing the creativity and efficiency views, depending on strategic objectives (including customer needs, global markets, and product features).

In this book, I have focused on in-depth case studies of leading Japanese companies to demonstrate the *knowledge integration dynamics* framework for companies to continually build new concept market positions and acquire new dynamic practical knowledge aimed at achieving future innovations. Innovative companies must deliberately implement the spiral knowledge integration process to continue creating their own new markets, and integrate internal and external knowledge inside and outside the company. In the knowledge society of the 21st century, the diverse knowledge (including various ideas and concepts, not technology alone) held by people is a new competitive capability, and becomes the creative source of products, services, and business models that have value for the customer. I consider that the framework of the knowledge integration firm confers new, value-laden insights for numerous practitioners aimed at achieving continuous innovation.

Bibliography

Abernathy, W. (1978). *The Productivity Dilemma*. Baltimore: Johns Hopkins University Press.

Afuah, A. (2001). Dynamic boundaries of the firm: Are firms better off being vertically integrated in the face of a technological change? *Academy of Management Journal*, 44(6), 1211–1228.

Afuah, N. and Bahram, N. (1995). The hypercube of innovation. *Research Policy*, 24, 51–76.

Ahuja, M., and Carley, K. (1999). Network structure in virtual organizations. *Organization Science*, 10(6), 741–757.

Albert, R., and Barabasi, A. (2000). Topology of evolving networks: local events and universality. *Physical Review Letters*, 85(24), 5234–5237.

Allen, T.J. (1977). *Managing the Flow of Technology*. Cambridge, MA: MIT Press.

Amabile, T., and Khaire, M. (2008). Creativity and the role of the leader. *Harvard Business Review*, October, 100–109.

Amasaka, K. (2004). Development of Science TQM, a new principle of quality management: effectiveness of strategic stratified task team at Toyota. *International Journal of Production Research*, 42(17), 3691–706.

Amburgey, T., William, K., and Barnett, P. (1993). Resetting the clock: the dynamics of organizational change and failure. *Administrative Science Quarterly*, 38(1), 51–73.

Anderson, P. (1999). Complexity theory and organization science. *Organization Science*, 10(2), 216–232.

Aristotle (350BCE/1980). *The Nicomachean Ethics.* (D. Ross, Trans.). Oxford: Oxford University Press.

Aston, W. (2006). *NIHONGI: Chronicles of Japan from the Earliest Times to A.D. 697.* New York, US: Cosimo Classics.

Auerswald, P. and Branscomb, L. (2003). Valleys of Death and Darwinian Seas: financing the invention to innovation transition in the United States. *The Journal of Technology Transfer,* 28(3–4), 433–451.

Balakrishnan, S., and Wernerfelt, B. (1986). Technical change, competition and vertical integration. *Strategic Management Journal,* 7, 347–359.

Baldwin, Y., and Clark, B. (2000). *Design Rules, Vol. 1: The Power of Moduarity.* Cambridge, MA: MIT Press.

Barabasi, A. (2002). *Linked: The New Science of Networks.* Cambridge, MA: Perseus Books Group.

Barney, J., and Hansen, M. (1994). Trustworthiness as a Source of Competitive Advantage. *Strategic Management Journal,* 15, Special Issue (Winter, 1994), 175–190.

Barney, J. (1991). Firm resources and sustained competitive advantage. *Journal of Management,* 17(3), 99–120.

Bateson, G. (1979). *Mind and Nature.* New York: Brockman, Inc.

Baum, J.A.C., Rowley, T.J., and Shipilov, A.V. (2004). The small world of Canadian capital markets: statistical mechanics of investment bank syndicate networks. *Canadian Journal of Administrative Sciences,* 21(4), 307–325.

Benner, M., and Tushman, M. (2003). Exploitation, exploration, and process management: the productivity dilemma revisited. *Academy of Management Review,* 28(2), 238–256.

Benson, J. (1977). Organization: a dialectical view. *Administrative Science Quarterly,* 22, 221–242.

Boland, R., and Tenkasi, R. (1995). Perspective making and perspective taking in communities of knowing. *Organization Science,* 6(4), 350–364.

Bookchin, M. (1990). *The Philosophy of Social Ecology: Essays on Dialectical Naturalism.* US: Black Rose Books Ltd.

Braha, D., and Bar-Yam, Y. (2004). Information flow structure in large-scale product development organizational networks. *Journal of Information Technology,* 19(4), 234–244.

Brown, J.S., and Duguid, P. (1998). Organizing knowledge. *California Management Review,* 40(3), 90–111.

Brown, J.S., and Duguid, P. (2001). Knowledge and organization: a social-practice perspective. *Organization Science,* 12(6), 198–213.

Brown, S.L., and Eisenhardt, K.M. (1995), product development: past research, present findings, and future directions. *Academy of Management Review,* 20(2), 343–378.

Brown, S.L., and Eisenhardt, K.M. (1997). The art of continuous change: linking complexity theory and time-paced evolution in relemtless shifting organizations. *Administrative Science Quarterly,* 42, 1–34.

Burgelman, R., and Sayles, R. (1986). *Inside Corporate Innovation: Strategy, Structure, and Managerial Skills.* US: Free Press.

Burgelman, R. (1983). A process model of internal corporate venturing in the diversified major firm. *Administrative Science Quarterly*, 28(2) 223–244.

Burgelman, R. (1984). Designs for corporate entrepreneurship in established firms. *California Management Review*, XXVI(3), 154–166.

Burgelman, R., and Grove, A. (2001). *Strategy Is Destiny: How Strategy–Making Shapes a Company's Future*, US: Free Press.

Burgelman, R., Christensen, C., Wheelwright, S., and Maidique, M. (2003). *Strategic Management of Technology and Innovation.* US: McGraw Hill.

Burt, S. (1992). *Structural Holes: The Social Structure of Competition.* Cambridge, MA and London: Harvard University Press.

Burt, R. (1997). 'The contingent value of social capital. *Administrative Science Quarterly*, 42(2), 339–365.

Cambell, A., and Park, R. (2005). *The Growth Gamble.* US and Canada: Nicholas Brealey Publishing.

Capra, F. (1996). *The Web of Life: A New Scientific Understanding of Living Systems.* New York: Anchor Books.

Carlile, P. (2002). A pragmatic view of knowledge and boundaries: boundary objects in new product development. *Organization Science*, 13(4), 442–455.

Carlile, P. (2004). Transferring, translating, and transforming: an integrative framework for managing knowledge across boundaries. *Organization Science*, 15(5), 555–568.

The Kojiki: Records of Ancient Matters. (B.H. Chamberlain, Trans.). Tokyo: Tuttle Publishing.

Chen, C., and Sewell, G. (1996) Strategies for technological development in South Korea and Taiwan: the case of semiconductors. *Research Policy*, 25, 759–783.

Chesbrough, H. (2003). *Open Innovation.* Boston, MA: Harvard Business School Press.

Chesbrough, H. (2006). *Open Business Models: How to Thrive in the New Innovation Landscape.* Boston MA: Harvard Business School Press.

Chiang, J. (1990). Management of national technology programs in a newly industrialized country — Taiwan. *Technovation*, 10, 531–554.

Christensen, C., and Bower, L. (1996). Customer power, strategic investment, and the failure of leading firms. *Strategic Management Journal*, 17, 197–218.

Christensen, C.M. (1997). *The Innovator's Dilemma: When New Technologies Cause Great Firms to Fail.* Boston, MA: Harvard Business School Press.

Christensen, C.M., and Raynor, M. (2003). *The Innovator's Solution.* Boston, MA: Harvard Business School Press.

Christensen, M., Raynor, M., and Verlinden, M. (2001). Skate to where the money will be. *Harvard Business Review*, 79(10), 72–83.

Clark, B. (1985). The interaction of design hierarchies and market concepts in technological evolution. *Research Policy*, 14(2), 235–251.

Coase, R.H. (1993). The nature of the firm: Influence. In O.E. Williamson, and S.G. Winter, (Eds.), *The Nature of the Firm* (61–74). New York: Oxford University Press.

Cohen, D., and Prusak, L. (2000). *In Good Company: How Social Capital Makes Organizations Work*. Boston, MA: Harvard Business School Press.

Cole, R., and Cole, S. (2007). *Social Stratification in Science*. Chicago: University of Chicago Press.

Coleman, J. (1988). Social capital in the creation of human capital. *American Journal of Sociology*, 94, 95–120.

Como, M. (2007). *Shotoku: Ethnicity, Ritual and Violence in the Japanese Buddhist Tradition*. USA: Oxford University Press.

Cook, S., and Brown. J. (1999). Bridging epistemologies: the generative dance between organizational knowledge and organizational knowing. *Organization Science*, 10(2), 381–400.

Cramton, C. (2001). The mutual knowledge problem and its consequences for dispersed collaboration. *Organization Science*, 12(3), 346–371.

Das, T.K., and Teng, B. (2000) Instabilities of strategic alliances: An internal tensions perspective. *Organization Science*, 11(1), 77–101.

Davila, T., Epstein, M., and Shelton, R. (2006). *Making Innovation Work*. US: Wharton School Publishing.

Day, G., and Schoemaker, J. (2005). Scanning the Periphery. *Harvard Business Review*, 135–148.

Dewar, R., and Dutton, E. (1986). The adoption of radical and incremental innovations: an empirical analysis. *Management Science*, 32(11), 1422–1453.

Drucker, P. (2004). *Management Challenges for the 21st Century*. US: Harper Business.

Dyer, J., and Hatch, N. (2004). Using supplier networks to learn faster. *Sloan Management Review*, 45(3) 57–63.

Eisenhardt, K., and Brown, S. (1998). Time pacing: competing in market that won's stand still. *Harvard Business Review*, 59–69.

Eisenhardt, K., and Martine, J. (2000). Dynamic capabilities: what are they?. *Strategic Management Journal*, 21(10–11), 1105–1121.

Eisenhardt, K., and Sull, D. (2001). Strategy as simple rules. *Harvard Business Review*, 79, 106–116.

Faust, K. (1997). Centrality in affiliation networks. *Social Networks*, 19, 157–191.

Ferguson, C. (1990). Computers and the coming of the US Keiretsu. *Harvard Business Review*, 68(4), 55–70.

Fine, H. (1998). *Clock Speed: Winning Industry Control in the Age of Temporary Advantage*. US: Perseus Books.

Fine, H (2000). Clock speed-based strategies for supply chain design. *Production and Operations Management*, 9(3), 213–221.

Florida, R., and Kenny, M. (1990). Silicon valley and route 128 won't save us. *California Management Review*, 33, 68–88.

Florida, R., and Kenny, M. (1991). Should the US abandon computer manufacturing?. *Harvard Business Review*, 140–161.

Floyd, W., and Wooldridge, B. (1999). Knowledge creation and social networks in corporate entrepreneurship: the renewal of organizational capability. *Entrepreneurship Theory and Practice*, 23(3), 123–142.

Galbraith, J.R. (1973). *Designing Complex Organizations*. Reading, MA: Addison-Wesley.

Galbraith, J.R., and Nathanson, D.A. (1978). *Strategy Implementation: The Role of Structure and Process*. St Paul, MN: West Publishing.

Garcia, R., and Calantone, R. (2002). A critical look at technological innovation typology and innovativeness terminology: a literature review. *Journal of Product Innovation Management*, 19, 110–132.

Gawer, A., and Cusmano, M.A. (2004). *Platform Leadership*. Boston, MA: Harvard Business School Publishing.

Gersick, J. (1994). Pacing strategic change: the case of a new venture. *Academy of Management Journal*, 37, 9–45.

Giddens, A. (1984). *The Constitution of Society*. Berkeley, CA: University of California Press.

Giddens, A., and Pierson, C. (1998). *Conversation with Anthony Giddens: Making Sense of Modernity*. Oxford: Blackwell Publishers Ltd.

Gilder, G. (1988). The revitalization of everything: the law of the microcosm. *Harvard Business Review*, 66(2), 49–61.

Glasmeier, A. (1991). Technological discontinuities and flexible production networks: the case of Switzerland and the world watch industry. *Research Policy*, 20, 469–485.

Goold, M., and Campbell, A. (2002). *Designing Effective Organizations: How to Create Structured Networks*. US: Jossey-Bass.

Govindarajan, V., and Trimble, C. (2005). *Ten Rules for Strategic Innovations*. Boston, MA: Harvard Business School Press.

Graebner, M. (2004). Momentum and serendipity: how acquired leaders create value in the integration of high-tech firms *Strategic Management Journal*, 25(8/9), 751–777.

Granovetter, M. (1973). The strength of weak ties. *American Journal of Sociology*, 78(6), 1360–80.

Grant, R. (1996). Prospering in dynamically competitive environments: organizational capability as knowledge integration. *Organization Science*, 7, 375–378.

Grant, R. (1997). The knowledge-based view of the firm: implications for management practice. *Long Range Planning*, 30(3), 450–454.

Grant, R., and Baden-Fuller, C. (1995). A knowledge-based theory of inter-firm collaboration. *Academy of Management Best Paper Proceedings*, 38, 17–21.

Greenwood, R., and Hinings, C. (1993). Understanding strategic change: the contribution of archetypes. *Academy of Management Review*, 36(5), 1052–1081.

Hagel III, J., and Brown, J.S. (2005). Productive friction. *Harvard Business Review*, 83(2), 139–145.

Hamel, G. (1996) Strategy as revolution. *Harvard Business Review*, July–August, 69–82.

Hamel, G. (2000). *Leading the Revolution*. Boston, MA: Harvard Business School Press.

Hamel, G., and Prahalad, C.K. (1989) Strategic intent. *Harvard Business Review*, 67(3), 139–148.

Hamel, G. and Prahalad, C.K. (1993). Strategy as stretch and leverage. *Harvard Business Review*, 71(2), 75–84.

Hamel, G., and Prahalad, C.K. (1994). *Competing for the Future*. Boston, MA: Harvard Business School Press.

Hargadon, A. (2003). *How Breakthroughs Happen: The Surprising Truth About How Companies Innovate*. Boston, MA: Harvard Business School Press.

Harrigan, R. (1984). Formulating vertical integration strategies. *Academy of Management Review*, 9(4), 638–652.

He, Z., and Wong, P. (2004). Exploration vs. exploitation: an empirical test of the ambidexterity hypothesis. *Organization Science*, 15(4), 481–494.

Hegel, J., and Singer, M. (1999). Unbundling the corporation. *Harvard Business Review*, 77(2), March–April, 133–141.

Heller, T. (1990). Loosely coupled systems for corporate entrepreneurship: imaging and managing the innovation project/host organization interface. *Entrepreneurship, Theory and Practice*, 24(2), 25–31.

Henderson, R., and Clark, K. (1990). Architectural innovation: the reconfiguration of existing product technologies and the failure of established firms. *Administrative Science Quarterly*, 35, 9–30.

Hill, C., and Rothaermel, F. (2003). The performance of incumbent firms in the face of radical technological innovation. *Academy of Management Review*, 28(2), 257–247.

Hill, L., and Hoskisson, E. (1987). Strategy and structure in the multiproduct firm. *Academy of Management Review*, 12, 331–341.

Hippel, E. (1998). Economics of product development by users: the impact of "Sticky" local information. *Management Science*, 44(5), 629–644.

Holland, J. (1975). *Adaption in Natural and Artificial Systems*. US: University of Michigan Press.

Howell, J., and Higgins, C. (1990). Champions of technological innovation. *Administrative Science Quarterly*, 35, 317–341.

Huston, L., and Sakkab, N. (2006). Connect and develop inside Procter & Gamble's new model for innovation. *Harvard Business Review*, 84(3), 58–66.

Iansiti, M., and Levien, R. (2004). *The Keystone Advantage: What the New Dynamics of Business Ecosystems Mean for Strategy, Innovation, and Sustainability*. Boston, MA: Harvard Business School Press.

Insead, D., and Eisenhardt, K. (2001). Architecutural innovation and modular corporate forms. *Academy of Management Journal*, 44, 1229–1249.

Jelinek, M., and Schoonhoven, B. (1990). *The Innovation Marathon: Lessons from High Technology Firms*. Oxford, UK: Basil Blackwell Inc.

Johansson, F. (2004). *The Medici Effect*. Boston, MA: Harvard Business School Press.

Kanter, R. (1983). *The Change Masters*. New York: Simons & Schuster.

Kaplan, S., Murray. F., and Henderson, R. (2003). Discontinuities and senior management: assessing the role of recognition in pharmaceutical firm response to biotechnology. *Industrial and Corporate Change*, 12(4), 203–233.

Karmin, S., and Mitchell, W. (2000). Path-Dependent and path-breaking change: reconfiguring business resources following acquisitions in the US medical sector, 1978–1995. *Strategic Management Journal*, 21(11), 1061–1081.

Katz, R., and Allen, T. (1982). Investigating the Not Invented Here (NIH) syndrome: a look at the performance, tenure, and communication patterns of 50 R&D project groups. *R&D Management*, 12(1) 7–12.

Kauffman, A. (1995). *At Home in the Universe: The Search for Laws of Self-organization and Complexity*. London: Viking.

Kawai, H. (2003). *Mythology and Japanese Mind* (in Japanese), Iwanami, Tokyo, Japan.

Kim, W.C., and Mauborgne, R. (2005). *Blue Ocean Strategy*. Boston, MA: Harvard Business School Press.

King, A., and Tucci, L. (2002). Incumbent entry into new market niches: the role of experience and managerial choice in the creation of dynamic capabilities. *Management Science*, 48(2), 171–187.

Klein, B. (1988). Vertical integration as organizational ownership: The Fisher-Body-General motors relationship revisited. *Journal of Law and Economic Organization*, 4, 199–213.

Kodama M., and Ohira, H. (2005), Customer value creation through customer-as-innovator approach-case study of development of video processing LSI. *International Journal of Innovation and Learning*, 2(1), 175–185.

Kodama, M. (2001), Creating new business through strategic community management. *International Journal of Human Resource Management*, 11(6), 1062–1084.

Kodama, M. (2002). Transforming an old economy company through strategic communities. *Long Range Planning*, 35(4), 349–365.

Kodama, M. (2003). Strategic innovation in traditional big business. *Organization Studies*, 24(2), 235–268.

Kodama, M. (2004). Strategic community-based theory of firms: case study of dialectical management at NTT Docomo. *Systems Research and Behavioral Science*, 21(6), 603–634.

Kodama, M. (2005). Knowledge creation through networked strategic communities: case studies on new product development in Japanese companies. *Long Range Planning*, 38(1), 27–49.

Kodama, M. (2007a). *The Strategic Community-Based Firm*. UK: Palgrave, Macmillan.

Kodama, M. (2007b). *Knowledge Innovation — Strategic Management as Practice*. UK: Edward Elgar Publishing.

Kodama, M. (2007c). *Project-Based Organization in the Knowledge-Based Society*. UK: Imperial College Press.

Kodama, M. (2007d). Innovation through boundary managing — Case of Matsushita Electric Reforms. *Technovation*, 27(1–2) 15–29.

Kodama, M. (2007e). Innovation and knowledge creation through leadership-based strategic community: case study on high-tech company in Japan. *Technovation*, 27(3), 115–132.

Kodama, M. (2008). *New Knowledge Creation Through ICT Dynamic Capability: Creating Knowledge Communities Using Broadband*. USA: Information Age Publishing.

Kogut, B., and Zander, U. (1992). Knowledge of the firm, combinative capabilities and the replication of technology. *Organization Science*, 5(2), 383–397.

Kuratko, F., Montagno, V., and Hornsby, S. (1990). Developing an intrapreneurial assessment instrument for an effective corporate entrepreneurial environment. *Strategic Management Journal*, 11, 49–58.

Lampel, J., and Bhalla, A. (2007). Let's get natural: the discourse of community and the problem of transferring practices in knowledge management. *Management Decision*, 45, 1069–1082.

Lave, J. (1998). *Cognition in Practice*. Cambridge, UK: Cambridge University Press.

Lave, J., and Wenger, E. (1990). *Situated Learning: Legitimate Peripheral Participation*. Cambridge, UK: Cambridge University Press.

Lawrence, P., and Lorsch, J. (1967). *Organization and Environments: Managing Differentiation and Integration*. Cambridge, MA: Harvard Business School Press.

Lei, D., Hitt, M., and Goldhar, J. (1996). Advanced manufacturing technology: organizational design and strategic flexibility. *Organization Studies*, 17(3), 501–523.

Leifer, R., McDermott, M., O'Connor, C., Peters, S., Rice, M., and Veryzer, W. (2000). *Radical Innovation: How Mature Companies Can Outsmart Upstarts*. Harvard Business School Press.

Leonard-Barton, D. (1992). Core capabilities and core rigidities: a paradox in managing new product development. *Strategic Management Journal*, 13(8), 111–125.

Leonard-Barton, D. (1995). *Wellsprings of Knowledge: Building and Sustaining the Sources of Innovation*. Boston, MA: Harvard Business School Press.

Levin, S. (1999). *Fragile Dominion*. US: Perseus Publishing.

Levinthal, D. (1991). Organizational adaptation and environmental selection-interrelated processes of change. *Organization Science*, 2(1), 140–145.

Levinthal, D. (1997). Adaptation on rugged landscapes. *Management Science*, 43(7), 934–950.

Levinthal, D., and March, G (1993). The myopia of learning. *Strategic Management Journal*, 14, 95–112.

Levinthal, D., and March, G. (1988). Organizational learning. *Annual Review of Sociology*, 14, 319–340.

Lichtenberg, F. (1992). *R&D Investment and International Productivity Differences*. National Bureau of Economic Research Inc.

Lin, L., and Kulatilaka, N. (2006). Network effects and technology licensing with fixed fee, royalty, and hybrid contracts. *Journal of Management Information Systems*, 23(2), 91–118.

Malone, T., and Crowston, K. (1994). The interdisciplinary study of coordination. *ACM Computer Surveys*, 26, March, 87–119.

March, J. (1991). Exploration and exploitation in organizational learning. *Organization Science*, 2(1), 71–87.

March, J. (1996). Continuity and change in theories of organizational action. *Administrative Science Quarterly*, 41, 278–287.

Markides, C. (1997). Strategic innovation. *Sloan Management Review*, 38(2), 9–23.

Markides, C. (1999). *All the Right Moves: A Guide to Crafting Breakthrough Strategy*. Boston, MA: Harvard Business School Press.

Markides, C. (1998). Strategic innovation in established companies. *Sloan Management Review*, 39(3), 31–42.

Marten, G. (2001). *Human Ecology*. US: Earthscan Publication Ltd.

Martines, L., and Kambil, A. (1999). 'Looking back and thinking ahead: effects of prior success on managers' interpretations of new information technologies. *Academy of Management Journal*, 42, 652–661.

Masutani, F. (1971). Buddhism (in Japanese). Tokyo, Japan: Chikuma Shobo.

Maturana, H., and Varela, F (1998). *The Tree of Knowledge*. Boston and London: Shambhala.

Meyer, A., Gaba, V., and Colwell, K. (2005). Organizing far from equilibrium: nonlinear change in organizational fields. *Organization Science*, 16(5), 456–473.

Miles, M.P., and Covin, J.G. (2002). Exploring the practice of corporate venturing: some common forms and their organizational implications. *Entrepreneurship Theory and Practice*, 26(1), 21–40.

Mintzberg, H., Ahlstrand, B., and Lampel, J. (1998). *Strategy Safari: A Guided Tour Through the Wilds of Strategic Management.* US: The Free Press.

Mintzberg, H., and Walters, J. (1985). Of strategies deliberate and emergent. *Strategic Management Journal*, 6, 357–272.

Mintzberg, H. (1973). *The Nature of Managerial Work.* New York: Harper and Row.

Mintzberg, H. (1978). Patterns in strategy formation. *Management Science*, 24, 934–948.

Mitchell, W. (1989). Whether and when? Probability and timing of incumbents' entry into emerging industrial subfields. *Administrative Science Quarterly*, 34, 208–234.

Mizuno, H. (1971). *Basic of Buddhism* (in Japanese). Tokyo, Japan: Syujyunnsya.

Moore, J.F. (1993). Predators and prey: a new ecology of competition. *Harvard Business Review*, 71(3), 75–86.

Morel, B., and Ramanujam, R. (1999). Through the looking glass of complexity: the dynamics of organizations as adaptive and evolving systems. *Organization Science*, 10(3), 278–293.

Morone, G. (1993). *Winning in High-Tech Markets.* Boston, MA: Harvard Business School Press.

Motter, A.E. (2004). Cascade control and defense in complex networks. *Physical Review Letter*, 93, 1–4.

Nadler, A. (1995). *Discontinuous Change: Leading Organizational Transformation.* US: Jossey-Bass.

Nahapiet, J., and Ghoshal, S. (1998). Social capital, intellectual capital, and the creation of value in firms. *Academy of Management Review*, 23(2), 242–266.

Nelson, R., and Winter, S. (1982). *An Evolutionary Theory of Economic Change.* Boston, MA: Harvard University Press.

Newman, M.E.J. (2004). Fast algorithm for detecting community structure in networks *Physical Review E*, 69(6), 1–5.

Nickerson, J.A., and Silverman, B.S. (2003). Why firms want to organize efficiently and what keeps them from doing so: inappropriate governance, performance, and adaptation in a deregulated industry. *Administrative Science Quarterly*, 48(3), 433–465.

Nisbett, R. (2003). *The Geography of Thought.* New York: The Free Press.

Nishiguchi, T., and Beaudet, A. (1998). The Toyota group and the Aisin fire. *Sloan Management Review*, 40(1), 49–59.

Nohria, N., and Garcia-Pont, C. (1991). Global strategic linkages and industry structure. *Strategic Management Journal*, 12 (Summer Special Issue), 105–124.

Nonaka, I., and Takeuchi, H. (1995). *The Knowledge-Creating Company.* New York: Oxford University Press.

Nonaka, I., Toyama, R., and Konno, N. (2000). 'Ba' and leadership: a unified model of dynamic knowledge creation. *Long Range Planning*, 33, 5–34.

Norgaard, R. (1994). *Development Betrayed.* London, UK: Routledge.

Nutt, P., and Backoff, R. (1997). Organizational transformation. *Journal of Management Inquiry*, 6, 235–254.

O'Connor, G., Leifer, R., Paulson, P. and, Peters, P. (2008). *Grabbing Lightning: Building a Capability for Breakthrough Innovation*. US: Jossey-Bass.

O'Connor, G., Ravichandran, T., and Robeson, D. (2008). Risk management through learning: management practices for radical innovation success. *Journal of High Technology Management Research*, 19(1), 78–82.

Orlikowski, W.J. (2002). Knowing in practice: enacting a collective capability in distributed organizing *Organization Science*, 13(3), 249–273.

Orr, J. (1996). *Talking about Machines: An Ethnography of a Modern Job*. Ithaca, NY: ILP Press.

Osono, E. (2004). The Strategy-making process as dialogue. In H. Takeuchi, and I. Nonaka (Eds.), *Hitotsubashi on Knowledge Management* (247–286). Singapore: John Wiley and Sons (Asia)

Ouchi, G. (1980). *Theory Z: How American Business Can Meet the Japanese Challenge*. MA: Addison-Wesley.

Owen-Smith, J., and Powell, W.W. (2004). Knowledge networks as channels and conduits: the effects of spillovers in the Boston biotechnology community. *Organization Science*, 15(1), 5–22.

O'Connor, C., and Rice, P. (2001). Opportunity recognition and breakthrough innovation in large established firms. *California Management Review*, 43(2), 95–116.

O'Connor, G. (2006). Open, Radical Innovation: Toward an Integrated Model in Large Established Firms. In H. Chesbrough, W. Vanhaverbeke, and J. West (Eds.), *Open Innovation; Researching a New Paradigm*. UK: Oxford University Press.

O'Connor, G. (2008). Major innovation as a dynamic capability: a systems approach. *Journal of Product Innovation Management*, 25, 313–330.

O'Connor, G., and DeMartino, R. (2006). Organizing for radical innovation: an exploratory study of the structural aspects of RI management systems in large established firms. *Journal of Product Innovation Management*, 23, 475–497.

O'Reilly, C., and Tushman, M. (2004). The ambidextrous organization. *Harvard Business Review*, 82, April, 74–82.

Padula, G. (2008). Enhancing the innovation performance of firms by balancing cohesiveness and bridging ties. *Long Range Planning*, 41(4), 395–415.

Peltokorpi, V., Nonaka, I., and Kodama, M. (2007d). NTT Docomo's launch of i-mode in the Japanese mobile phone market: a knowledge creation perspective. *Journal of Management Studies*, 44(1), 50–72.

Peng, K., and Nisbett, R.E. (1999). Culture dialectics and reasoning about contradiction. *American Psychologist*, 54, 741–54.

Phillippi, D. (1977). Kojiki. Tokyo: University of Tokyo Press.

Pisano, G. (1991). The governance of innovation: vertical integration and collaborative arrangements in the biotechnology industry. *Research Policy*, 20(3), 237–249.

Pisano, P. (2006). *Science Business.* Boston, MA: Harvard Business School Press.

Porter, M. (1980). *Competitive Strategy: Techniques for Analyzing Industries and Competitors.* New York: Free Press.

Prigogine, I. (1996). *The End of Certainty.* New York: The Free Press.

Qiang, L., and Bianca, B. (2006). Process development: a theoretical framework. *International Journal of Production Research,* 44(15), 2977–2996.

Raynor, M. (2006). *The Strategy Paradox: Why Committing to Success Leads to Failure.* Australia: Currency Press.

Roethlisberger, F., and Dickson, R. (1939). *Management and the Worker.* Cambridge, MA: Harvard University Press.

Roethlisberger, F. (1977). *The Elusive Phenomena: An Autobiographical Account of My Work in the Field of Organizational Behavior at the Harvard Business School.* Boston, MA: Harvard Business School Press.

Ryle, G. (1949). *The Concept of Mind.* London, UK: Hutchinson.

Sanchez, R., and Mahoney, T. (1996). Modularity, flexibility, and knowledge management in product and organizational design. *Strategic Management Journal,* 17, 63–76.

Sanchez, R. (1996). Strategic product creation: managing new interactions of technology, markets, and organizations *European Management Journal,* 14, 121–138.

Santos, F.M., and Eisenhardt, K.M. (2005). Constructing markets and organizing boundaries: entrepreneurial action in nascent fields Working paper, INSEAD.

Schilling, M., and Phelps, C. (2007). Interfirm collaboration networks: the impact of large-scale network structure on firm innovation. *Management Science,* 53(7), 1113–1127.

Schilling, M., and Steensma, H. (2001). The use of modular organizational forms: an industry-level analysis. *Academy of Management Journal,* 44, 1149–1168.

Schon, A. (1983). *The Reflective Practitioner.* New York: Basic Book.

Schon, A (1987). *Educating the Reflective Practitioner.* San Francisco: Jossey-Bass.

Schutz, A. (1932). *Der Sinnhafte Aufbau der Sozialen Welt.* Berlin: Springer.

Selzanick, P. (1957). *Leadership in Administration.* US: Harper and Row.

Shah, P. (2000). Network destruction: the structural implications of downsizing. *Academy of Management Journal,* 43(1), 101–112.

Shannon, C., and Weaver, W. (1949). *The Mathematical Theory of Communications.* Urbana: University of Illinois Press.

Shapiro, C., and Varian, H.R. (1998). *Information Rules.* Boston, MA: Harvard Business School Press.

Schein, E. (1985). *Organizational Culture and Leadership.* San Francisco: Jossey-Bass.

Shibata, T., and Kodama, M. (2007) Knowledge integration through networked strategic communities — cases of Japan. *Business Strategy Series,* 8(5), 394–400.

Shibata, T., Yano, M., and Kodama, F. (2005). Empirical analysis of evolution of product architecture Fanuc numerical controllers from 1962 to 1997. *Research Policy*, 34(1) 13–31.

Simon, A. (1996). *The Architecture of Complexity: Hierarchic Systems*. In *The Science of the Artificial* (3rd ed.). Cambridge, MA: MIT Press.

Skyrrme, D.J. (2001). *Capitalizing on Knowledge: From e-business to k-business*. London: Butterworth-Heinemann.

Smith, S., and Tushman, M. (2005). Managing strategic contradictions: a top management model for managing innovation streams. *Organization Science*, 16(5), 522–536.

Spender, J.C. (1992) Knowledge management: putting your technology strategy on track. In T.M. Khalil, and B.A. Bayraktar, (Eds.), *Management of Technology*, 3, 404–413. Norcross, GA: Industrial Engineering and Management Press.

Spender, J.C. (1990). *Industry Recipes: An Enquiry into the Nature and Sources of Managerial Judgement*. Oxford: Basil Blackwell.

Stacey, R. (1996). *Complexity and Creativity in Organizations*. San Francisco, Berett-Koehler Publishers.

Stacey, R. (1995). The science of complexity: an alternative perspective for strategic change process. *Strategic Management Journal*, 16(6), 477–495.

Star, S.L. (1989). The structure of Ill-Structured Solutions: Boundary objects and heterogeneous distributed problem solving. In M. Huhns, and I.L. Gasser, (Eds.), *Readings in Distributed Artificial Intelligence*. Menlo Park, CA: Morgan Kaufman.

Strong, J. (2007). *The Experience of Buddhism: Sources and Interpretations (Religious Life in History)*. USA: Wadsworth Pub Co.

Sturgeon, T. (2002). Modular production networks: a new American model of industrial organization. *Industrial and Corporate Change*, 11(3), 451–496.

Sutcliffe, K.M. (2000). Organizational environments and organizational information processing. In F.M. Jablin, and L.L. Putnam, (Eds). *The New Handbook of Organizational Communication*, 197–230. Thousand Oaks, CA: Sage.

Sydow, J., and Windeler, A. (1998). Organizing and evaluating interfirm networks: a structurationist perspective on network processes and effectiveness. *Organization Science*, 9(3), 265–284.

Takazawa, H. (1996). *What is 'Wa' for Japanese* (in Japanese). Tokyo Japan: Hakuto Syobo.

Teece, D. (2001). Strategies for managing knowledge assets: the role of firm structure and industrial context. In I. Nonaka, and D.J. Teece (Eds.), *Managing Industrial Knowledge: Creation, Transfer and Utilization*. London: Sage Publication.

Teece, D. Pisano, G., and Shuen, A. (1997). Dynamic capabilities and strategic management. *Strategic Management Journal*, 18, 509–533.

340 *Knowledge Integration Dynamics*

Teece, D. J. (1998). 'Capturing value from knowledge assets. *California Management Review*, 40(3), 55–76.

Tripsas, M., and Gavetti, G. (2000). Capabilities, cognition, and inertia: evidence from digital imaging. *Strategic Management Journal*, 21, 1147–1161.

Tsoukas, H. (1997). Forms of Knowledge and Forms of Life in Organizational Context. In R. China (Eds.), *The Realm of Organization*. London: Routledge.

Tushman, M. (1979). Work characteristics and subunit communication structure: a contingency analysis. *Administrative Science Quarterly*, 24, 82–98.

Tushman, M., and Romanelli, R. (1985). Organizatinal evolution: a metamorphosis model of convergence and reorientation. *Research in Organizational Behavior*, 7(2), 171–222.

Tushman, M.L., and Anderson, P. (1986). Technological discontinuities and organizational environments. *Administrative Science Quarterly*, 31, 439–465.

Tushman, M.L., and O'Reilly, C.A. (1997). *Winning Trough Innovation*. Cambridge, NA: Harvard Business School Press.

Tushman, M., and Nadler, D. (1978). Information processing as an integrating concept in organizational design. *Academy of Management Review*, 3(3), 613–624.

Tushman, M.L. (1977). Special boundary roles in the innovation process. *Administrative Science Quarterly*, 22, 587–605.

Van de Ven, A., and Poole, S. (1995). Explaining development and change in organizations. *Academy of Management Review*, 20(5), 510–540.

Vanhaverbeke, W., and Peeters, N. (2005). Embracing innovation as strategy: the role of new business development in corporate renewal. *Creativity and Innovation Management*, 14(3), 246–257.

Von Bertalanffy, L. (1960). *Problems of Life*. New York: Harper Touchbooks.

Von Bertalanffy, L. (1968). *General Systems Theory*. New York: Braziller.

Von Bertalanffy, L. (1972). General System Theory: A Critical Review. In J. Baishon, and G. Peters (Eds.), *Systems Behavior* (29–49). London: Open University Press.

Walker, G., Kogut, B., and Shan, W. (1997). Social capital, structural holes and the formation of an industry network. *Organization Science*, 8(2), 109–125.

Wasserman, S., and Faust, K. (1994). *Social Network Analysis: Methods and Applications*. New York: Cambridge University Press.

Watts, J. (2003). *Six Degrees: The Science of a Connected Age*. New York: W.W. Norton and Company.

Watts, J., and Strogatz, S. (1998). Collective dynamics of 'small-world' networks. *Nature*, 393(4), 440–42.

Weick, K (1995). *Sensemaking in Organizations*. London: Sage Publication.

Weick, K.E. (1979). *The Social Psychology of Organizing* (2nd ed.). Reading, MA: Addison–Wesley.

Wenger, E., McDermott, R., and Snyder, W.M. (2002). *Cultivating Communities of Practice*. Boston, MA: Harvard Business School Press.

Wenger, E.C. (1998). *Community of Practice: Learning, Meaning and Identity*. Cambridge: Cambridge University Press.

Wenger, E.C. (2000). Communities of practice: the organizational frontier. *Harvard Business Review*, 78(1), 139–145.

Wernerfelt, B. (1984). A resource-based view of the firm. *Strategic Management Journal*, 5, 171–180.

Westerman, G., McFarlan, W., and Iansiti, M. (2006). Organization design and effectiveness over the innovation life cycle. *Organization Science*, 17(2), 230–238.

Wheelwright, S., and Clark, K. (1992). *Revolutionizing Product Development*. New York: Free Press.

White, D., and Houseman, M. (2003). The navigability of strong ties: small worlds, tie strength, and network topology. *Complexity*, 8(1), 82–86.

Williamson, O.E. (1975). *Markets and Hierarchies: Analysis and Antitrust Implications*. New York: Free Press.

Williamson, O.E. (1981) The economics of organizations: the transaction cost approach. *American Journal of Sociology*, 87(3), 548–557.

Williamson, O.E. (1985) *The Economic Institutions of Capitalism*. New York: Free Press.

Winter, S. (2000). The satisficing principle in capability learning. *Strategic Management Journal*, 21(10–11), 981–996.

Winter, S. (2003). Understanding dynamic capabilities. *Strategic Management Journal*, 24(10), 991–995.

Zollo, M., and Winter, G. (2002). Deliberate learning and the evolution of dynamic capabilities. *Organization Science*, 13(3), 339–351.

Author Index

Subject Index